Advance Praise for the Book

'At one level, *Dharmanomics* is an oxymoron. Economic models assume that individuals act in their self-interest, and societal well-being results as a by-product. In contrast, central to the concept of Dharma is the injunction to individuals to act righteously in pursuit of societal welfare. Individual happiness results as a by-product. In this book, Sriram Balasubramanian brilliantly argues that there is no such contradiction and that ancient Dharmic kingdoms had in fact harmonised these two seemingly conflicting strands. To buttress his thesis, Sriram takes us on a travel from the Cholas, Pallavas and Pandyas of South India to Southeast Asian kingdoms like Cambodia. He analyses how these empires structured their economies around Dharma, focusing on agriculture, trade and governance. This book is a work of deep scholarship that is sure to trigger an enlightened debate on Dharmanomics and its potential relevance for the future'

Dr Duvvuri Subbarao, Former Governor,
Reserve Bank of India

'An unusual but outstanding book about a period of Indian history on which no worthwhile research has, so far, been done. The linkages between contemporary economics and Kautilya's famous treatise, the *Arthashastra*. This book, which focusses on "Dharmanomics" makes a persuasive, compulsive read for researchers, commentators and those interested in the legacy and evolution of our economic history'

Dr N.K. Singh, Chairman,
15th Finance Commission

'India has a long established tradition of thinking about governance and economics that goes back thousands of years. To the extent we refer to it at all today, we do so as a historical curiosity. What Sriram attempts here is to credibly re-establish the thread as a living tradition. Readers may or may not agree with his specific interpretations, but the idea of re-establishing the chain is ambitious and necessary'

Sanjeev Sanyal, Writer, Economist and Member,
Prime Minister's Advisory Council,
Government of India

'This book, a sequel to *Kautilyanomics for Modern Times*, explores the much-needed aspects of Dharmanomics, including an overview of the Dharmic capitalism framework of the earlier book and also the development of the idea of Dharmanomics, which is economics based on the idea of Dharma in empires and kingdoms in the south such as those of the Pallavas, Pandyas, Cholas and Vijayanagara. In addition to a historical perspective of empires such as the Cholas, this book provides a much-needed analysis of its economic models, focusing on the corporate guilds (srenis), trade, governance and other aspects and the underlying role of Dharma in the functioning of these institutions. It also focuses on the encompassing Dharmic ecosystem stemming from the temples and how it influenced agriculture, trade and local industries. A comparison of economic activities such as trade between the Chola and Vijayanagara empires has also been attempted. Hindu culture had embedded itself in many countries of Southeast Asia and this book tries to highlight not only economic trade, but also the geo-political alliances between the kingdoms in South India and those of Southeast Asia over many a century. A large amount of research has gone into the writing of this book, with the author having travelled extensively and read voluminously. The outcome is a much-needed attempt at looking at the political and economic history of empires and kingdoms of South India which have hitherto not received the attention they deserve'

Dr Chitra Madhavan, Historian

'In ancient yogic practices, mudras or hand gestures bring together various combinations of our fingers for desired energetic configurations. While the thumb denotes our ego or our identity, the middle finger represents artha or wealth, and the ring finger represents Dharma or virtue/morality. A profound aspect to these mudras is that one never sees just the thumb, representing the ego, and the middle finger, representing wealth, join without the ring finger, representing Dharma, joining the middle finger. This is but one manifestation of the eternal, yet profound, idea in Indian philosophy that artha and Dharma must go together. In other words, wealth acquired without virtue never creates lasting welfare for society. Not surprisingly, when one observes the economic models of capitalism in the West, the overwhelming rapaciousness inherent in them stems from the absence of Dharma in the pursuit of artha. I believe India's economic growth is essential for India to teach the world the profound civilisational idea that Dharma and artha have to be pursued synchronously for lasting human welfare. Sriram's brilliant book, *Dharmanomics*, which is based on rigorous scholarship, contributes to this endeavour by establishing the continuum of Dharma-based economic models in Indian thought for the last 5,000 years. The book is therefore an important contribution to the civilisational cause of India teaching the world how to create sustainable, equitable prosperity. Undoubtedly, a must-read for everyone!'

Dr K.V. Subramanian, Executive Director at the International Monetary Fund for India, Bhutan, Bangladesh and Sri Lanka

Dharmanomics

An Indigenous and Sustainable Economic Model

SRIRAM BALASUBRAMANIAN

BLOOMSBURY
NEW DELHI • LONDON • OXFORD • NEW YORK • SYDNEY

BLOOMSBURY INDIA
Bloomsbury Publishing India Pvt. Ltd
Second Floor, LSC Building No. 4, DDA Complex, Pocket C – 6 & 7,
Vasant Kunj, New Delhi, 110070

BLOOMSBURY, BLOOMSBURY INDIA and the Diana logo
are trademarks of Bloomsbury Publishing Plc

First published in India 2024
This edition published 2024

ISBN: PB: 978-93-56409-69-9; eBook: 978-93-56409-78-1
2 4 6 8 10 9 7 5 3 1

Typeset in Baskerville MT Std by Manipal Technologies Limited
Printed and bound in India by Thomson Press India Ltd

MIX
Paper | Supporting responsible forestry
FSC® C010615
FSC www.fsc.org

To Dr Nagaswamy, R.C. Majumdar, K.A. Nilakanta Sastri and R. Shamasastry—the four persons without whose work none of this would have become known to the public—and all the other Indic researchers who spoke truth to power.

धर्मो रक्षति रक्षितः।

Contents

॥श्रीगुरुभ्यो नमः ॥

हर हर शङ्कर जय जय शङ्कर!

Lord Brahma

Lord Ranganatha

One thousand Shiva lingams across the stream in various places over which the water flows

These three pictures were taken in Kbal Spean, which is located on the south-west slopes of the Kulen Hills in the north-east of Angkor in Banteay Srei District, Siem Reap Province, Cambodia. The uniqueness of this hilltop is that you can see a thousand Shiva lingams, Lord Ranganatha and Lord Brahma in equipoise. The Stung Kbal Spean river, after getting sanctified by flowing over these devatas, flows downstream, bifurcating into the Siem Reap River and the Puok River and, after passing through the plains and the Angkor temple complex (https://en.wikipedia.org/wiki/Kbal_Spean, accessed on 2 April 2024), finally flows into the Tonlé Sap Lake. Since this was the source river, the rulers wanted to ensure that it went through the divine devatas before entering the Greater Cambodia region. This was made akin to the formation and flow of the Ganges in Bharat, according to some accounts. The sculptures were created during the reigns of Suryavarman I and Udityadityavarman II, between the eleventh and twelfth centuries.

My pranam to this great civilizational marvel, which inspires researchers such as me every day!

Message from Dr M. Venkaiah Naidu
Honourable Former Vice President of India

Dharmanomics is an interesting book written by Sriram Balasubramanian, the well-known author of *Kautilyanomics for Modern Times*, the bestselling book on India's economic history. The book, an organic spinoff from his research on the earlier book, explores the evolution of the economic policies of Kautilya through the centuries, across various Hindu kingdoms of the ancient period. These include Kambuja Desa (current-day Cambodia, according to many historians) and the Chola, Pallava, Pandya and Vijayanagara empires, all of which had a powerful economic foundation in ancient Bharat.

Sriram Balasubramanian traces the development of Kautilya's economic policies by these kingdoms tailored to their own geopolitical situations, but firmly rooted in Dharma. It is evident from a cursory reading of his book that Dharma is the common thread that binds the economic policies of many of the ancient kingdoms of Bharat. This work reveals that Kautilya's economic philosophy, and his view of Dharmic capitalism, was implemented in all the ancient kingdoms. It tells us that Dharma was not only a powerful element of economic policies but it also played a critical role in governance in all these kingdoms.

Sriram Balasubramanian discusses the centrality of Dharma in the Saraswati–Sindhu period and how it led to the overall prosperity of our ancient civilisation. Similarly, the great Chola empire and their economic paradigms, built on Dharma, are discussed at length in the book. We find an interesting insight into ancient corporate guilds of the period known as Srenis. Once again, we see that Dharma is the central pivot around which governance, trade and all other institutions in the economy revolve. These concepts are further highlighted in the chapter on the Pallavas, the Pandyas and the Vijayanagara empire while discussing the contrasts and commonalities.

The chapter on the Indic history of Kambuja Desa and the Dharmic element at its core, which also discusses economic models of the country at length, is insightful and makes for an engaging read. We also find a detailed discussion on other kingdoms in Southeast Asia, such as Champa (modern-day Vietnam) and Java (Indonesia), as also Thailand, all of which have economic models similar to that of Kambuja Desa with their own variations.

The reader will be fascinated by descriptions of how geopolitical alliances, economic trade flow and areas of agriculture and industry functioned in the Southeast Asian kingdoms of the time. The overarching rubric is Dharma, on which diverse features of the economy in all these kingdoms is founded. The central framework of Dharma as the core principle in these economic models is supported by a range of references to primary and secondary evidence. Sriram Balasubramanian's *Dharmanomics* is a well-researched work and constitutes an important contribution and an insightful addition to the body of knowledge on the history of ancient Bharat, especially from the standpoint of economic philosophy and the all-embracing concept of Dharma.

Acknowledgements

THIS BOOK HAS BEEN a very intense exercise for me. Unlike my earlier books, it involved an extensive amount of research over many years and across many eras. That needed a lot of time. In addition, an equivalent amount of time was required to ensure everything was appropriate. For all that, I owe a deep sense of gratitude to many people. First, to my immediate family—my wife, Lakshmi; my son, Skanda; and my parents, R. Balasubramanian and Sharada Balasubramanian. Despite not being subject matter experts in this field, their earnestness, unwavering support and good intent are priceless.

I would like to thank some of the doyens of Indology and archaeology who have tirelessly researched these topics. Dr Nagaswamy, R.C. Majumdar, K.A. Nilakanta Sastri and Shamasastry are stalwarts in their own right. The massive amount of information that they have collated for younger people such as me is amazing, to say the least. The sheer passion, diligence and, in some cases, audacity to interpret the ancient manuscripts, inscriptions and archaeological finds many years ago is extremely inspiring. My pranams to all these scholars.

I am very honoured and privileged to have received a special message for the book from the former Vice President of Bharat Dr Venkaiah Naiduji. His kind words and acute observations on the book were admirable to say the least. My sincere thanks to him and his office for facilitating this.

There are also many others to thank. My publishers, Bloomsbury, to start with. I had worked with Praveen Tiwari during the publication of my previous book, followed by Nitin Valecha, who has carried the baton forward. The main editor, Sanjiv Sarin, has been a delight to work with. Given his track record of editing some very successful books, his valuable insights have really streamlined and refined the content and style of the book. Other folks who have been supportive include Krishan Chopra, editor-in-chief of Bloomsbury. His cooperation has been a key factor in the successful publication of this book.

As part of the research for this book, I had the opportunity to interact with a variety of scholars and friends. On top of this list is the late Dr Nagaswamy, the doyen of Indic archaeological research for decades in southern Bharat. His relentless zeal for Indic research and his valuable thoughts were a true inspiration for this book as well. The next is Professor Kalyanaraman from the Saraswati–Sindhu Centre and an ardent researcher of the Indus seals and inscriptions. His passion and drive for relentlessly learning about ancient Bharat surely motivates several young people. The chapter on Saraswati–Sindhu civilization in this book is co-authored with him—he is an encyclopaedia on Indus inscriptions. Other scholars whom I have to thank include Dr K.R.A. Narasaih, Dr Chitra Madhavan, Jeysundhar (Indian Foreign Service), T.S. Krishnan, Kanakalatha Mukund and Nandita Krishna. In addition, I owe my gratitude to Dushyant Sridhar-ji, renowned upanyasam expert, and a good friend of mine. Our travels to Cambodia and visits to many of the sites mentioned in this book were very helpful, along with his valuable lectures on the subject. Despite his expertise on Dharmic Puranas, he always greets my work with respect, humility and admiration. I also want to thank J.R. Rao, a colleague and mentor, who is based at the International Finance Corporation (IFC). He was one of the first to read the manuscript and give his frank and constructive comments. I would also like to thank Dr Badri Narayanan Gopalakrishnan—trade economist and NITI Aayog fellow—for his feedback on the manuscript.

I would be remiss if I don't thank Dr N.K. Singh, prominent academic and policymaker; Dr Duvurri Subbarao, former RBI governor; Dr K.V. Subramanian, executive director at the International Monetary Fund; Dr Vikramaditya Khanna from the University of Michigan, Ann-Arbor; Dr Chithra Madhavan, widely acclaimed historian; and Sanjeev Sanyal, leading economist and popular historian, for their generous help.

N.K. Singh was kind enough to endorse this book. His lifetime of public service in academia and policymaking is second to none. Dr Subbarao also kindly consented to give an endorsement for this book despite his busy schedule. His towering persona adds more credibility to the book. Dr K.V. Subramanian has been a supporter of my work and has creditably written about ancient scriptures in his economic surveys as the Chief Economic Advisor. Dr Khanna has been a keen admirer of my work and I am collaborating with him on several interesting projects. His work on Srenis a decade ago remains one of the most definitive explorations of the subject. Dr Chithra Madhavan is an eminent historian whose illustrious work on south Bharatiya history has been an inspiration for many. Her endorsement of the book was a pleasant surprise, for which I am extremely grateful. I would also like to thank Sanjeev Sanyal, member of the Prime Minister's Economic Advisory Council, for his endorsement of this book. His support for my work (for more than a decade now) has continuously motivated me to pursue my research. I am also grateful to the late

S. Viswanathan (SV) of the *Industrial Economist* magazine. His nurturing of my interest in economics and public affairs was foundational to my writing and economic careers.

I cannot end this section without thanking, acknowledging and dedicating this book to my late grandmother, Jambakam Ramamurthy. It has been almost six years since she passed away, yet she remains with me, guiding me every second of the day. Without her grace, kindness and upbringing, none of this would have been possible.

Copyright Acknowledgements

I would like to thank the following people for permission to reproduce copyright material:

E. Lusting for images and extracts from his book *Power and Pragmaticism in the Political Economy of Angkor* (Sydney: University of Sydney, 2009).

George Coedès for extracts from his book *The Indianized States of Southeast India* (Canberra: Australian National University Press, 1968).

Kanchi H.H. Sri Chandrashekharendra Saraswati for extracts from his book *Hindu Dharma: The Universal Way of Life* (Delhi: Bhartiya Vidya Bhawan, 1995).

K.A. Nilakanta Sastri for extracts from his books *Pandya Kingdom: From the Earliest to the Sixteenth Century* (London: Luzac & Co., 1929) and *The History of South India: From Prehistoric Times to the Fall of Vijayanagar* (London: Oxford University Press, 1966).

N.P. Chakravarti for extracts from his book *Epigraphia Indica* (Calcutta: University of Calcutta, 1933).

R.C. Majumdar for images from his books *Corporate Life in Ancient India* (Poona: The Oriental Book Agency, 1922) and *Inscriptions of Kambuja* (Calcutta: University of Calcutta, 1922).

Swami Tejomayananda for extracts from his book *Dharma Shastras: Way to Peace, Prosperity and Purity* (Mumbai: Central Chinmaya Misson Trust, 2022).

Prof. S. Kalyanaraman for images from his articles:

'Bharata Maritime Trade of Śrēṣṭhin Khār "Guild-Master", Sarasvati-Sindhu Civilization, Cire Perdue (lost-wax) Metalcasting Artificers'.

'Bronze-Age Financial System, Indus Script Corpora'.

'Chanhudaro (चान्हूदड़ो), Tin-Bronze Age Industrial Manufacturing Hub of Sarasvati-Sindhu Civilization, Evidence from Archaeology & Indus Script Decipherment'.

'Contributions of Sarasvati Civilization to Tin-Bronze Revolution of 3rd Millennium BCE'.

'Roots of International Gold Standard, 2nd Millenium BCE'.

'Stoneware Bangles Are Assigned Responsibilities in Sreni Guild, Corporate Form'.

'Treasure Guard, Maritime Boat, Warehouse Armour, Metalwork Guild Master, Daybook'.

N. Karashima, Y. Subbarayalu and P. Shanmugam, 'Nagaram during the Chola and Pandyan Period: Commerce and Towns in the Tamil Country A.D. 850–1350', *Indian Historical Review* 35 (1) 2008, p. 1–33.

Vikramaditya Khanna for extracts from his article 'The Economic History of the Corporate Form in Ancient India' (2005).

Assumptions Made in the Book

The following assumptions have been made in the book:

1) Words such as frameworks and models have been used interchangeably for the sake of convenience for the common reader. The author acknowledges the academic differences but has done this for ease of reading. Similarly, Srenis and guilds have been interchangeably used for convenience though I have retained the latter as much as possible.
2) All dates which do not have any denomination attached to it are considered by default to be CE dates. For example, if its written 5th century, it is assumed to be the 5th century CE.
3) Dating of all the historical figures have been sourced to the key books that have been referenced. The author is not a dating expert yet and neither is this book focused on the dating aspect of history. As such, any differences (if any) in dating is well reserved for dating experts.
4) This book does not refer to the pre-ce phase of economic history except for the Saraswati–Sindu civilization and Kautilya's Arthashastra. The author is cognizant of the differences in perspectives on pre-ce Sangam age, early Cholas, Pallavas and Pandyas history and this book does not deal with those issues since it is beyond the scope of the book.
5) There are references to my previous book, *Kautilyanomics for Modern Times*. In most places, I have referred the ideas from that book as succinctly as possible. If readers feel the need to know more, I would request you to read the book at your convenience.

Introduction

As I was completing my book *Kautilyanomics for Modern Times*, I contemplated what to do next. In my mind, I already had a trilogy in mind—*Kautilyanomics for Modern Times*, a sequel to showcase the continuity of the Dharma-based economic models in the common era (CE), and the relevance of these Dharma-based ideas and frameworks for Viksit Bharat. While the research intent and work had started in the mind, the details of *Dharmanomics* were still a bit hazy. Moreover, I first wanted to see how *Kautilyanomics* performed and review the feedback from the readers.

Kautilyanomics was declared a national bestseller by the bookstores and ranked number one on Amazon India for economic history in 2022. Its success led to a natural demand from the readers and well-wishers for a sequel. So the hazy outline I had of the next book had to take a more concrete shape. Dharmic capitalism was central to the previous book and I intuitively believed that it was not the end of the story—that Kautilya's version of Dharmic capitalism was merely the starting point of the economic philosophy that would continue to be implemented in many kingdoms in the common era. This belief was based on several experiences I had on this subject. Let me explain it a little.

Almost a decade ago, I had the good fortune of interacting with the Indologist and archaeologist, Dr R. Nagaswamy on the important subject of Kambuja Desa (current-day Cambodia). I was told to meet him by His Holiness

Vijayendra Saraswati Swamigal (Bala Periva) of the Kanchi Mutt and to explore the mention in an R.C. Majumdar book about the journey of a Kanchi pandit to Cambodia. Despite his advanced years (even then), Dr Nagaswamy's reactions were razor sharp, and he shared many interesting ideas. He believed that there was a thriving and prosperous Hindu civilization in Cambodia, whose existence had largely been ignored by Bharatiya historians. He said, 'Almost every village in Cambodia had a Shiva lingam—you can see their remains even today.' We couldn't pursue the discussions further, but the ideas stayed stuck in my inner consciousness for a long time.

Coincidentally, at that time, I was going through three interesting books. The first was *Kambuja Desa* by the renowned historian R.C. Majumdar, which I was reading for the second time. The book was a masterpiece and served as a very important guide for this book. The second was K.A. Nilakanta Sastri's brilliant treatise *History of South India*, which illustrates how prosperous the Cholas, Pallavas and Pandyas were during their reigns. The third was an audiobook. I was listening to the Tamil novel *Ponniyan Selvan*, which was adapted into a movie in 2022. All these three literary experiences further intrigued me about this subject, given that Angus Maddison's dataset on economic history already showed that Bharat was the most prosperous country in the world during that period.

It was clear to me that the common thread among all these kingdoms was the role of Dharma. Dharma seemed to be omnipresent and appeared to play a key role in the governance of these kingdoms. This made me ask the natural question, 'What was the importance of Dharmanomics in the functioning of these kingdoms and how important was it in the factors that led to the dominance of these kingdoms?'

While historians have highlighted the role of Dharma in general, I recognized early that they never discussed it as the foundation for studying economic models and thinking in ancient times. This was not just due to the lack of economic or financial competence of these historians, but due to their sheer contempt for the past, in general. If Rajaraja Chola could build the world-renowned Brihadisvara temple in Tanjore which could withstand more than six earthquakes due to its robust architecture, to the amazement of modern-day engineers, isn't it obvious that he would have had a decent understanding of the economics behind building the temple? Wouldn't the Cambodian King Suryavarman II, who built the world's largest temple, Angkor Wat, have at least some understanding of economics? Given that Greek writers such as Megasthenes had been in awe of the Mauryan empire, which had an economic philosophy pioneered by Kautilya (which I have discussed in my earlier book), can't we reasonably expect the subsequent kingdoms, based on Dharma, to take the economic philosophy a notch higher?

The answers to these questions are obviously in the affirmative but, unfortunately, very little literature exists on these topics. Not only did this motivate me to study this subject further, it also made me realize the importance of dealing with this theme. I felt it was necessary that the story of the continuation of Kautilya's ideas and the central focus on Dharma should be told to the readers, especially the young, who are eager to know more about this subject. The more we discover, the more we learn that economists of yesteryears had a vision that was far ahead of their times. The importance of this also goes beyond the mundane need for a sequel; 'continuum' is central to the endurance of such systems.

Why is it so important for a continuum to be established? First, this would identify a common thread in the economic governance of successful kingdoms in the Common Era. Given that modern-day capitalism itself is just about two hundred years old, a model which has been used for many centuries could add further credibility to Dharmanomics, in general. Second, it would establish a qualitative 'time series' for researchers to understand and analyse such frameworks. The length of the time series would be an important benchmark for people to assess its importance and relevance. Third, it would also reiterate the foresight that our ancestors had and the sustainability of such a model in the long run. More importantly, having established a qualitative time series for all these years, I hope to use them as a benchmark for the third part in this trilogy series to use these ideas and their relevance to Viksit Bharat.

This book examines the need to establish the common thread and Sreni Dharma followed by the time series. The discussion begins with a chapter on the definitions and contours of Dharmanomics. It includes detailed descriptions of the Kautilyan Dharmic Capitalism (KDC) and the Dharmic ecosystem. It provides an overview of the Dharmic capitalism framework which we discussed in *Kautilyanomics for Modern Times* and showcases the evolution of the notion of Dharmanomics, that is, economics based on the idea of Dharma in the kingdoms being discussed. Subsequently, I move backwards from Kautilya's time in the third century BCE to the Saraswati–Sindhu civilization. In *Kautilyanomics for Modern Times*, I had started off with an introduction about ideas from our ancient texts such as the Ramayana and Mahabharata and their imprint on Kautilya's *Arthashastra*. In a similar vein, the chapter focuses mainly on the Saraswati–Sindhu period and argues on the centrality of Dharma in the prosperity of the civilization. The chapter further discusses maritime trade and commerce, the international gold standard of those times and why some of the more modern economic ideas such as industrialization could have been a pre-Kautilyan phenomena.

Chapter 4 focuses on the Cholas—the grand empire that spanned many countries—and their economic framework. Besides providing a historical perspective, the chapter includes a detailed analysis of the Srenis (corporate guilds), trade, governance and the intrinsic role of Dharma in facilitating the functioning of these institutions. In addition, I also look into the role of communities, the broader Dharmic ecosystem emanating from the temples and its impact on conventional economic pillars such as agriculture, manufacturing and economic trade. Chapter 5 discusses the Pallavas, Pandyas and the Vijayanagar empire, though a bit more briefly, highlighting and expanding some of the trends mentioned in the Cholas chapter. In these chapters, I also make an attempt to draw a subtle distinction about how the other empires varied from the Cholas in their economic philosophies and also their pertinent commonalities. For example, what was the extent of maritime trade during the Cholas as compared to the Vijayanagar empire? How were the economies structurally different? What were some of the areas that were emphasized more in a particular kingdom compared to other kingdoms? As a natural continuum of this, I subsequently move to the kingdoms in Southeast Asia.

Given my travels to Cambodia, the focus of the Southeast Asian kingdoms begins mainly with Kambuja Desa, that is, modern-day Cambodia. Chapter 6 discusses the fascinating Indic history of Kambuja Desa and details the origins of Indic rule, its roots in contemporary southern Bharat and its Dharmic core. The chapter also mentions the various types of economic models in the country and argues in detail about the temple-based economic model and its centrality to economic success in areas such as manufacturing, trade and agriculture. This specific focus on such a model is unique to Southeast Asia and its gradations exist in other countries of the region. Other chapters include kingdoms in Champa (modern-day Vietnam) and Java (Indonesia) along with Thailand, which have unique variations compared to the Cambodian model, yet have some important similarities. Through this process, the chapters also try to highlight the important aspects of continuous economic trade and the geopolitical interactions/alliances between the southern Bharat CE kingdoms and the Southeast Asian kingdoms, over these years.

In each of these chapters, I look at expanding the Dharmanomics framework. I explain how each of the components of Dharmanomics has evolved in these empires. This includes summaries of how agriculture, trade, labour and other features of the economy evolved during those times. These are supplemented by both primary (inscriptions) and secondary evidence that is available. In Chapter 7, titled, 'Dharmanomics through 5,000 Years', I connect all the previous chapters and establish the common connection of Dharmanomics in the kingdoms referred. Deducing from this, I try to also establish the qualitative 'time series' that I mentioned earlier. This then leads to the final chapter which summarizes all these ideas and shows the continuity of prosperous economic civilizations based on the idea of Dharma as their foundation.

It is imperative to emphasize the primary and secondary research done on the subject. First, I was keen to visit some of the places where these kingdoms existed to have a soulful connection with history. Besides travelling in my home state of Tamil Nadu, which included travelling to Thanjavur, Kanchipuram, Uthiramerur, Kumbakonam and Govindapuram, I also travelled extensively in

Cambodia. I spent a few weeks there to understand the temple architecture, look at the vast swathe of research material available there and appreciate the extensive Dharmic connections in the place.

Second, I conducted a large amount of secondary research on the subject. Reading inscriptions and their interpretations and cross-referencing them with others while ensuring that the context and circumstances were not diluted was a long exercise. Numerous books and research works played a key role, but I will name only a few—R.C. Majumdar's *Kambuja Desa*, *Inscriptions of Kambuja*, *Hindu Kingdoms of the Far East* and *Corporate Life in Ancient India*; Nilakanta Sastri's *History of Southern Bharat* and *Cholas*; G.E. Coedes's *Hindu Kingdoms of Southeast Asia*; Eileen Lusting's *Power and Pragmaticism in the Political Economy of Angkor*; Kenneth Hall's *Maritime Trade and State Development in Early Southeast Asia*; and Dr Nagaswamy's *Dharma Yoga* and *Vedas and History*.

Third, keeping the focus on the economic history was a difficult yet fascinating exercise. Much of the literature regarding inscriptions is poetic in nature. To distil its ideas and express them in a simplified form, put together common themes from the set of available inscriptions and then articulate them in a coherent framework was not an easy task. Many people supported me in this effort and I have shared my gratitude to them in the acknowledgements.

Compared to *Kautilyanomics for Modern Times*, this book is a less analytical and more at-ease read, though with similar levels of analytical rigour. One of the main reasons is that my previous book had many sections which dealt with datasets and data in the current era. The availability and veracity of this data made it easier to do rigorous quantitative work. In this book, the scope to perform such quantitative analysis is lesser, though I have still done some limited analysis. On the other hand, this book will be a lighter read compared to the earlier book. This is a deliberate attempt to ensure that the book reaches a wider section of readers—not just an audience interested in economics and finance, but also general readers who are interested in the history of our culture.

This book does not propose that Dharmanomics is the only way for an economy to function. Far from it. At the same time, it raises some important questions which, frankly, baffle me. Why haven't any of our economists or historians made a serious effort to discuss the wide range of historical material available, either from a standpoint of economic history or historical narrative? Why don't school textbooks and academic curriculum have a single paragraph, if not entire chapters and books, on this subject? Why do we take the quasi-Western narrative as the norm for everything, especially in sciences and history? Just to put things in perspective, all the kingdoms mentioned in this book existed at least 300–400 years before Adam Smith's *Wealth of Nations*! There are questions galore and someone had to set the ball rolling. I do hope I have played a small part in this.

Last but not the least, one of the main purposes of this book is to engage and enrich the general reader. I hope to expose the reader to a plethora of facts related to the subject—facts which have been barely mentioned in our academic discourse so far. By sharing the proposition called Dharmanomics along with the necessary evidence, I hope to induce the readers to debate and discuss the topic further. The more people debate and discuss, the better it will be for all of us. I see it as my swadharma to share this knowledge with everyone. Perhaps this is what made my book, *Kautilyanomics for Modern Times*, a national bestseller.

I leave you with two quotations that might make you ponder more on the subject. The Honourable Finance Minister Nirmala Sitharaman mentioned in her 2020

Budget speech[1] Indus scripts, Srenis and the continuous civilizational might that Bharat has had (all of which I will detail more in the book):

> The guilds of Saraswati–Sindhu civilization & the Harappan seals are remarkable. They belong to 3300 BCE. Words from the Indus script hieroglyphs have been deciphered. Commerce and trade related words show how India for a millennia is continuing as rich in skills, metallurgy, trade etc. 'Takara Kolimi' = Tin smithery, 'Sreni' = Guild, 'Sethi' = wholesale merchant, 'Poddar' = Assayer of metal into treasury.

The fact that the Honourable Finance Minister recognized and mainstreamed such economic–historical ideas serves well for a Viksit Bharat. Not only are these motivating for scholars such as me, they also symbolize a confident Bharat which can envision an economic framework for itself based on its ethos.

The second quotation is from R.C. Majumdar. It was written in 1953 as a part of the preface of his book *Inscriptions in Kambuja*:

> It is not difficult to account for this strange apathy or indifference to the rich store of Samskritam learning which Kambuja inscriptions offer to us. The study of ancient Indian culture in Southeast Asia is still in its infancy in India, mainly because the relevant literature is written mostly in foreign languages like French and Dutch, which are little cultivated in this country. In order to remove this difficulty, and to arouse interest in these studies among educated Indians, I planned, more than twenty-five years ago, a series of books on this subject under the general title, 'Ancient Indian Colonies in the Far East'.

More than seventy years later, the situation is no different in the study of these subjects in Bharat. I hope we use the positivity in the finance minister's budget speech and learn from R.C. Majumdar's quotation to make ourselves more indigenous in our approach to understanding economic history and using it for policymaking.

I wish this book arouses your interest about ancient economic models and the need to study and debate them for future generations—if it does, I would consider my efforts and this book to be a success.

Hope you enjoy reading *Dharmanomics*!

1

Sreni Dharma

THERE ARE SOME FOUNDATIONAL elements of Dharmanomics and the most important of them are the Srenis, which were central to economics and finance in ancient Bharat. They were, by far, the most significant institutional drivers of economic growth and prosperity in the Dharmic kingdoms in the last 5,000 years or more. The sustenance of the institution of Srenis was not merely by chance but due to the structural and organizational elements that enhanced their value. Moreover, the institution's integral role in Dharmanomics, which I will detail in the next chapter, cannot be overemphasized. I will discuss Srenis in this chapter in a question-and-answer format for easier understanding.

Q. *What were the Srenis?*

A. Srenis (śreṇiḥ) were the earliest form of collective groups that were engaged in commercial activities. They are defined as 'a legal entity composed of a group of people who were normally engaged in a similar trade'.[1] They were inclusive in nature, that is, they involved all jatis and communities in their organization. They served as egalitarian groups that functioned as the fulcrum for the business community to promote and protect commercial activities, mainly maritime trading, across countries. Not only did they facilitate the processes of maritime trading, they also simultaneously served as financial institutions and business bodies.

Q. *How long were Srenis in existence? In brief, what is their history?*
A. Srenis existed for thousands of years and many inscriptions and incidents validate this. I will go in a reverse chronological order on the evidence related to the presence of Srenis. Some of the most recent evidence of Srenis is seen in the Cholas, Pallavas and Vijayanagar empires. I will explore that in detail in subsequent chapters. The Gupta dynasty (around 240–550 CE) embraced Srenis and Sreni Dharma like few other civilizations.[2] Due to the expanding trade and technological developments during that era, there was an incentive to promote Srenis since they were instrumental in economic prosperity. There was a notable increase in the number of Srenis (150 by some counts) in this period and also in the sources of the members, which highlights the importance of Sreni Dharma in commerce and governance.

The first important evidence about the presence of Srenis is in the *Arthashastra*. Kautilya mentions the presence of Srenis and their role in trade and commerce on multiple occasions. While Kautilya was suspicious of large private entities such as Srenis, their role was critical for the cohesion of the Mauryan State. Despite tight regulation and some level of suspicion, there was an expectation 'for the monarch to apply Sreni Dharma to internal Sreni matters and encourage Srenis to be active participants in the credit markets providing loans and deposits'.[3] The presence of Srenis was seen as important for economic growth and Sreni Dharma was seen as a key foundation for that.

There have been mentions of Srenis in the *Rig Veda* and *Brihadaranyaka Upanishad*, among others. A mention in the *Brihadaranyaka Upanishad*, which was dated around 800 BCE, serves as important evidence about the presence of Srenis. Furthermore, as I show in the chapter on Saraswati–Sindhu civilization, there is evidence of both Srenis and Sreni Dharma during the period of Indus civilization. Based on the inscriptions found, we can safely say that Srenis existed much earlier than 3500 BCE. There are other ancient texts too where there is evidence of not just the presence of these guilds but their entire organizational structure as well. Figure 1.1 is an example from Brihaspathi's teachings.

FIGURE 1.1 Example from Brihaspathi's Teachings

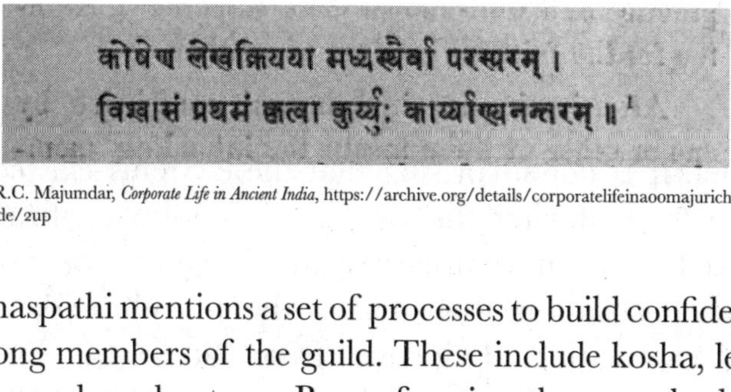

कोषेण लेखक्रियया मध्यस्थैर्वा परस्परम् ।
विश्वासं प्रथमं कृत्वा कुर्य्युः कार्य्याण्यनन्तरम् ॥ [1]

Source: R.C. Majumdar, *Corporate Life in Ancient India*, https://archive.org/details/corporatelifeinaoomajurich/page/n5/mode/2up

Brihaspathi mentions a set of processes to build confidence among members of the guild. These include kosha, leka-kriya and madyastana. By performing these methods of filtering members, it was expected that confidence among the members would be built. According to these guidelines, this sense of mutual confidence was considered to be one of the first steps in the formation of a guild. This shows a detailed structural and organizational understanding of the existence of Srenis and their sustenance. In the next few paragraphs, we will see the level of detail and sophistication in these guilds, which seem equivalent to the structures in today's developed economies.[4]

Q. *What was so special about these entities?*

A. In an era of enterprise and commerce considered primitive by present-day historians, it is interesting to learn about three very distinct features of Srenis that stand out. First, these institutions were mainly run by a group of people who were a part of the private commercial enterprise and did not belong to the monarchy or entities of the state. Given that private enterprise in itself is espoused as a modern-day concept, it is amazing to know that not only did private entities exist, they had representatives who were leading organizations that promoted the goals of private enterprise as a block, beyond the territorial boundaries as defined in those times. Second, Srenis had a very important role in enhancing, sustaining and promoting economic prosperity. Kautilya's *Arthashastra* mentions several instances of Srenis and their role in commerce. Given that Kautilya lived around the third century BCE and that Srenis seemed to have existed since many years earlier, it is not surprising that these Srenis existed in some form during the Saraswati–Sindhu civilization as well. Last, it is precisely this longevity of Srenis as an institution that makes them both endearing and captivating. Evidence from Saraswati–Sindhu civilization to Kautilya to the Common Era kingdoms, all seems to show the sustenance of the Srenis as organizational entities. The longevity of 5,000 years or more is something that very few similar systems can boast in human history.

Q. *What was the governance structure of the Srenis?*

A. The governance of the Srenis was a very important feature and is central to the theme of this book. The Srenis were governed mainly by the principles of Sreni Dharma, which consisted of broad principles which were protected and promoted by these entities and their members.

Examples of these principles include the following:

> The manager or president of a guild was called a śreṣṭhin. This position is comparable to the Chairman of Board of Directors in a modern corporation. The Indus script hieroglyph which signifies a śreṣṭhin was a squirrel. In Gupta age (second century to fifth century), śreṣṭhins, sārthavahas, prathamakulikas (head of a local guild) and prathamakāyastha (head accounts officer) figured in the town and district councils. Early Buddhist texts refer to the head of a guild as the jetthaka or pamukkha. For example, the head of garland makers was called the 'malakara jetthaka' and the head of the carpenters was the 'vaddhaki jetthaka'.[5]

These principles, based on Sreni Dharma, were used in creating the organizational structure of the Srenis. The organizational structure is shown in Figure 1.2.

FIGURE 1.2 Organizational Structure of Srenis

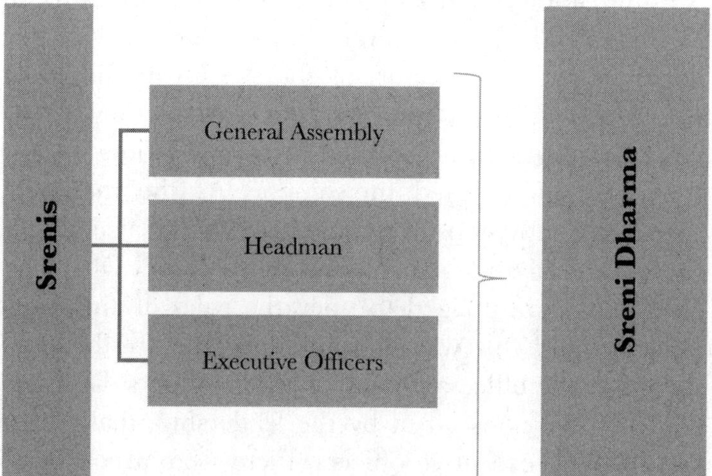

Source: Author's representation

The general assembly was considered to be the overarching organization which voted to elect the headman and executive officers through a democratic process. In some instances, there were almost a thousand people in an assembly, so it was a large, umbrella organization. The most important feature of the general assembly was that it was highly democratic. Democracy was not a post-French Revolution phenomenon but existed thousands of years earlier. The general assembly had to first come to an agreement about the principles that would govern the Sreni, that is, the Sreni Dharma. These principles had to be debated and discussed, with a consensus document presented to the monarch for a symbolic approval. This approved Sreni Dharma would often be documented as the sthitipatra[6] for general circulation (I will detail some of the contours of the Sreni Dharma in subsequent paragraphs).

Once it was approved, this Sreni Dharma served as the basis for electing people for leadership positions within the Sreni. These included the headman (śreṣṭhin) and executive officers of the guild as shown in Figure 1.2. The headman was the main authority to take decisions with the support of the executive officers for whom qualifications were prescribed, which they had to meet before they were elected to their positions. While the headman enjoyed the support of the monarch, there were provisions to remove him via the assembly if there were any major violations of the Sreni Dharma.[7] Members were obliged to obey the rules of the Sreni Dharma and this was monitored by the śreṣṭhin and the executive officers. If any of the members disagreed with the decisions taken by the leadership, that is, the śreṣṭhin and executive officers, there were a couple of ways of redressal. The member or members could go to the monarch with the necessary proof of wrong actions by the leadership or they could appeal to the general assembly itself for the removal of the concerned officers.

These aspects—structure, election of leaders, redressal mechanisms—indicate the far-sighted management style of the Srenis, which was way ahead of its time. First, the democratic nature of the entire exercise is something worth recognizing. The emphasis on the larger assembly taking key decisions through a democratic process was an impressive concept by itself in those times. Second, the emphasis on decentralization of decision making was also quite novel. While the monarch had an overarching role in terms of recommending the headman, his role in selection and deselection was fairly limited, unless there were special circumstances.

All these functions were similar to what a private sector Fortune 500 shareholder-driven company would do in today's times. Such democratically elected constitutional set of values were foundational to the governance of the Srenis.

There are many such similarities between the governance of Srenis and contemporary concepts of corporate governance. A brief comparison between Srenis and contemporary corporations, sourced from the brilliant paper by Prof. Khanna, is shown in Table 1.1.

TABLE 1.1 Srenis and Modern Systems

Characteristics Which Exist in Modern-Day Corporations	**Were present in Ancient Bharatiya Srenis?**
Separate entity	Yes
Centralized management	Yes
Transferability of interest	Probably yes
Limited liability	Probably not
Election and removal of management through a democratic process	Yes
Duty of care	Yes

Characteristics Which Exist in Modern-Day Corporations	**Were present in Ancient Bharatiya Srenis?**
Liability insulation	Yes
Ease of formation	Yes
Ease of registration with the state	Yes
Need for state approval	Yes
Ease of entry and exit	Yes for both, but with some conditions and obligations
Sharing of assets and liabilities	Yes—according to prescriptions in Sreni Dharma
Independence of the Board/Committees	Likely yes
Voting regulations	Yes
Transparency and disclosure of conflict of interest	Likely yes
Opportunity for open debate for shareholders	Yes but with certain sensible restrictions

Source: Vikramaditya Khanna, 'The Economic History of the Corporate Form in Ancient India', p. 26

In Table 1.1, we can observe the far-sighted nature of Srenis as organizations in their similarities to modern systems.

Q. *In the context of economics and finance, what were the other roles of Srenis?*

A. Srenis had a variety of roles beyond the standard one of being commercial guilds. They evolved depending on the type of political denomination in a particular state or region. Irrespective of this, one key role of the Srenis was to serve as financial institutions. There is reasonable evidence to suggest that Srenis served as commercial banks for their members and also for non-members. Kautilya's *Arthashastra* makes many observations about Srenis and one of the most interesting one is the fact that the Srenis were providing the equivalent of a letter of credit to its members.[8]

Furthermore, their reputation for being stable and honest enhanced their standing among the populace so much so that the monarch, elites and common people started depositing their money with the Srenis. They used the interest accrued from such deposits for charitable and social causes. For example, in a second-century inscription in Mathura,[9] there is a mention of two endowments, each worth 550 silver coins, with two guilds, whose interest payment was used to pay two needy Brahmins. A second-century inscription found in Nasik shows a record of 2,000 karshapanas with an interest rate of 1 per cent per month for providing clothes to bhikshus.[10] Srenis also made substantial profits, similar to how banks profit today, from the difference between the interest rate charged for loans issued by them and the interest rate they paid on deposits.

Q. *What was the level of autonomy that the Srenis had with regard to the state?*

A. The autonomy of the Srenis was a very important feature that distinguished them from other institutions. Srenis were quite autonomous, with the state having very little control over their functioning. Their regulations and operations were determined by their Sreni Dharma, which was determined by the general assembly. The general rules of law and order were applicable to them but, besides that, they were quite free to explore the opportunities available within the established norms. Instead of restrictions, Srenis and their commercial interests played an important role in the formulation of state policy. For example, as we will see in more detail in later chapters, during the Chola era, the Ainnuruvar Sreni was one of the largest and most extensive Srenis that ever existed. Ainnuruvar had extensive trading arrangements with Southeast Asian countries, including empires like Shailendras (Indonesia), Kedar (Malaysia), Kambuja (Cambodia) and Champa (Vietnam), among others. During the reign of Rajendra Chola I, there was a trading dispute with the Shailendras. This triggered Rajendra Chola I to conquer them to ensure that commercial trade continued without any hindrance to the Ainnuruvar.[11] There are many such stories which show the influence of Srenis on geographical, economic and political strategies.

Q. *Given that the Srenis existed from at least 3000* BCE *onwards, their continuity and sustenance are incredible, especially in the context of the never-ending wars and changes in rulers during this period in Bharat. What was the key to the success of the Srenis?*

A. The single biggest factor that enabled the Srenis to succeed was the umbilical cord called Sreni Dharma. There are a variety of reasons for this. First, the democratic nature of the creation of Sreni Dharma for most of the Srenis was very vital to their sustenance. The fact that the members could choose and re-evaluate the Sreni Dharma depending on the context, situation and external conditions indicates that there was a continuous assessment of its relevance. The bottom-up approach of ideating the Sreni Dharma also ensured that there was a collective ownership and commitment to the sustenance of the Sreni. Second, the institutional strength of Sreni Dharma ensured that the rulers had a certain confidence in the institution's governance principles even if they may have reservations about its role. For example, even though Kautilya had reservations about such powerful external organizations, he was shrewd enough to understand the solid foundation of the Srenis. Hence, he was open to incorporating their needs in the broader governance framework.

2

Dharmanomics

KAUTILYANOMICS FOR MODERN TIMES provides an important perspective about Kautilya's *Arthashastra* and his economic framework for Bharat. More importantly, the book also highlights the economic model that Kautilya had followed, based on the idea of Dharma, that is, Dharmic capitalism. In Figure 2.2, I illustrate the entire structure of Dharmic capitalism with a focus on ethics, responsibilities and harmony. As Kautilya mentioned, these ideas emanated much before him and he was a mere messenger in articulating some of them. In this book, we will revisit the concept of Dharmic capitalism under a broader ambit, which includes a wider definition of Dharma, a focus on the Dharmic ecosystem and also the wide set of principles of such a system. All this constitutes the broader economic philosophy called Dharmanomics which is the central theme of this book.

Dharma

Dharma is a multi-dimensional word. I will start with a very crucial shloka that defines it:

> धृतिः क्षमा दमो-अस्तेयं, शौचम् इन्द्रिय-निग्रहः ।
> धीः विद्या सत्यम् अक्रोधो दशकं धर्म-लक्षणम् ॥ मनुस्मृतिः ॥6.92॥
> dhṛtiḥ kṣamā damo-asteyaṁ śaucam indriya-nigrahaḥ |
> dhīḥ vidyā satyam akrodho daśakaṁ dharma-lakṣaṇam
> ||Manusmṛtiḥ 6.92||

The shloka says that Dharma is defined by patience; forgiveness; control over the mind; non-stealing; cleanliness of body, mind and soul; restrain of the senses; proper use of intellect; proper knowledge of God, soul and nature; honesty; and control over anger. As the phrase 'dharayate iti dharma' connotes, Dharma sustains, integrates and holds everything together. This includes activities at the individual as well as the collective (community) level that together bring prosperity to all. It encompasses the 'way of life' of Dharmic civilization and communities.

A visual representation of this explanation is shown in Figure 2.1. The figure also tries to show the role of Dharma as an instrument which looks beyond the state and market economy as explained in my book *Kautilyanomics*.

FIGURE 2.1 Dharma Explained

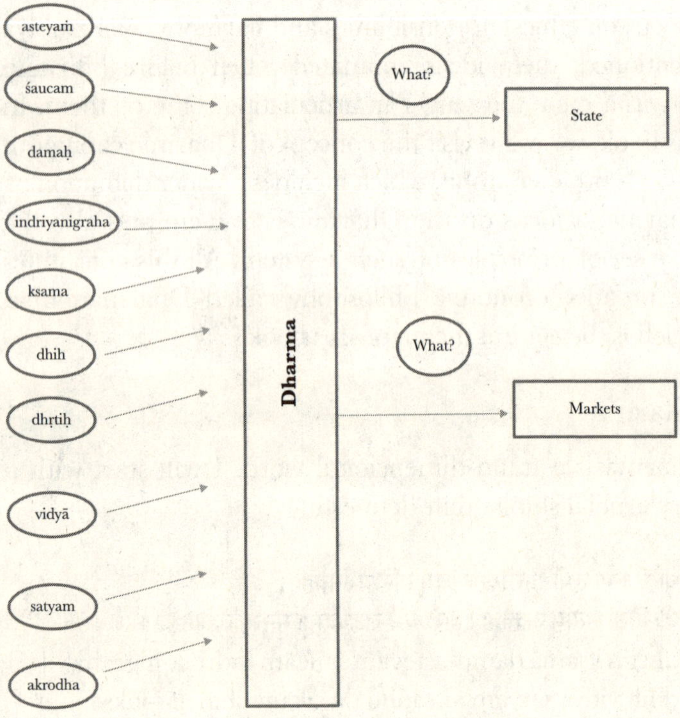

Source: Author's representation

There is a plethora of literature defining, explaining and characterizing Dharma's components, mainly in the context of the spiritual world. Even from a materialistic viewpoint, there are numerous definitions and interpretations. Yet the subject is so sacred that even for a materialistic definition, it needs someone of great stature who preaches and practises a Dharmic way of life. As my father often says, it is important for people to practise than preach on such subjects. While this is generally applicable to spirituality, I shall extend that need of having 'subject matter experts' on Dharma to economic policy discussions.

His Holiness Sri Chandrashekharendra Saraswati, known fondly as 'Maha Periava' to devotees such as I and my family, has written and spoken in many forums about Hindu Dharma. The book *Hindu Dharma*[2] which summarizes his views on a variety of issues, also shares his views related to Samanya Dharma, which has offered very useful inputs for this book. Swami Tejomayananda from the Chinmaya Mission is one of the most profound thinkers on this subject. His book *Dharma Shastras*[3] is a must-read for anyone interested in the subject. The book deals with the sheer breadth and multi-dimensional nature of the subject in a simple yet profound way.[4] I will use snippets from the chapters on Samanya Dharma in His Holiness Maha Periava's and Swami Tejomayananda's books which explain some of the words equivalent to 'Dharma' so as to present a more comprehensive picture. Table 2.1 gives a few of the explanations.

TABLE 2.1 Meaning of Dharma

Meaning of Dharma[5]	**Explanation Provided by the Books**
Dhṛtiḥ	Fortitude or steadfastness; consistently and steadily walking the noble path of Dharma so as to bring transformation in one's life.

Meaning of Dharma[5]	**Explanation Provided by the Books**
Kṣamā	Forgiveness; *ksama jnanasya bhushanam*—forgiveness is the ornament of knowledge.
Damah	Control over our senses.
Asteyaṁ	Non-stealing.
Śaucam	Inner cleanliness (antahsuddhi) and outer cleanliness (svacchata); this should involve activities which are clean both internally as well as externally. For example, if one is keeping one's neighbourhood clean, he/she should seek to also be clean internally, thus benefitting the society.
Indriya nigrahah	Control over the indiryas such as jnanendriyas and karmendriyas. They can be referred as our sense organs (eye, ears, nose, tongue, skin) and organs of action (hands, speech, excretion, reproduction), respectively.
Dhīḥ	Buddhi, that is, discriminative intellect and having viveka. Viveka refers to observing, analysing, discriminating and understanding an entity's nature in order to gain knowledge.
Vidyā	Knowledge; there are many forms of vidya including sahitya (literature), sangita (music), kala (art), vijnana (science), darsanam (philosophy), etc. Buddhi should be used to gain all this knowledge.
Satyaṁ	Speaking the truth in the right context—the act ensuring that satyam upholds, integrates and sustains the welfare of the people. सत्यं ब्रूयात् प्रियं ब्रूयान्न ब्रूयात् सत्यमप्रियम् । प्रियं च नानृतं ब्रूयादेष धर्मः सनातनः ॥ १३८ ॥ *satyaṃ brūyāt priyaṃ brūyānna brūyāt satyamapriyam* | *priyaṃ ca nānṛtaṃ brūyādeṣa dharmaḥ sanātanaḥ* || 138 || He shall say what is true, and he shall say what is agreeable; he shall not say what is true but disagreeable; nor shall he say what is agreeable but untrue; this is the eternal law. (138)[6]
Akrodha	Free of anger

Source: Kanchi H.H. Sri Chandrashekharendra Saraswati, *Hindu Dharma: The Universal Way of Life*; Swami Tejomayananda, *Dharma Shastras*

Swami Tejomayananda sums this well:

> These ten basic values represent a broad spectrum of similar noble values, like love, compassion, shradda and so on. These constitute Dharma and purify our mind. When these values are followed in our individual life, family life, in organizations and the nation, there will be structural integration and harmony.[7]

As the readers of *Kautilyanomics* would recall, from a definitional standpoint, the notion of Dharma in the book revolved mainly through the lens of ethics, responsibilities and harmony. I shall stay with that in this book as well for the sake of simplicity. However, I want to add that this was not an out-of-the-blue construct—it was a reasonably well thought out process based on the scriptural definition of Dharma. Table 2.1 (through Swamiji's insights) presents the broad definitions of the various meanings of Dharma (please do note the word 'broad' because every definition in the table can be a book in itself). Table 2.2 contains the components bucketed into ethics, responsibilities and harmony.

TABLE 2.2 Classification of the Components of Dharma

Ethics	**Responsibilities**	**Harmony**
Satyam	Dhṛtiḥ	Indriya nigrahah
Asteyaṁ	Śaucam	Akrodha
Dhīḥ	Kṣamā	Damah
Vidyā		

Source: Author's own analysis

Let me clarify the thought process that I used to classify the core tenets of Dharma into the buckets of ethics, responsibilities and harmony. I should have mentioned this in the previous book, but this is a good opportunity to highlight it. I have done this assessment and classification to make it easier for the English-educated Bharatiyas to absorb such a complex topic. There could definitely be other ways of classification which retain the essence of Dharma and I am open to feedback from readers and critics. It is important to highlight this because the reader needs to understand that my thoughts are not static—they are in a continuous state of evolution based on research and facts that keep coming up. I firmly believe that we have to reassess our views and positions based on all the new and valid ideas and propositions that are presented.

Dharmanomics

For the purpose of this book, the moot questions are—What is Dharmanomics? What are its components? How do we go about analysing Dharmanomics in this book?

For easier and simpler understanding, let us express this through Equation 1:

> Dharmanomics =f (KDC, Dharmic ecosystem, Sreni Dharma)

Dharmanomics is defined as a function of Kautilyan Dharmic Capitalism (KDC), the Dharmic ecosystem and Sreni Dharma. I will define these terms now.

Kautilyan Dharmic Capitalism

For those who are not familiar with my first book *Kautilyanomics for Modern Times*, the model representing Kautilyan Dharmic Capitalism is shown in Figure 2.2. In the model, I have condensed the definitions of Dharma to ethics, responsibilities and communal harmony. These are mapped to the broad themes of a rule-based yet non-intrusive state, wealth creation via global outlook and sustainable growth and welfare. These themes are based on clean administration, clean institutions, enforcement of rules, driver of economic growth, having a global outlook, social welfare and well-being, and ensuring sustainable growth through the prism of societal, familial and environmental responsibilities.

FIGURE 2.2 Kautilyan Dharmic Capitalism

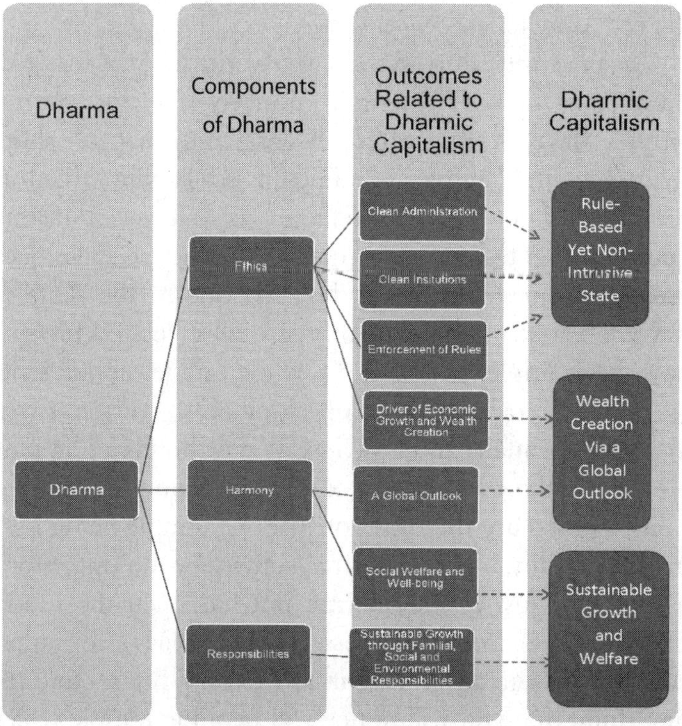

Source: Sriram Balasubramanian, *Kautilyanomics for Modern Times* (Bloomsbury, 2022)

Dharmic Ecosystem

Dharmic ecosystem is a new concept in the context of economic policy, but I believe it is a much-needed inclusion. Dharmic ecosystem primarily refers to the institutions that are created as a result of the Dharmic way of life and their effects on the socioeconomic policies of a particular geographical area. To explain this, let us take an example of a temple. The temple is perhaps the single-most important institution that has been set up to represent and enable the Dharmic way of life. Besides being a religious establishment, the temple, by its mere presence, functions as a Dharmic institution and plays a very important socioeconomic role. It serves as an important driver of economic stimulus and has also been a force multiplier for the economy for many centuries.

Consider the Ram Mandir in Ayodhya. As a result of the construction of the temple, a variety of socioeconomic entities have been created. A large number of shops related to the temple—dealing in pooja items, clothes such as traditional saris, artefacts—as well as restaurants, guest houses, transport companies and so on have been created. Tourism has been boosted due to the visits of devotees, roads and other infrastructure related projects have been implemented and a whole range of industries have benefited from these developments. We see a new airport; new malls and a variety of new hotels being built along with the construction of the Ram Mandir. All these things, which are the result of just one temple being built in the holy city, boost economic activity by multiple times. This is not just a one-off case but has been the model of economic progress across all our villages for many centuries. Go to any village in any part of Bharat and the first thing that you will notice will be a big temple which is central to that village. Much of the economic activity in the village would be an offshoot of the temple. In Tamil Nadu, where I come from, there are multiple temples in the same village, which serve as the central economic hubs for that village.

Though I will discuss this in further detail in subsequent chapters, it is important to highlight here that there is significant inscriptional evidence[8] from Thanjavur, Srirangam, Kalahasti, Tirupati and several other places to suggest that in all the Common Era kingdoms that I will discuss—from the Chola period to the Vijayanagar empire—the temple was supported significantly by the state and, as a consequence, it played a very crucial role in the economic and developmental activities of the region as a whole. Not only did the temple play the role of a religious institution, it was one of the key employers in the state besides being one of the largest drivers of economic growth of that era.[9]

I have to add here that it is amusing that economists studying Bharat have barely tried to understand the temple economy, which has been so central to economic activity in Bharat for thousands of years. Much of the informal sector, which contributes to about 70–75 per cent of the economy, is a result of the Dharmic ecosystem in some form or the other. Yet, there is negligible research on the subject. Forget understanding this, even acknowledgment of this fact comes with endless riders. However, the practical reality of economic activities is for all of us to see. Unless we study the contours of this ecosystem, it is impossible to understand or comprehend the broad operations of the Indian economy.

Hence, it is important to understand and explore this phenomenon which I call the Dharmic ecosystem. Similar to the temple, in practice, there are a variety of other activities that fall under the ambit of the Dharmic ecosystem. For this book, I will limit our discussions to the temple and its offshoots (the economic benefits that are triggered due to the functioning of the temple) as a proxy for the Dharmic ecosystem.

Sreni Dharma

As explained in the previous chapter, Sreni Dharma played a very important role in organizing, catalysing and sustaining economic activities for thousands of years. In the context of Dharmanomics, it is an important component as mentioned in Equation 1. Right from the Cholas to the Pallavas, Pandyas, Kambuja Desa and even the Champa empires, Srenis played a prominent role in ensuring economic prosperity. Besides their role as business guilds, they played a multitude of other roles including being key trade financiers and banks in most of the Common Era kingdoms that I discuss in this book.

Q. *How do we assess Dharmanomics in the various kingdoms?*
A. The primary argument of this book is that there has been an economic model for the last 5,000 years that is based on the idea of Dharma and its related ecosystems. Dharmanomics is an economic system which positions Dharma beyond the binary of the state and the market (unlike modern-day capitalism) and is growth-centric, sustainable, global and most importantly, has a 5,000-year history of successful implementation. This model is represented in different forms in different Common Era kingdoms and in this book I try to illustrate and represent it as vividly as possible. In addition, through this process, I make an attempt to pull together the commonalities of these frameworks and present their uniqueness. I also make an attempt to highlight the common inspirations for these economic models and the evidence to suggest the same.

So how does one show all this in a simple yet comprehensive manner? The best way would be to do it through the three key parameters—the KDC model, the Dharmic ecosystem and Sreni Dharma—mentioned in Equation 1 earlier. The underlying assumption here is that this model of KDC serves as a good foundation for the frameworks in the various kingdoms that I am exploring in this book. An exact replica would naturally be impossible for any two frameworks, but the commonalities in the underlying principles are what I am trying to assess here. By describing economic philosophies, economic trends or frameworks and policies in Common Era kingdoms that were similar to the KDC, I establish a qualitative congruence among these policies. This applies to the second parameter, that is, the Dharmic ecosystem as well. By highlighting examples of the presence and the importance of the Dharmic ecosystem to the economy of the Common Era kingdoms, I hope to add another dimension to the Dharmanomics story. Similarly, I will explore the presence of Srenis and Sreni Dharma in the case studies of the Common Era kingdoms.

In the subsequent chapters, I will also focus on the Saraswati–Sindhu civilization, the Cholas, other kingdoms in the South including Pallavas, Pandyas and Vijayanagar, Kambuja Desa and other Southeast Asian kingdoms, such as Champa and Java. In the first half, the focus will be on the similarities with the KDC model and its principles. In the second half, for the Southeast Asian kingdoms, I will focus more on the Dharmic ecosystem and its centrality to their economic models. The method for all this is purely evidence based. The evidence and inscriptions available, especially for the Southeast Asian kingdoms: in much more detail clearly illustrate the Dharmic ecosystem, so I will use that as the focus in those chapters. The KDC model is mentioned in these chapters as well, but its emphasis is lower. The idea is to provide a holistic picture of Dharmanomics in these kingdoms and showcase their various gradations within the broader Dharmic umbrella.

3

Saraswati–Sindhu Civilization

THE CONTOURS OF DHARMANOMICS have been changing continuously, over many centuries. While most of this book provides a sequel to *Kautilyanomics for Modern Times*, that is, the shape of the economy in civilizations after Kautilya's time, there is considerable evidence to suggest that many of these systems existed before Kautilya. It is in this context that we focus on the Saraswati–Sindhu civilization and try to decipher the key economic models and principles based on Dharma that existed then.

The scholarly interpretations of the Indus seals include those by the late Iravathan Mahadevan[1], along with the likes of A. Parpola and others, which tilt towards Dravidian linkages to the scripts. Some others have identified the seals to be mainly tags and labels for identification purposes. Individuals like Prof. B.V. Subbarayappa have suggested that they could be merely of numerical values.[2] Prof. D.P. Sharma's recent presentations[3] illustrate the artistic elements of the S–S civilization along with its connections to the Dharma–dhamma traditions based on the works of Prof. Shinde and Prof. Wills. Prof. Mayank Vahia suggested recently that none of these could be validated by syntactic analysis including our interpretations.[4] Prof. Kalyanraman's work alludes to the Bharatiya principle

---

This chapter is co-authored with Prof. S. Kalyanaraman and is a part of a working paper series on the topic.

of *anvaya* and suggests that it is complete with graphemes of text scripts and field symbols. He also argues that the syntax-based approach is irrelevant in a wealth or accounting ledger system. All these represent a plethora of views on this subject.

This chapter is based on Prof. Kalyanraman's extensive work on interpreting the Indus seals for 30 years and more—I am not a subject matter expert on this yet and hold no pretence otherwise. Prof. Kalyanraman's lifelong work leads to the conclusion that the seals represent an accounting control system for maritime trade which was a precursor to Kautilya's *Arthashastra*. Each grapheme (each Indus script) represents a word from ancient Bharat in the context of the Sreni maritime trade. This accounting, financial and economic ecosystem has been continuing in various forms for centuries since then. While we don't get into the details of interpretations in this chapter and have only made references to the overarching philosophical, socioeconomic projections that seem logical and backed by evidence, we acknowledge that there could be other interpretations—which are a work-in-progress—of the seals. We respect all the other research material on the subject—this chapter is our perspective of the subject given the evidence available at the moment.

We will first have a quick overview of the Saraswati–Sindhu civilization, the centrality of Sreni Dharma to the economic activities at that time, its impact on trade routes and maritime trade, the idea of industrialization at scale taking roots in those times—thousands of years before the Anglo-Saxons—and the role of financial institutions. The sustainability and the presence of Dharma will be the connecting thread for all these pillars of economic activity.

Introduction of Saraswati–Sindhu Civilization

The Saraswati–Sindhu civilization has been one of the oldest recorded civilizations. Ancient Hindu texts such as the Rig Veda mention about this civilization in great detail and recent archaeological excavations have also authenticated this. This civilization dated back to at least circa fifth millennium BCE. The Harappan civilization is also believed to have been on the banks of the holy river Saraswati. The Indus–Saraswati civilization flourished circa 2500 to 1700 BCE on the river valleys of Indus and Saraswati. The drying up of the Saraswati River led to the migration of people living there.[5]

This civilization was formed in the backdrop of the world's largest mountain range called the Himalayas, millions of years ago. As mentioned here:[6]

> The Hindu Kush Himalayan (HKH) region extends 3,500 km over all or part of eight countries from Afghanistan in the west to Myanmar in the east, affecting air and water circulation systems, and impacting the weather conditions in the region. Today it is the source of ten large Asian river systems—the Amu Darya, Indus, Ganges, Brahmaputra (Yarlung Tsangpo), Irrawaddy, Salween (Nu), Mekong (Lancang), Yangtse (Jinsha), Yellow River (Huanghe), and Tarim (Dayan). Drawing warm air from the south, which cooled and precipitated as torrential rainfall, the Himalayas created the monsoons and a fertile area in the Northwest that may well be 'the land of seven rivers' described in the Vedas.

Over the years, these communities from the Hindu Kush Himalayan area settled in the fertile plains and valleys and developed an ecosystem which was far advanced for those times. It included developing new industries and skills such as pottery, metallurgy and agriculture, among others. They also developed some of the most profound and detailed town planning systems that humanity has seen in that era. This made them one of the greatest civilizations in the ancient world, with an estimated population of 5 million people.

This civilization is known as the Indus Valley civilization, that is, the Saraswati–Sindhu (S–S) civilization since it flourished in the basin of the Indus River and the erstwhile Saraswati River (Ghaggar–Hakra River) which flowed through Northwest Bharat. This is also referred to as the Harappan civilization and the dating of its origins is a work-in-progress. While it is considered to have flourished around 3500 BCE, some recent carbon dating attempts date the Harappan civilization to almost 7000 BCE,[7] much earlier than the previous estimates. Figure 3.1 depicts the geographical stretch of this civilization.

FIGURE 3.1 Saraswati–Sindhu Civilization

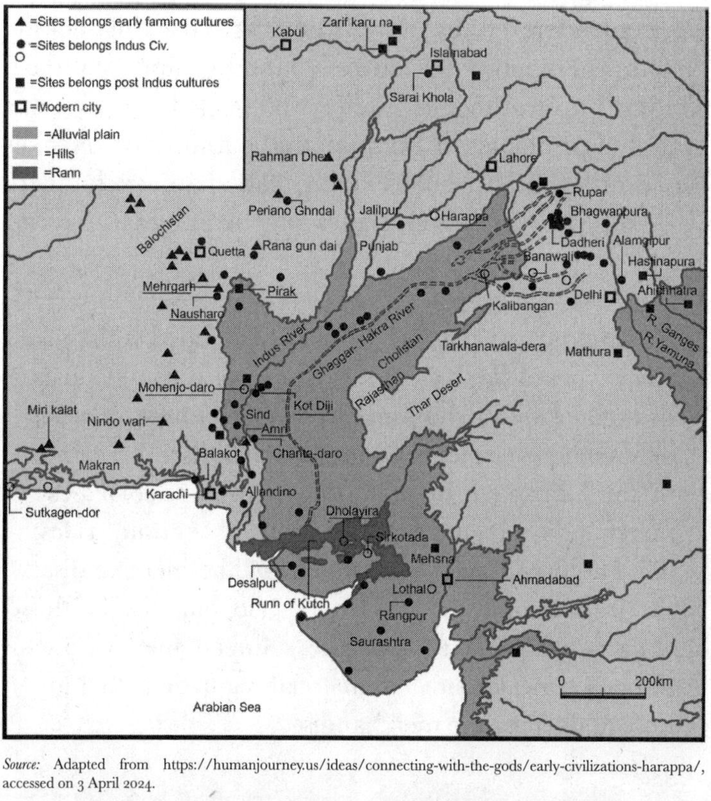

Source: Adapted from https://humanjourney.us/ideas/connecting-with-the-gods/early-civilizations-harappa/, accessed on 3 April 2024.

The people of the S–S civilization had a wide range of trading and commercial engagements with Iran, Central Asia and the rest of the world. They exported gold, timber, iron, tin and a variety of other products to Mesopotamia and other countries. They were also masters of urban and rural town planning, which involved sophisticated drainage systems. They were considered to have the world's best technology for ship building, sailing and transportation. There have been several archaeological finds of products from the S–S civilization including the recent (2023) finds in Ganweriwala and Mohenjo-daro (in Pakistan) and of course, the Rakhigarhi findings located in Haryana, near New Delhi.[8] In addition to their expertise in commerce and product manufacturing, they also had several scientific achievements to their credit. They were considered to be one of the first to use the decimal system, geometry for town planning and standard weights for trading of their products. Their systems included principles of taxation and a multitude of taxes for commodities that were being traded and exchanged. For example, a research paper on the subject in *Nature* says:

> Commodity packages are generally stamped with only a few types of information: (i) Names of the individuals or organizations who were the manufacturers, owners, or intended recipients of the merchandise; (ii) Names of the individuals or organizations who endorsed the merchandise regarding fulfilment of certain rules; (iii) The origin and destination(s) of the merchandise; (iv) Information about the type and quantity of the commodity packed inside the stamped merchandise package; (v) Types of commercial regulations that are duly fulfilled by the merchandise.[9]

In addition, research also affirms that Indus seals were used as revenue-stamps and as licences issued to tax collectors or merchants. They also represented the licence fee/slabs through their reverse numerical metrological expressions. Most of all, the civilization provided us with the Indus script which is one of the most marvellous scripts that the world has ever produced.[10]

The S–S civilization was not only a divine-oriented civilization, given its geographical borders aligned to the Himalayan belt and its mention in the holy Rig Veda, but also a civilization which was far ahead of its time in terms of technology, urban and rural town management, maritime and overland trade of a variety of products, manufacturing, industrialization, international gold standard, corporate guild management, technology and science.

In the following chapters, I hope to showcase some of these economic achievements in the context of the S–S civilization and propose a new theory on the role of Dharma in being the foundation and a catalytic force behind the prosperity that was present in the S–S civilization thousands of years ago.

Centrality of Dharma in the Prosperity of the S–S Civilization

Given the prosperity of the S–S civilization, it is obvious for us to ask the basic question—What led to these levels of unprecedented prosperity in ancient times? The complexity of the structures and the scalability of the civilization tends to indicate that there was a detailed thought process to this progress rather than an abstract, out-of-the-blue or fortuitous development. This was obviously a calibrated and well-thought-out economic model that had its foundations in the idea of Dharma. This is highlighted through two important economic vehicles of that time—Sreni (श्रेणि:), the principles of Sreni Dharma which we will illustrate further in this section and the concept of balutēdāra (बलुतेदार) which we will be highlighting in further sections.

Economic activities in the S–S times were mainly of three types—trade, agriculture and state-driven activities. Trade was a very important pillar of the economy and was mainly driven by corporate guilds called Srenis.

> न त्वं प्रकृतयः सर्वः श्रेणिमुख्यश्च भूषितः
> *Na tvāṃ prakṛtayaḥ sarvāḥ śreṇīmukhyāśca bhūṣitāḥ*
> (Rām.2.26.14; Ms.8.41; Bhāg.2.8.18)

The guild in ancient Bharat was not merely the means for the development of arts and crafts. Through autonomy and freedom accorded to it by the law of the land, it became a centre of strength and abode of liberal culture and progress, which truly made it a power and ornament of the society.[11]

There were many similar groupings, such as gana, pani, puga, vrata, samgha and nigama, which were businesses or communities. These were mainly controlled by non-state actors, that is, people who were not officers or a part of the administration but were those who were involved in the commercial trading activities—merchants, traders and businessmen of all kinds. All these activities were people-to-people and independent of the state. We will detail all this in further chapters in the context of the S–S civilization.

Srenis in Saraswati–Sindhu Civilization

We dealt with the basics of Srenis in the previous chapter. It is important to highlight the evidence of Srenis thriving even during the S–S civilization for two reasons. First, it will establish the longevity of the Sreni as an economic and financial institution. Second, it will establish a level of continuity in economic parameters and policies from the time of the S–S civilization to thousands of years later.

In Figure 3.2,[12] we see the Indus script of a steersman in a chart of the bell smelter and the in-charge of a warehouse of a smithy forge equipment. The manufacture of the bangles and the maritime guard seal is evident on the pot for the bangles. The manufacture of these bangles was coordinated and orchestrated by a Sreni whose functioning was by Dharma Saṁjñā. These industrial scale bronze age activities had thirty-two artificers segregated by professional expertise within a Sreni. These badges were worn by members or merchants of that particular Sreni. The thirty-two Dharma Saṁjñās are mentioned in the box titled 'Dharma Saṁjñā'.

FIGURE 3.2 Indus Script of a Steersman

Source: S. Kalyanaraman, 'Stoneware Bangles Are Assigned Responsibilities in Sreni Guild, Corporate Form,' June 2023, https://www.academia.edu/102787853

Dharma Saṁjñā

'Dharma Saṁjñā, Badges of Responsibility'—Artificers of Śreṇiḥ[13]

1. Head of a guild working with gold beads, ingots, implements, iron (metalwork) warehouse (m2078)
2. dul koḍ karṇaka 'metal casting workshop accounting scribe'; this is a shell bangle (m1647)
3. kancu 'bell-metal' (ingot-maker) (m1646)
4. crucible steel button (m1645)
5. dul khaṇḍa kamari 'metalcasting implements maker blacksmith' (m1642)
6. koṟu 'sprout' rebus koṟu 'bar of metal' kolimi 'smithy, forge' (m1641)
7. Alloymetal implements (maker) blacksmith workshop, head of guild (m1639)
8. kuṭila kamari kāmathā 'Bronze workshop warehouse, mint working of blacksmith' (m1638)
9. kancu koḍ 'bell-metal workshop' (m1637)
10. koṭhārī m. 'storekeeper', (Gujarati. Bhojpuri) kuṭhiyārī (Hindi), kamari khaṇḍa implements (maker) blacksmith (m1635, m1636)
11. dul mẽṛhẽt khaṇḍa 'cast iron implements furnace'—blacksmith working with cast iron implements furnace (m1633)
12. karṇika 'helmsman' cargo of: ayas 'alloymetal', ṭaṁka 'stamped-coin', karaḍā करडा 'bar-form arrangement' (m1632)
13. koṭhārī m. 'storekeeper' (Gujarati, Bhojpuri) kuṭhiyārī (Hindi) (m2079)
14. dul 'metal casting' khār खार् 'blacksmith' karaṇī 'supercargo, scribe' कर्णिक 'steersman' helmsman (Balakot-6)
15. Wealth, possessions ledger of tin, alloymetal, metalcasting blacksmith (m1629)

16. khātī 'wheelwright' (working with) dhăvaḍ 'smelter', muhãbhaṭa 'ingot furnace' (m1659)
17. goṭā 'gold-braid' khaṇḍa 'implements' karaṇī 'accounting, scribe, supercargo' (m1631)
18. Working of blacksmith, mineral ore iron smelter, karaṇī 'scribe, supercargo' (m1630)
19. iron ingot furnace (smelter), metals manufactory (m2080)
20. khār खार् 'blacksmith' (m1628)
21. śrēṣṭhin khār 'blacksmith guild-master' (m1634)
22. dhatu mūhā mẽṛhẽt 'mineral iron ore smelting' khār खार् 'blacksmith' (m1648, m1643)
23. crucible button ingot smith (m1644)
24. khār खार् 'blacksmith' (m2081, m2082)
25. Metalcasting blacksmith (m2083, m2084, m2085)
26. Brazier. katthīl 'bronze (8 parts copper and 2 parts tin)' + dhātu 'mineral' (h2574)
27. Copper, metal ingot maker (h2575)
28. Mineral, stones, gem-setter (h2576)
29. Metalswork with tryambaka 'three coppers' (h98-3516/8667-01)
30. Metalcasting, metal infusion worker (h1008)
31. Warehouse-keeper (h1009)
32. ṭhākur 'blacksmith' + kod 'workshop' + mũhã' bun-ingot' (h1010)

These Dharma Saṁjñās illustrate the level of detail that the guilds had for the activities and responsibilities of their members. Given that this was for very specialized activities dealing with metal manufacturing, it is noteworthy that the nomenclature and contours of Dharma were enshrined in the psyche of ancient Bharat. This also shows that the underpinning of Dharma were central to economic activities in ancient times.

Other Frameworks Inspired by Srenis

The role of Dharma was further reinforced in subsequent and customized frameworks across ancient Bharat. The principles of Dharma were reflected in socioeconomic models and organizational entities in kingdoms after the Saraswati–Sindhu period and continued to kingdoms after 1 CE as well. An example of this was balutēdāra, which I detail next for further understanding.

The system of बलुतेदार (balutēdāra) is considered 'a remarkable egalitarian, equitable sociocultural system, unparalleled in civilizational history, respecting the dignity of work and professions in society'.[14] It provided a profound process for sharing of janapadas wealth among the masses with predominant roots in contemporary Maharashtra. Figure 3.3 contains an Indus inscription highlighting a balutēdāra. This system and its components are shown in this quotation:

> बलुतें balutēṃ refers to a share of the corn and garden-produce assigned for the subsistence of the twelve public servants of a village.... A share of the dues of the hereditary officers of a village, such as पाटील, कुळकरणी &c...[was specified]. A public servant of a village [was] entitled to बलुतें. There are twelve distinct [public servants] from the regular Government officers पाटील, कुळकरणी &c.; viz. सुतार, लोहार, महार, मांग (These four constitute पहिली or थोरली कास or वळ the first division. Of three of them each is entitled to चार पाचुंदे, twenty bundles of Holcus or the thrashed corn, and the महार to आठ पाचुंदे); कुंभार, चाम्हार, परीट, न्हावी constitute दुसरी or मधली कास or वळ, and are entitled, each, to तीन पाचुंदे; भट, मुलाणा, गुरव, कोळी form तिसरी or धाकटी कास or वळ, and have, each, दोन पाचुंदे. Likewise there are twelve अलुते or supernumerary public claimants, viz. तेली, तांबोळी, साळी, माळी, जंगम, कळवांत, डवऱ्या, ठाकर, घडशी, तराळ,

सोनार, चौगुला. Of these the allowance of corn is not settled. The learner must be prepared to meet with other enumerations of the बलुतेदार (e.g. पाटील, कुळ- करणी, चौधरी, पोतदार, देशपांड्या, न्हावी, परीट, गुरव, सुतार, कुंभार, वेसकर, जोशी; also सुतार, लोहार, चाम्हार, कुंभार as constituting the first-class and claiming the largest division of बलुतें; next न्हावी, परीट, कोळी, गुरव as constituting the middle class and claiming a subdivision of बलुतें; lastly, भट, मुलाणा, सोनार, मांग; and, in the Konkaṇ, yet another list); and with other accounts of the assignments of corn; for this and many similar matters, originally determined diversely, have undergone the usual influence of time, place, and ignorance. Of the बलुतेदार in the Indápúr pergunnah the list and description stands thus: First class, सुतार, लोहार, चाम्हार, महार; Second, परीट, कुंभार, न्हावी, मांग; Third, सोनार, मुलाणा, गुरव, जोशी, कोळी, रामोशी; in all fourteen, but in no one village are the whole fourteen to be found or traced. In the Panḍharpúr districts the order is: पहिली or थोरली वळ (1st class); महार, सुतार, लोहार, चाम्हार, दुसरी or मधली वळ (2nd class); परीट, कुंभार, न्हावी, मांग, तिसरी or धाकटी वळ (3rd class); कुळकरणी, जोशी, गुरव, पोतदार; twelve बलुते and of अलुते there are eighteen. According to Grant Duff, the बलतेदार are सुतार, लोहार, चाम्हार, मांग, कुंभार, न्हावी, परीट, गुरव, जोशी, भाट, मुलाणा; and the अलुते are सोनार, जंगम, शिंपी, कोळी, तराळ or वेसकर, माळी, डवऱ्यागोसावी, घडशी, रामोशी, तेली, तांबोळी, गोंधळी. In many villages of Northern Dakhaṇ the महार receives the बलुतें of the first, second, and third classes; and, consequently, besides the महार, there are but nine बलुतेदार. The following are the only अलुतेदार or नारू now to be found; सोनार, मांग, शिंपी, भट गोंधळी, कोर-गू, कोतवाल, तराळ, but of the अलुतेदार & बलुतेदार there is much confused intermixture, the अलुतेदार of one district being the बलुतेदार of another, and vice versa. (The word कास used above, in पहिली कास, मध्यम

कास, तिसरी कास requires explanation. It means Udder; and, as the बलुतेदार are, in the phraseology of endearment or fondling, termed वासरें (calves), their allotments or divisions are figured by successive bodies of calves drawing at the कास or under of the गांव under the figure of a गाय or cow.[15]

FIGURE 3.3 Indus Inscription Highlighting a Balutēdāra

Source: https://www.academia.edu/104986216

Through these examples, we have shown instances of the Sreni and Sreni Dharma's role in enabling economic progress in the S–S civilization. Given the timeframe of ancient Bharat, it definitely gives us an idea of the role of Sreni Dharma in economic policy and trade.

Maritime Trade and Commerce

International trade has been a very common feature among the ancient communities of Bharat. Trade and commerce were an important component of the economic model in ancient times. In the previous section, we looked at the role of Dharma and its centrality in the economy in ancient times. In this section, we deal with how some of these pillars of Dharma and its contours were connected with maritime trade.

There is considerable evidence to suggest the presence of maritime trade during that period. Many scholars (e.g., Sanjeev Sanyal[16]) have written about this and the Indus script evidence. We need to identify three elements to further bolster the presence of maritime trade and commerce in those times:

1. Evidence of institutions, components and operational elements of maritime trade
2. Evidence of materials that were traded and trade routes used during those times
3. Evidence of institutional linkages, that is, Srenis, to trade and its occurrence

1. Evidence of institutions and operational elements of maritime trade

Figure 3.4 contains an Indus script graphic and provides evidence of a maritime treasury guard and the guild metal used in cargo.

FIGURE 3.4 Indus Script Graphic

Maritime Treasury Guard, guild metal implements cargo, Mohenjo-daro pectoral m1656

lo 'overflow' *kaṇḍa* 'pot' Rebus: लोखंड *lōkhaṇḍa* 'metal implements, metalware'

ṭaṁka, ṭaṅga 'thigh' Rebus: *ṭaṅka* 'mint, stamped coin'

kanṭāḷa 'double-bag' Rebus: *kāṭhāḷ* 'maritime' कण्ठाल 'boat'

पाठ *pāṭha, peṭā* 'back, belly'

Rebus: *phaḍā, paṭṭaḍe* 'metals manufactory'

mlekh-mukha 'goat-face' Rebus: *mleccha-mukha* 'copper'

kār 'ear' Rebus: *khār* 'blacksmith'

singhin 'forward-thrusting, spiny-horned' + खोंड *khōṇḍa* 'young bull'

Rebus: *singi* 'ornament gold' + कोंड *kōṇḍa* 'circular hamlet, मौजा or guild'

māñjhī 'centre, middle' rebus: *mañji* Cargo boat with a raised platform' *vartaka* 'duck' Rebus: *vartaka* 'merchant'

सांगड *sāṅgaḍa* 'a body formed of two or more parts' Rebus 1: જંગડિયો *jangaḍiyo* 'military guard who accompanies treasure into the treasury'

ചങ്ങാതംപcaṅṅātam čaṇṇāδam (Tdbh.; സംഘാതം) 1. Convoy, guard; responsible Nāyar guide through foreign territories. ച. പോരുകപto accompany as such. ച. പോന്നപ വാരിയർ, എന്നെപച'വുംപ കൂട്ടിപഅയച്ചുപRebus 2: *sanghāṭa, jangada, jaṅgala* 'maritime double-canoe, cargo boat, catamaran'

kanṭhāla 'churning vessel' Rebus: : *kāṭhāḷ* 'maritime' *kunda* 'lathe' *kundan* 'fine-gold, Kubera's treasure'

Source: https://www.academia.edu/104986216

The Indus script in Figure 3.4 tells us about the presence of a maritime treasury guard who accompanies the treasure into the treasury through a cargo boat or catamaran. These facts indicate the existence of institutional stakeholders—maritime treasure guards, cargo boats for trade, armaments—who were taking part in the maritime trade process.

2. Evidence of materials that were traded and trade routes used during those times

There were a plethora of goods that were traded during the S–S civilization. An example of an assortment of goods is shown in Figure 3.5.[17]

FIGURE 3.5 A Cache of Beads of Various Raw Materials Being Traded

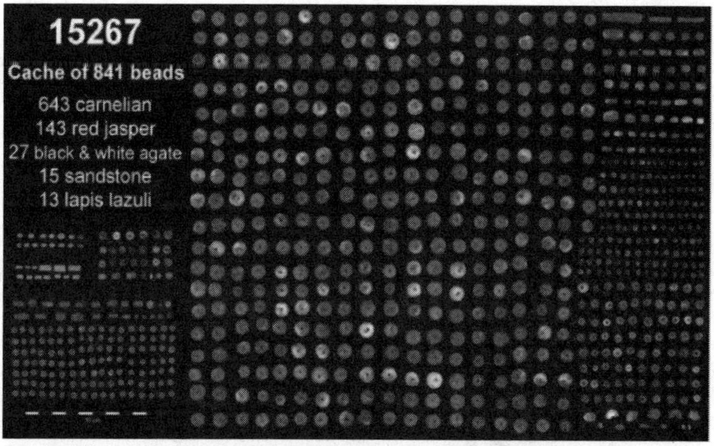

Source: https://www.academia.edu/82503984/Bharata_maritime_trade

These metals are examples of products that were traded through the S–S channel. Trade was not restricted to the borders of Bharat. It has been established that many global traders were using this route and trading with S–S. An example of this is the connection between the S–S and Israel and the trade linkages which were established during those times. This has been indicated in the Indus script examples found in Mohenjo-daro, as shown in Figure 3.6.

FIGURE 3.6 Global Trade Linkages

Source: S. Kalyanaraman, 'Contributions of Sarasvati Civilization to Tin-Bronze Revolution of 3rd millennium BCE,' https://www.academia.edu/37367694

Here is a quotation which adds to Prof. Kalyanaraman's pictorial evidence:

> The fact that a Mohenjo-daro prism tablet shows, on one side, a boat carrying oxide ingots, establishes the Meluhha-Cypriot link. The administrative unit in Cyprus transacting seafaring trade in copper and tin ingots may have acted as intermediaries for trade from Meluhha or community of Meluhha traders settled in Cyprus handling imports from Meluhha. Meluhha had received the tin (cassiterite) from the largest tin belt of the globe in Ancient Far East in the basins of Himalayan rivers, Irrawaddy-Salween, Mekong River Basins which had accumulated cassiterite as placer deposits after grinding down granite rocks of the river basins. Secondly it is probable that both metals necessary in the making or bronze were distributed by an administrative complex centred in Cyprus. Although the source of the tin is unknown, it passed through Cyprus where it received the markings, which are also found on copper ingots of LBA date.[18]

3. Evidence of institutional linkages, that is, linkage of Srenis to trade and its occurrence

We have discussed in the previous chapter about Srenis and their extensive survival as an institution for thousands of years. We have also dealt with Srenis in the S–S civilization. This establishes the importance of Srenis to trade and its existence in the S–S era.

Industrialization

The advent of industrialization in Bharat was not a British phenomenon of the 1800s but was evident thousands of years earlier during the S–S era. It is natural for one to ask this question—If there was trade based on the routes and the Sreni Dharma as mentioned earlier, what were the industrial products that were traded? How were they manufactured and on what scale?

Manufacturing was an important component of the economy in those times. While the scale and size of modern-day industries is much larger, there is considerable evidence to suggest that the idea of manufacturing and industrial activity at scale was present during the S–S times. This is corroborated by the evidence of many Indus scripts and their interpretations. The urban centres of the S–S carried many industrial activities with the major industries being textiles, construction and pottery making. There were also centres which specialized in a particular artifact. For example, Nagwada in Gujarat was known for jewellery production and Kuntasi for bead making. Bead making required techniques of sawing, flaking, grinding and boring, all of which are not easy to perform. The fact that such manufacturing processes existed in those times in such an organized manner is in itself very impressive.

Metal Manufacturing

There were metal manufacturing workshops in the S–S era. Indus scripts show evidences of metal casting mints and metal manufacturing workshops as shown in Figure 3.7.

FIGURE 3.7 Metal Manufacturing

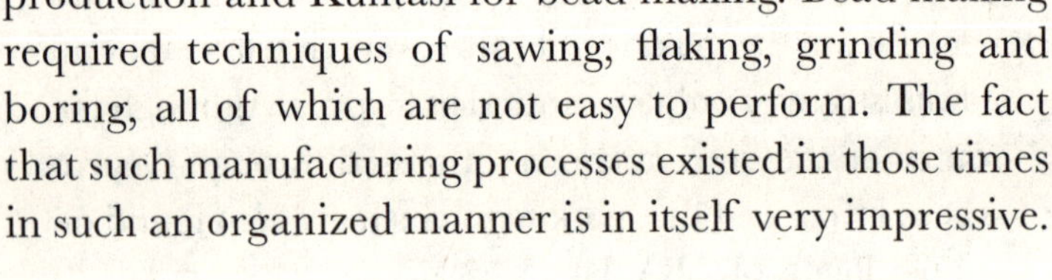

Sign 267. *kanac* 'corner' rebus: *kancu* 'bell-metal' PLUS Sign 99. sal 'splinter' rebus: sal 'workshop'. Thus, bell-metal workshop.

Sign 59. *ayo* 'fish' rebus: *aya* 'iron' *ayas* 'alloy metal' (RV)

Source: https://www.academia.edu/43438213

There are about thirty-one inscriptions that showcase that kara was the revenue shared by the Srenis in a common treasury of फड (phaḍa) in Meluhha vocable: *Ta.* paṭṭaṭai, paṭṭaṟai anvil, smithy, forge. *Ka.* paṭṭaḍe, paṭṭaḍi anvil, workshop. *Te.* paṭṭika, paṭṭeḍa anvil; paṭṭaḍa workshop (DEDR 3865). Thus फड (phaḍa) signifies metals manufacturing in a metals manufacturing plant which consisted of many types of artificers including smiths and other types such as ornament and refined gold jewellery. Such metal factories used a variety of metals including iron. Figure 3.8 shows an example of an Indus script which clearly indicates the deposit of iron in this metal workshop.

FIGURE 3.8 Indus Script Indicating Deposit of Iron

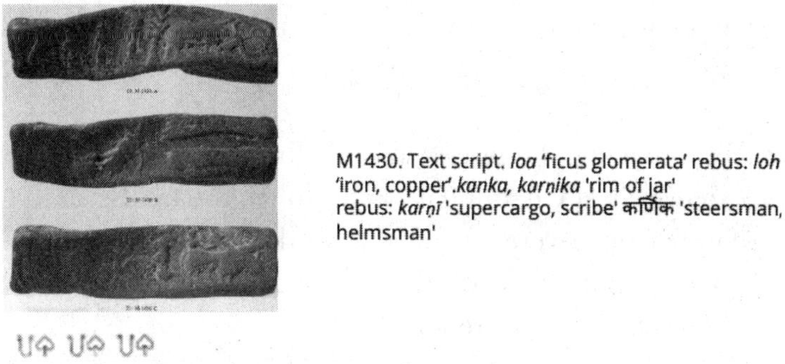

Source: https://www.academia.edu/102731194

Iron deposits have also been found in many other excavations related to the S–S era. For example, in this discovery from the Chanhudaro (Figure 3.9)—considered to be the manufacturing capital in the S–S era—excavation, we can see the 'snarling iron' which is dated somewhere around the S–S era.

FIGURE 3.9 Snarling Iron

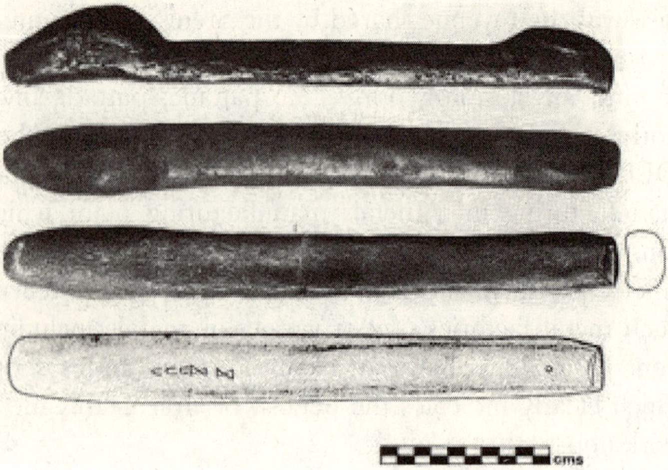

Source: https://www.academia.edu/43438213

Another secondary source to cross-verify some of this is a quotation:

> For building houses, baked bricks were used extensively at Chanhudaro and Mohenjo-daro. Several constructions were identified as workshops or industrial quarters and some of the buildings of Chanhudaro might have been warehouses.[19]

Metals were also used by common folks for a variety of activities. As shown in Figure 3.10, priests used a variety of metal equipment to perform their yagnas on a grand scale. Figure 3.11 depicts a wide range of common utensils which were made of metal in various shapes including cylindrical and rectangular shapes.

FIGURE 3.10 Examples of Metal Use

Figure 6.8 Vase from Bactria with men dressed as the Seated Man (L.950) and possibly the Priest-King (after Ardeleanu-Jansen 1991)

FIGURE 3.11 Common Utensils

Source: https://www.academia.edu/101263226

This is an important observation related to the scalability of such production units—since common people were using these metal products for their daily activities, it would mean that there would have been a metal industry which had to supply different kinds of metal products in large numbers.

Tin Manufacturing

Tin manufacturing was also quite prominent during that time. There is considerable evidence to suggest that it was done on a large scale at multiple locations within the S–S belt. There were many traders who traded tin, bronze, iron and other metals. Excavations in Mesopotamia have discovered that the tin came from the Far East and from the S–S area.[20] This research has helped us to conclude that the trading routes from the Far East (Hanoi in contemporary Vietnam) went all the way to Haifa in Israel. To highlight the extent of possible tin manufacturing, the quote from Prof. Kalyanraman's paper mentioned earlier would suffice:

> While speculations have been on the sources of tin, now Indus Script evidences that the source for the tin is the Ancient Far East, Himalayan river basins of Mekong, Irrawaddy and Salween rivers. These river basins constitute the largest tin belt of the globe. Geological studies have proved that the cassiterite (tin mineral ore) have been created and accumulated as placer deposits because the three great Himalayan rivers—Mekong, Irrawaddy, Salween—traversed through regions with granites which have been ground down by the incessant flows of the perennial glacier-fed rivers to create the cassiterite (tin ore) deposits of the Ancient Far East. This tin resource from the largest tin belt of the globe, powered the Tin Bronze Revolution

> from 4th millennium BCE through the interventions of seafaring merchants and metalworkers of Ancient Far East and Ancient India (Meluhha) who delivered pure tin ingots to the regions in Ancient Near East. This is evidenced by the discovery of tin ingots inscribed with Indus Script, from Haifa shipwreck of ca. 2nd millennium BCE. The Indus Script writing system was also used in the Ancient Far East on Dong Son/Karen Bronze drum tympanums and bronze bodies of drums which evidence Indus Script hieroglyphs/hypertexts.[21]

Based on the interpretations of Indus scripts, this shows that not only was tin manufacturing thriving in the S–S region, but also that it was an integral part of an ancient trading network that spanned from the Far East to Israel. This also indicates the presence of tin manufacturing facilities and their scalability, given its trading potential across many countries.

International Gold Standard

The gold standard is a monetary system in which the standard economic unit of account is based on a fixed quantity of gold. While being largely abandoned during the Great Depression, it was reintroduced post the Second World War and was considered to be the pillar of the international monetary system.[22] In 1971, the US government moved away from the convertibility of the US dollar into gold. The gold standard was inspired by many historical precedents in the Anglo-Saxon world. However, there is evidence to suggest that thousands of years prior to this, in the S–S civilization, the roots of the international gold standard existed. Besides the role of Dharma in enabling commerce, maritime trade and industrialization, this was an important component of the S–S economy, which we will show in the subsequent examples of Indus scripts and Tamil inscriptions.

Six-Angled Grapheme Coins

Coins were used widely in ancient Bharat. There were many facets of these coins, which were used as barter for commercial transactions in trade, both internally and externally. An example of this were the punch marked coins (PMC) that have been found with Indus script, as shown in Figure 3.12.

FIGURE 3.12 Punch Marked Coins

Source: S. Kalyanaraman, 'Bronze-Age Financial System, Indus Script Corpora', https://www.academia.edu/101263226

These five PMCs signify mint work with iron, molten cast copper, iron implements, ingots and furnace work. They include six-angled (षट्-कोण) grapheme (वज्र) coins whose numerous variants, belonging to the S–S period and beyond, have been found across Bharat. An example of the variations is shown in Figure 3.13.

FIGURE 3.13 Six-Angled Grapheme Coins

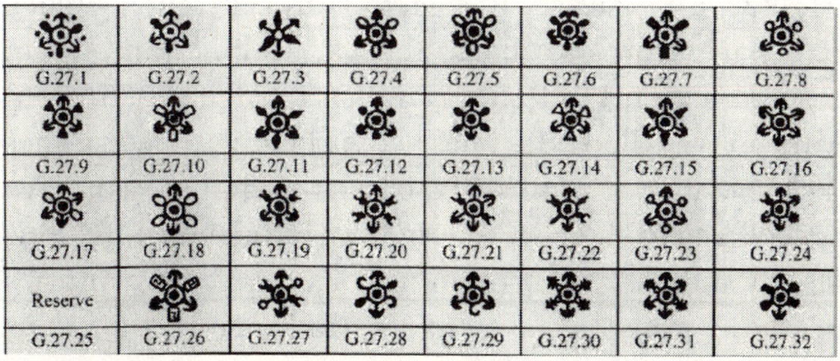

Source: S. Kalyanaraman, 'Roots of International Gold Standard, 2nd m. BCE,' 2023, https://www.academia.edu/100830813

Interestingly enough, these variants can be mapped across various parts of Bharat based on their usage.

FIGURE 3.14 Six-Angled Coins Locations

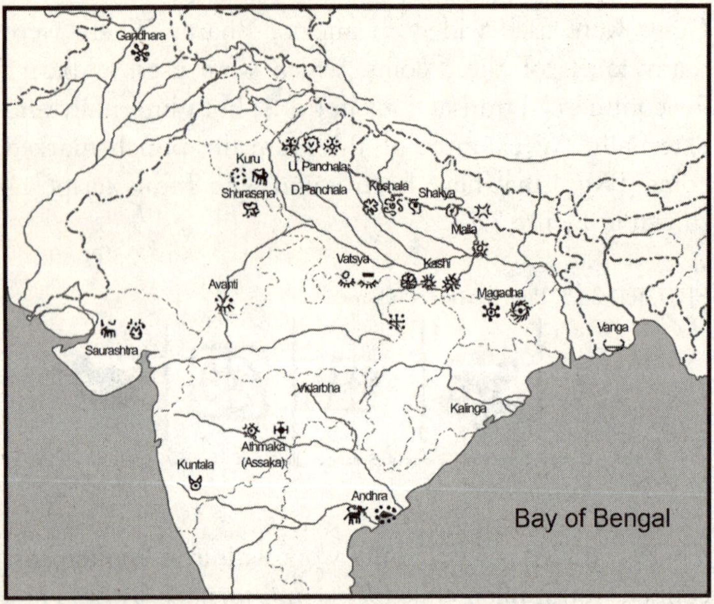

Source: Adapted from S. Kalyanaraman, 'Roots of International Gold Standard, 2nd m. BCE', 2023

As seen in Figure 3.14, different forms of the six-angled grapheme coins have been found in contemporary Gujarat (Saurashtra), Karnataka (Kuntala and Ashmaka), Andhra, Avanti and Vanya (in current Madhya Pradesh), Magada (in current Bihar), Panchala, Kuru, Koshala, Shakya, Mala, Krathi (all in current Uttar Pradesh), Gandhara (Afghanistan) and Vanga (West Bengal). These coins belong to later times (usage evidence from 600–500 BCE to 300 CE) but have precedents in the S–S six-angled grapheme coins. This clearly indicates the continuity of usage over centuries of these coins as payment for trade, given that their source existed in the S–S period.

Varaha and the Possible Inspiration for the Gold Standard

An important extension of the six-angled coins was the symbolism associated with Varaha, which has been the embodiment of wealth in ancient Bharat. The following Tamizh quotation is an example:

> வராகன்[1] வராகரூபியான திருமால். (பிங்.)
> மூன்றரர ரூபாய் மதிப்புள்ளதும் பன்றிமுத்திரர ககாண்
> டதுமான ஒரு வரகப் கபான்நாணயம். (அரு. நி.)
> வராகன் , விராகன்
> *1. varākan̲, n. Varāha. Viṣṇu, in His boar-incarnation;*
> *2. Pagoda, a gold coin = 3½ rupees, as bearing the image of a boar;*
> *3. a gold-coin with the figure of a boar, a pagoda worth 3½ rupees (Fabricius)*
> புள்ளிவராகன் *puḷḷi-varākan̲, n. id. +. Star Pagoda = 3½ rupees;* மூன்றரரரூபாமதிப்புள்ளகபான்னாணயவரக.[23]

The Tamizh inscriptions show that Varaha was also used as a barter in trade extensively in the southern parts of Bharat. Besides the religious connotations of Varaha, that is, Varaha Roopam as the consort of Lord Vishnu, its materialistic connotations resembled that of a symbolic standard for financial transactions akin to the gold standard. This was used in practice as गद्याण (gadyāṇa) which had several variations similar to the six-angled grapheme coins. These included other nomenclatures and variations such as bhairava-gadyāṇa, lokki-gadyāṇa, aṅka-gadyāṇa, gāva-gadyāṇa, komarina-gadyāṇa, priyaśrāha-gaja-malla-gadyāṇa, ambili-gadyāṇa, jagadalaṃ -gadyāṇa and so on.[24] These are further corroborated by the pictorial evidence as shown in Figure 3.15.

FIGURE 3.15 Calling Card of a Goldsmith

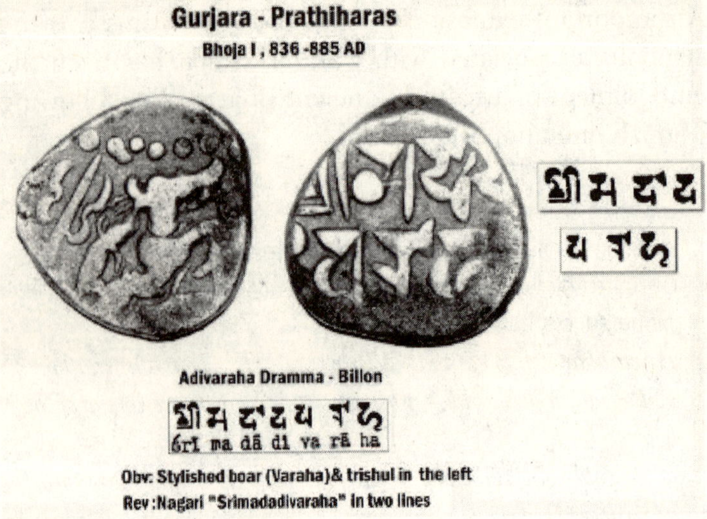

Source: https://www.academia.edu/100830813

Figure 3.15 shows a professional calling card of a goldsmith during the Gurjara–Pratihara dynasty. It gives the Varaha inscriptions in the coins as a matter of identification. There is a stylized boar (Varaha) and a trishul on the left and the Srinandiavaraha on the right in two lines. This clearly shows that there was a substantial usage of metal coins—so much so as to have a goldsmith making such a pictorial calling card indicating his or her expertise. It also shows that the Varaha symbol was used for prominent trade transactions in the period related to the calling card (836–885 CE). This also illustrates the continuity of the usage of the Varaha symbol for commercial transactions given that the date range on this calling card is thousands of years from the Tamizh inscriptions.

All these—the six-angled grapheme coins and the Varaha coins—represent several trends. First, they clearly show that these coins were used for transactions across different parts of Bharat and not just restricted to the S–S region. Second, the existence of these coins, which were used for transactions, also implies that the Dharma-based Srenis as well as trade and movement of manufactured goods were a pan-Bharat phenomena during and after the S–S period. Last, despite the subtle variations in the design of these coins, there is a common presence of the six-angled grapheme or the Varaha symbol across the coins found in various parts of contemporary Bharat. This could not have happened without a coordinated monetary model where people had a common understanding of the value of these coins. In simple terms, the commonality of currency that we attribute today could have been replicated, in those days, as a commonality of a base coin (such as the six-angled grapheme) for financial transactions. This could be the modern-day equivalent of a common currency benchmark such as the gold standard that has been used in trade and financial transactions.

Dharmanomics Tantra

In this chapter, so far we have looked at the essence of the S–S civilization—its history and its glorious developmental zeal, the role of Sreni Dharma in promoting economic prosperity, maritime trade and industrialization during that era and the role of the international gold standard.

The roles of both Sreni Dharma and KDC were evident in the discussions. We saw that Sreni Dharma was quite active during the S–S period, especially with the examples of Dharma Saṁjñā and बलुतेदार (balutēdāra), which showed the well-established principles of Sreni Dharma in the S–S period. This was instrumental in the functioning of the Srenis, who were the key drivers of economic growth since they were catalysing trade, manufacturing and, to an extent, agricultural exports and imports as well. To that extent, it is reasonable to conclude that Sreni Dharma was an important part of the economic systems of the S–S period.

As far as the KDC is concerned, obviously there are no inscriptional evidence or references to it since the S–S era was far earlier than the Kautilyan era. In fact, there is a distinct possibility that Kautilya himself could have learnt from the S–S era about economic systems! There are many principles which were common between the KDC and the S–S era. Similar to the KDC, in the S–S era, there was a big emphasis on trade and engagement with the rest of the world on commerce—the presence of an international dollar-type currency is an example—and production of goods and services were reasonably common as shown by tin and iron manufacturing. Sustainable growth was also mentioned in the S–S era, similar to the KDC. However, the role of the state, its institutions and the ethical discourse thus far around their functioning are things that we do not see in the S–S era. This could be mainly because the evidence has not been uncovered yet since the events took place thousands of years ago, prior to even Kautilya. Given that S–S had such detailed drainage systems and governance mechanisms to facilitate them, there had to be a governance system to run the economy, too.

All this shows that there was significant prosperity during the S–S period, and the principles behind Dharmanomics played an integral part in this economic prosperity.

Dharmanomics in the Chola Period

The next chapter in this book deals with the Cholas, but we want to provide some context on the possible continuity that existed from the S–S age to the Cholas and other Southern Bharatiya kingdoms as well.[25] While there have been many debates on the origins of Bharatiyas, there are some key economic traits that are common and visible from the S–S era to the Common Era kingdoms in southern Bharat.

First, the manufacturing ability of Bharatiyas is exemplified by the concept of simhanika—an artificer who manufactures rice, oil and other such items—which is mentioned by Kautilya in the *Arthashastra*[26] and is also seen in the Indus inscriptions of the S–S civilization. Remnants of some of this expertise of artificers can be seen in recent discoveries in Telangana.[27] This is in addition to the tin trade, which we mentioned earlier, which spanned from Bharat to Israel. The tin trade via the Mekong delta was one of the defining moments of metal alloy (bronze) revolution as well. All these broadly indicate the continuity of the expertise in the industrial complex domain, starting with the bronze–tin revolution during the S–S period and its continuation until much later times.

Second, in terms of textiles, there was a reasonable amount of continuity of techniques and skills. For example, the textiles produced in the Gujarat and Maharashtra regions find resonance in the Batik tradition of Indonesia. Similarly, the silk-weaving expertise of Kashi continues till today in the silk-weaving traditions of Kanchipuram in southern Bharat.

Third, the continuity also is seen from a civilizational standpoint. For example, there is a reference to पांड्या (pāṇḍyā) in Indus inscriptions which has been correlated with members of *vēḷir* in Sangam literature poems.[28] Besides, there were alloy-metal artisans who moved from the S–S civilization to continue their craft in Swamimalai, which was the presiding deity of Eraka Subrahmanya. Here 'Eraka' refers to metal infusion or metal cast method to make bronze and panchaloha (or panchadhatu), that is, five metals of divine idols.

Last, we had mentioned many of the S–S ideas which find resonance in Common Era kingdoms and even in today's times. Examples include the Srenis, coinage and the gold standard, among others. Another example of this is the concept of 'jangada', which was a principle of trade transactions during the S–S time, based on invoicing of trade transactions on a prior approval basis. This concept continues till date in Bharat as evidenced by a more contemporaneous judgment of the Bombay High Court.[29]

Thus, the civilizational continuity from the S–S civilization to the Common Era kingdoms seems to be a natural phenomenon. While I have been fairly brief in this book, it is important to be aware of these elements as I discuss the Cholas and the others in the rest of this book.

4

Cholas

THE CHOLAS[1] WERE ONE of the most successful empires that Bharat has ever seen. Their reign extended from southern Bharat all the way to north Bharat and extended to Southeast Asia via alliances with empires in contemporary Indonesia, Cambodia, Thailand and Vietnam, among others. In this chapter, we will explore the history of the Chola empire, its economic framework and the role of Dharmanomics.

> The Yeuch-chi opened up the commerce between India and the Roman Empire. Here, as in Central Asia, the trade had been merely incidental and subject to depredations of numerous savage tribes. The existence of a unified power in Indus Valley and Afghanistan made possible regular trade from the Ganges to Euphrates. The rapid growth of such trade was indicated by coinage of Yueh-chi kings in India ... In Southern India, where there was an active Roman maritime trade, there was no native gold coinage, the Roman being sufficient.
>
> — *Periplus of the Erythrean Sea,* first century CE[2]

History of the Chola Kingdom

Before I delve into the history of the Chola empire, it is important to understand the chronology of the Tamizh kingdoms in southern Bharat in the Common Era. This is important for a variety of reasons. First, it shows that the vast empires that existed before and after the Cholas were equally prosperous and had a vision to promote trade and prosperity in the region. Second, given that most of these kingdoms propagated and practised Dharmic values, it shows the continuity of the Dharmic ethos in the economic construct of these kingdoms. Irrespective of who ruled the land, the emphasis on Dharmic ideals and the necessity to promote commerce and prosperity were a few constants all through the period. It is also important to note that these kingdoms were constantly at war with either each other or with other kingdoms, yet the importance of Dharmic values and the continuity of the economic growth and prosperity were not inhibited by any means. The Dharmic values were concurrent and continuous because the rulers and, more importantly, the people had faith in them. Thus, there was an amazing continuity of these value systems for hundreds of years at a stretch. Table 4.1 contains the chronology of the Tamizh kingdoms in the common era.[3]

TABLE 4.1 Chronology of the Tamizh Kingdoms in the Common Era

Era (CE)	**Rulers**	**Key Characteristics**
50–300	Sangam age, which was ruled mainly by Chola, Chera and Pandya kings with very little dominance by any side.	Part of the famed Sangam age which gave birth to great literature and also had substantial maritime trade with Romans and the rest of the world.
300–550	An interim period where there is a lack of historical clarity on who ruled during this time.	Key phase when master literary works such as *Silapadikaram*, *Manimekalai* and *Thirukkural* were believed to have been written.

Era (CE)	**Rulers**	**Key Characteristics**
550–900	Rise of the Pallava kings, who had their capital at Kanchipuram, and also the rise of the Pandya kings with Madurai as their capital.	Revival of Hindus through the Bhakti movement after the rise of Buddhism and Jainism during the earlier period. This was also a period when there was a simultaneous rise of Hindu kingdoms in Southeast Asia including Kambuja (Cambodia), Champa (Vietnam), Srivijaya (Indonesia) and Kedar (Malaysia).
900–1279	Age of the Cholas with the rise of Parantaka followed by Sundara Chola, Rajaraja I, Rajendra I, Kulottunga I, Vikrama Chola and Kulottunga II. Figure 4.1 gives the names of the kings with the dates of their reign.	One of the most prosperous periods of Tamizh and Bharatiya history. Large temples, massive trade infrastructure and a thriving maritime trade was established during this period. The reign of the Cholas extended all the way to the north of the Vindhyas and included all the southern states and also Southeast Asia.

Any discussion of the Tamizh kingdoms in the common era would not be complete if we do not look at the reign of the Cholas in depth. Figure 4.1 shows the Chola dynasty with the rulers and their respective close families.

FIGURE 4.1 The Chola Dynasty

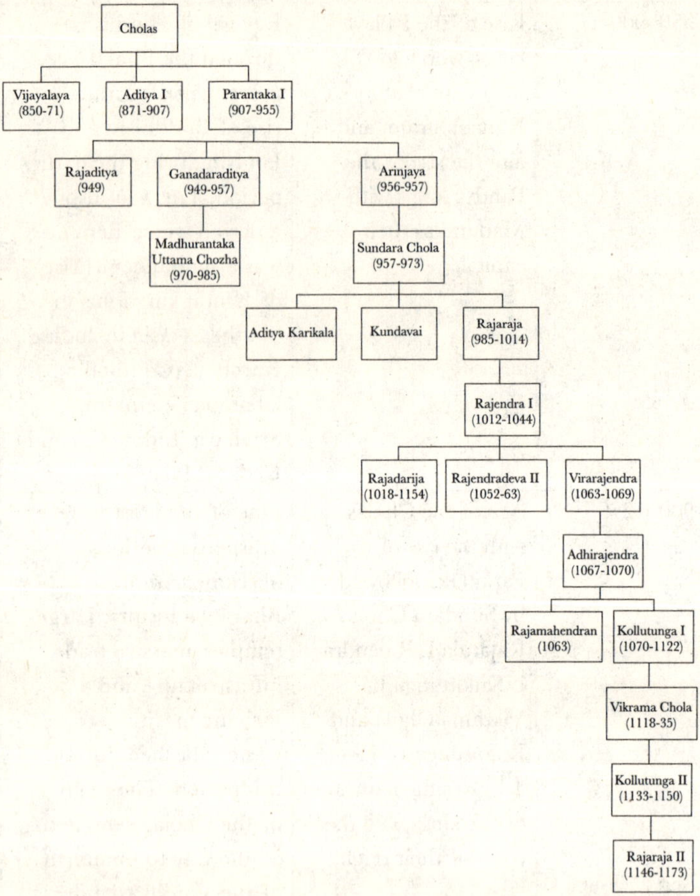

Source: Author's analysis

Table 4.2 gives a summary of all the Chola rulers from 848 to 1279 and their major contributions.

TABLE 4.2 Chola Rulers and Their Major Contributions

Chola King	**Era (CE)**	**Contribution**
Vijayalaya Chola	848–891	He was known by the title of 'Parakesarivarman' and was the founder of the post-Pallava Chola empire. Among his accomplishments were building the Choleeswaram temple in Pudukkottai.

Chola King	**Era (CE)**	**Contribution**
Aditya I	870–907	He was the son of Vijayalaya—popularly known by the surname 'Kodandarama'—who extended the Chola territories by the conquest of the Pallavas and occupied the Western Ganga Kingdom. He was known to have built 108 temples for Shiva along the banks of the Kaveri.
Parantaka Chola I	907–950	He was known by the title of 'Maduraiyum Elamum Konda Parakesarivarman', meaning 'Parakesarivarman who conquered Madurai and Sri Lanka'. Many contemporary tales and folklore mention his name and attribute increasing political success to him.
Gandaraditya Chola	950–957	A king who was known to be involved in building and contributing to temples and was known as 'Merkey elundarulina devar'—the 'king who was pleased to go west'.
Arinjaya Chola	956–957	Arinjaya had various pseudonyms such as 'Arikulakesari' and 'Arikersari' and his rule is subject to further research due to a lack of substantial evidence on how his reign was.
Sundara Chola	957–970	He was known through the famous novel and movie *Ponniyin Selvan*, in popular parlance, he was also known as 'Madurantaka Sundara Chola' and 'Parantaka Chola II'. Various literary feats in Samskritam and Tamizh literature were initiated during his reign.
Uttama Chola	970–985	He was an important character in the novel *Ponniyin Selvan* and also in real life. He was the son of the illustrious Sembiyan Mahadevi.
Rajaraja Chola I	985–1014	He was perhaps the most famous king in Tamizh history and was considered to be one of the most illustrious rulers of the land. His legacy still stands tall with the Brihadisvara Temple in Thanjavur which is one of the largest Hindu temples. Besides his military powers which led to international victories, he also promoted literature with the Tamil poets Appar, Sambandar and Sundarar which were collected and made into one compilation called *Thirumurai*.

Chola King	Era (CE)	Contribution
Rajendra Chola I*	1012–1044	He was the son of the illustrious Rajaraja, and took forward his father's legacy manyfold. Not only did he conquer Southeast Asia, he also went till the north of the Vindhyas and built a new capital city in Tanjore called 'Gangaikonda Cholapuram' to commemorate his victory after defeating Mahipala, the Pala king of Bengal and Bihar. Besides his conquests in Southeast Asia, he also built a 16 mile long and 3 mile wide artificial lake which was one of the largest man-made lakes in India.
Rajadhiraja Chola	1044–1054	He was known as 'Vijaya Rajendra Chola' and ensured continuity of territorial influence of the Cholas in Sri Lanka, Vengi and Kalinga among others.
Rajendra Chola II	1054–1063	He played a central role in the battle of Koppam which was a pivotal war for the Cholas.
Virarajendra Chola	1063–1070	The younger brother of Rajendra Chola II and was a patron of many Tamizh literature, arts and culture during his reign.
Athirajendra Chola	1070–1070	A lot of anxiety and unrest was seen during his rule.
Kulothunga Chola I	1070–1122	Another prominent king whom we will discuss later in the book. His name means 'exalter of his race' and he was established lordship over Kedah (in Malaysia) during his reign.
Vikrama Chola	1118–1135	He was called 'Tyagasamudra', and was a great patron of the Chidambaram temple.
Kulothunga Chola II	1133–1150	He was known for his good governance and his ability to maintain peace and tranquillity during his rule.
Rajaraja Chola II	1146–1173	He started the construction of the renowned Airavateswarar Temple at Darasuram near Kumbakonam. He built the prowess of the Chola navy from east to west of the coastline.
Rajadhiraja Chola II	1166–1178	His reign was considered to be the time which saw the evolution of local chieftains to significant power brokers in the reign.

Chola King	Era (CE)	Contribution
Kulothunga Chola III	1178–1218	He gained great victories in wars against the Hoysalas, Pandyas of Madurai, Cheras of Venad, the Sinhala kings of Eelam (Ceylon), as well as the Chodas of Velanadu and Nellore. He commissioned the Sarabeswara temple at Thirubuvanam near Kumbakonam, and also built the mukha-mandapa of Sabhapati, the gopura of Goddess Girindraja (Sivakami) and the verandah around the enclosure (prakara harmya) in the Siva temple at Chidambaram.
Rajaraja Chola III	1216–1256	During his rule, the Cholas lost most of the control of their territories south of the river Kaveri. Their hold on the Vengi territories in the north started slipping with the emergence of the Hoysala power.
Rajendra Chola III	1246–1279	During his reign of the Chola empire, the Pandyas destroyed the fort and the outer wall of the temple at Gangaikonda Cholapuram.

Source: 'Chola Dynasty', https://www.jagranjosh.com/general-knowledge/list-of-chola-ruler-and-their-contributions-1508933575-1

*The reign of Rajendra Chola has always fascinated people because of the vast areas that he conquered. I have illustrated those areas through a picture and the explanation of the map in Figure 4.2.

FIGURE 4.2 Naval Expeditions of the Cholas

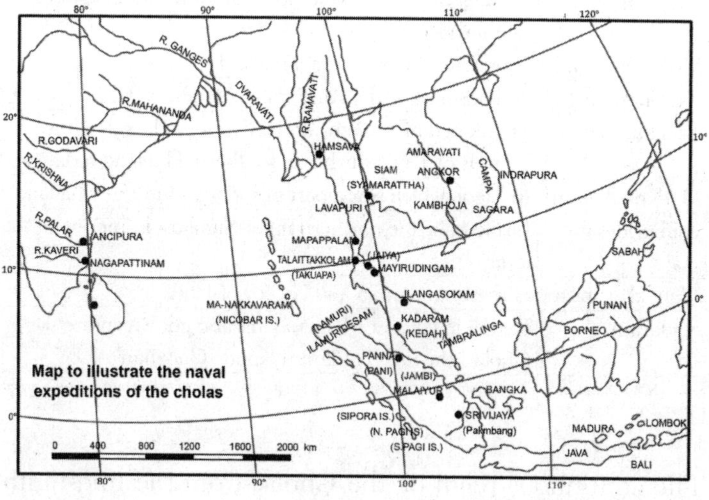

Source: Adapted from 'Lord of the Ocean', https://porridgemagazine.com/2022/05/21/lord-of-the-ocean-aneeta-sundararaj/

While the Cholas conquered several Southeast Asian countries, there is little evidence to suggest that they ruled these places themselves. Most of the conquests were a result of the activities of the commercial Srenis and the need to ensure that there was smooth trade in the continent. In some cases, the conquests were in defence of the allies of the Cholas in the region. The main purpose of the alliances they forged was to encourage trade and commerce. We will look at some of the finer details of these expeditions in a later chapter. Meanwhile, the places that Rajendra Chola conquered as per the inscriptions are mentioned in Table 4.3.

TABLE 4.3 Conquests of Rajendra Chola

Places	**Comments**
Srivijaya	Pelambang
Pannai	On the east coast of Sumatra (Indonesia), facing Malacca in current Malaysia
Malaiyur	Jambi, which was called Malaiyur in the seventh century
Mayirudingam	A part of current Malaysia
Ilangsogam	Langasuka kingdom, which was a Hindu–Buddhist kingdom and was in control of parts of current Malaysia
Mappaplam	Considered to be the city of Papphalama mentioned in the *Mahvamsa*; thought to be in the Talaing region of southern Myanmar
Mevilimbangam	Somewhere in southern Thailand
Vallaipanduru	Perhaps part of the Panduranga empire in Champa
Talaittakolam	Mentioned by Ptolemy and is considered to be at the isthmus of Kra, which is in southern Thailand today
Madamalingam	In Ligor, which was a part of today's southern Thailand
Ilaimuridesam	Likely to be the northern tip of Sumatra in Indonesia today
Manakkavaram	Current Andaman and Nicobar Islands
Kadaram	Kedah in current Malaysia; this also got Rajendra Chola I the title 'Kadaram Konda Chozhan'

Source: N.P. Chakravarti, ed., *Epigraphia Indica*, vol. 22, 1933, p. 146, https://archive.org/details/in.ernet.dli.2015.69621/page/n195/mode/2up

The continuous reign of the Cholas from the mid-ninth century to almost the end of the thirteenth century is shown in Table 4.2 through the rulers and their achievements. It is important to acknowledge the continuous dominance of the Cholas for such a long time and not just their huge achievements in terms of trade, economy and the vast regions that they conquered. The amazing continuity was not an accident. It was the consequence of a carefully integrated ecosystem that ensured such a continuous rule, with a high degree of prosperity. We will see in the subsequent sections how the economic policies, principles and prosperity were at the centre of this continuity.

Economy During the Chola Era

As mentioned, the Cholas dominated southern Bharat from the mid-ninth century until about the end of the thirteenth century, though their origins date much earlier. The most dominant phase of the Cholas was during the reigns of Rajaraja Chola and Rajendra Chola. The world renowned Brihadisvara temple was among the many marvellous structures built during this period. Naturally, such a dominant and multi-continent encompassing regime would have an economic model that would be responsible for the prosperity of the kingdom. There are three important components of the economics of the Cholas—underpinning of Dharma as a philosophical and socioeconomic construct, presence of Srenis, and the vast maritime trade networks which were anchored by the first two components. We will discuss each of these in this chapter.

Dharma as a Philosophical and Socioeconomic Construct

The Bedikhal inscription says that Dharma of the Veera Valanja (who pursued Dharma, artha and kaama by the sale and purchase of articles and whose sole delight was the distribution of goods to the needy), were lords of Ayyavole (identified with Aihole). It mentions other information similar to the Kamudi inscription.

Contours of Economic Trade

There was an all-encompassing Dharmic philosophical foundation on which economic activity was based during the Chola era. While agriculture played an important role in economic activities, the novelty that the Cholas brought in was the emphasis on maritime trade, like no other earlier kingdom. The scale, complexity and the organizational depth of the trade associated with Cholas is fascinating, to say the least. We will look at some of these elements, beginning with the organizational structure of trade during the Chola era.

There was a well-organized relationship between the key stakeholders—local communities producing goods including the Srenis, artisans in the hinterland and the trading centres on the coasts. The seamless interaction between these key stakeholders through organizational entities such as the nagaram, naadu and pattinam were vital for the successful trade ventures of the Cholas.

FIGURE 4.3 Components of the Chola Economic Model

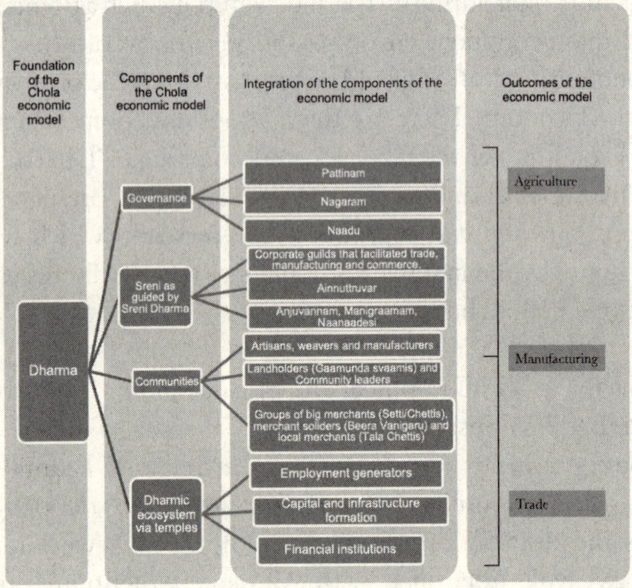

Source: Author's analysis

As shown in Figure 4.3, the principle of Dharma was foundational to the three components of the Chola economic model. These components were governance, Srenis and the communities. Governance was further sub-divided into the concept of pattinam (coastal towns), nagaram (inland towns) and naadu (a state in today's parlance). The Srenis were further divided into corporate guilds that facilitated trade, manufacturing and commerce that included Ainnuruvar, Anjuvannam, Manigraamam and Naanaadesi. Communities were further sub-divided into artisans, weavers and manufacturers, landholders, community leaders and groups of big merchants, merchant soldiers and local merchants. During the Chola regime, all these were integrated into a seamless system to ensure that trade and commerce worked smoothly and flourished.

Governance

The success of the civic administration and governance of the Chola empire was an important reason as to why it was so successful economically. Before we venture into the contours of economic administration, let us understand the broader governance mechanisms of the Cholas.

Uthiramerur Inscriptions

A very important and substantive evidence of the governance system is found in the famous inscriptions in the Vaikunta Perumal temple in Uthiramerur village near Kanchipuram.[4] These inscriptions serve as an important reminder of how advanced the governance was during the Chola period. Even though most of these inscriptions are about political governance, they help us understand some of the underlying thematic nuances of the governance model of the Cholas.

These inscriptions cover the reign of Parantaka Chola I, who ruled during 907–956, that is, a few decades before Rajaraja Chola's reign. These inscriptions refer to the twelfth and fourteenth year of his reign and are in Tamizh grantha, which is mostly about events around the tenth century. These inscriptions provide a vivid picture of the political governance at the village level with the mahasabhas and sabhas—large and small gatherings in villages, respectively—being central to the governance. There are also minute details about a constitution of sorts which included electoral systems (also called the Kudavolai electoral systems)[5] including description of wards, qualifications of candidates, constitution of committees with elected members and so on.[6]

In addition, these inscriptions also indicate a well thought out process and structure for a Dharma-based governance model at the village level. They also give detailed minutes of what had transpired. For example, let us look at this quotation from an inscription:

> சோழ நாட்டுப்புறங் கரம்பை நாட்டு ஸ்ரீ வாங்க நகரக்கரஞ் செய்கை கெண்ட யக்ரமவித்த பட்டனாகிய சோமாசி பெருமாள்

This quotation says that the general assembly met in Purangarambainadu of the Chola country in the august presence of Karanjai Kondaya Kramavitha Bhattan alias Somasiperumal of Srivanga nagar. The location, people and the members of the assembly have all been mentioned in the inscriptions.

There were also references to the method of conducting elections, eligibility of candidates, committees of elected candidates and their terms and also the implementation of rules so that candidates do not game the system. The inscriptions indicate that each village was segmented into kudumbu (குடும்பு) or wards and each of these wards had a single representative in the general assembly. There were thirty wards in the Uthiramerur Chaturvedimanaglam, that is, Uthiramerur village. People from each of these wards would choose a particular person from their ward to represent them through a 'pot-ticket' (குடவோலை) system. There were criteria that candidates had to meet to be eligible to run for representatives of these wards. An example of this is shown below in Table 4.4 for reference. Only a few examples of the criteria are mentioned here and not the complete list as found in the inscriptions.

TABLE 4.4 Criteria for Candidates[7]

Criteria for Eligibility	**Criteria for Disqualification**
Candidate should be above 35 years of age and below 70 years (எழுபது பிராயத்தின் கீழ் முப்பத்தைந்து பிராயத்தின் மேற்[illegible]ார்)	Candidate who has been a part of the committees for the last three years and has not submitted his or his relatives' accounts appropriately (மூவாட்டினிப்புறம் வாரியஞ் செய்து கணக்குக் காட்டாதே இருந்தாரையும்)
Candidate should have expertise in the business/qualifications to run a business and be known for their virtuous deeds (அவர்களிலும் கார்யத்தில் நிபுணராய் ஆகாரமு டையாரானாரை யேய் கொள்வதாகவும்)	Candidate who has stolen or taken away things inappropriately from others (பரத்ரவியம் அபகரித் தானையும்)
Candidate should have purity, i.e., honesty in economic dealings/earnings and a pure soul/mind (அர்த்த சௌசமும் ஆன்ம சௌசமும் உடையாராய்)	Candidate who is considered to be impulsive/rash (சாகசிய ராயிரைப்பாரையும்)
Candidate should own a house which is built legally (தன் மனையிலே அகம் மடெுத்தக் கொண்டிரப்பானை)	Candidate whose relatives (ranging from close to distant) have been defaulters or have violated the law in some form or the other

Source: N. Karashima, Y. Subbarayalu and P. Shanmugam, 'Nagaram during the Chola and Pandyan Period: Commerce and Towns in the Tamil Country A.D. 850–1350', *Indian Historical Review*, 35 (1) 2008, p. 1–33, https://journals.sagepub.com/action/showCitFormats?doi=10.1177%2F037698360803500101&mobileUi=0,

Similar to the selection criteria for candidates, there is also evidence regarding the mode of elections that were conducted in the villages. A sample summary is shown in Table 4.5, with the original Tamizh verses for reference.

TABLE 4.5 Modes of Elections

Inscriptions in Tamizh	**English Translation (not verbatim)**
ஆகா இச்சுட்டப்பட்ட இத்தனைவரையும் நீக்கி; இம்முப்பது குடும்பிலும் குடவோலைக்குப் பேர் தீட்டி	The names will be written for pot-tickets in the thirty wards, with the applicable exclusions.
இபன்னிரண்டு சேரியிலுமாக இக்குடும்பும் வெவ்வேறே வாயோலை பூட்டி முப்பது குடும்பும் வெவ்வேறே கட்டிக்குடம் புக இடுவதாகவும்	In the twelve streets of Uthiramerur, each of the wards shall prepare a ticket for the ward separately. All these tickets will be placed in a pot.
குடவோலை பறிக்கும் போது மகா சபைத் திருவடியாரை சபால விருத்தம் நிரம்பக் கூட்டிக் கொண்டு	During the process of drawing pot-tickets, a complete Mahasabha (Great Assembly) meeting needs to be convened with people of all eligible age groups being asked to attend.
அன்றுள்ளீரில் இருந்த நம்பிமார் ஒருவரையும் ஒழியாமே மகா சபையிலேரும் மண்டகத்தி லேயிருத்திக் கொண்டு	On that day, all the Nambinars (temple priests), without excluding anyone, should be asked to be seated in the inner hall of the Mahasabha.
அந்நம்பிமார் நடுவே அக்குடத்தை நம்பிமாரில் வருத்தராய் இருப்பா ரொரு நம்பி மேல் நோக்கி எல்லா ஜனமுங் காணுமாற்குலெடுத்துக் கொண்டு நிற்க	The eldest among the temple priests should stand up, lift the pot so that it is visible to all the people in the Mahasabha.

Inscriptions in Tamizh	**English Translation (not verbatim)**
பகலே யந்திர மறையாதானொரு பாலனைக் கொண்டு ஒரு குடும்பு வாங்கி மற்றொரு குடத்துகே புகவிட்டுக் குலைத்து அக்குடத்திலோரோலை வாங்கி மத்யஸ்தன் கையிலே குடுப்பதாகவும்	A young boy, who is not aware of the contents of the pot, will pick the packet representing one ward and transfer it to another empty pot and shake it. From this, the boy shall draw one ticket and give it to the madyastha (arbitrator).
அக்குடத்த வோலை மத்தியஸ் தன வாங்கும்போது அஞ்சு விரலும் அகல வைத்த உள்ளங்கையாலே ஏற்றுக் அவ்வேற்று வாங்கின வோலை	The arbitrator shall receive the ticket on the palm of his hand with five fingers open in order to indicate that his hand was empty and nothing had been hidden inside the palm.
வாசித்த அவ்வோலை அங்குள் மண்டகத்திருந்த தமபிமார் எல்லோரும் வாசிப்பாராகவும் வாசிப்பானாகவும் கொள்வானா கவும்	The arbitrator will read out the name on the ticket, followed by all the priests present in the inner hall.
வாசித்த அப்பர் திட்டமிடுவதாகவும் இப்பரிசே முப்பது குடும்பிலும் ஒரே பேர் கொள்வதாகவும்	The chosen person's name will be read and accepted. This process will be replicated for each of the thirty wards.

Source: Author's interpretations with inputs from source and inscriptions

In addition to the candidacy requirements and mode of elections, there were rules for the committees that elected members could be a part of, including the duration and structure. Some examples of the constitution of such committees are given in Table 4.6.

TABLE 4.6 Constitution of Committees

Inscriptions in Tamizh	English Translation
இக்கொண்ட முப்பது பேரினுந்தோட்ட வாரியமும் ஏரி வாரியமும் செய்தாரையும் விச்சையா வருத்தரையும் வயோவ்ருத்தர்களையும் சம்வத்ஸர வாரியராக கொள்வதாகவும்	Among the thirty men chosen, people with prior experience in the garden and lake/ tank committees and with additional knowledge will be included in the committees.
மிக்கு நினாருட்பன்னிருவரைத் தொட்ட வாரியங் கொள்வதாகவும்	Among the rest, twelve would be for the garden committee and remaining six would be for lake/tank committee.
நின்ன அறுவரையும் ஏரி வாரியமாகக் கொள்வதாகவும்)	These committees (garden and lake/tank committees) will be chosen.

The membership of all these committees came with a one-year term limit. The inscriptions clearly state that after 365 days, the members needed to retire from their roles. Not only did this ensure accountability, it clearly negated any tendency of clinging on to power for ever.

> இவ்வாரியம் செய்கின்ற மூன்று திறத்து வாரியப் பெருமக்களும் முன்னுற்றருபது நாளும் நிரம்பச் செய்து ஒழிவதாகவும்)
> (These wise men from these committees would hold office for 365 days and then retire subsequently.)

All these inscriptions mentioned here—on the selection of candidates, mode of election, structure of the village committees—represent an ecosystem which was akin to modern-day parliamentary democracy and the various committees that are set up in both the Lok Sabha and the Rajya Sabha in today's Bharat. Thus, we get a sense of the importance of the quality of governance and a track record of service delivery of the constituents.

Of course, these inscriptions refer to only one village where the scale was much smaller, but the underlying principles of a sabha, mahasabha, elections and a democratic method of electing candidates, all provide an idea about the democratic governance model based on Dharmic ideals. We will discuss more about this later in the book.

Economic Governance

There was a well-organized and efficient administration and transportation network to facilitate trade. There were three components of this—pattinam, nagaram and naadu. They were designed to ensure efficient movement of goods and services across the Chola empire.

Naadus played an important role in integrating the sabha (assemblies) and served as a vital link between the monarchy and the smaller village assemblies.[8] As a part of this system, they also had one nagaram which served as a hinterland hub for commerce. It served as a vertical connection for all the villages in the naadu and a horizontal connection with other nagarams. It was a link between commercial markets, villages, market towns and larger entities such as naadus/ managarams and ports.[9] The nagarams had authority over local trade since they collected taxes on commercial transactions in their areas. Moreover, these nagarams also represented things like kadai, angadi and perangadi, which were all different representations of market scenes which are seen even today in contemporary Tamil Nadu. They also reflected an interesting socioeconomic trend of urban–rural continuum which is mentioned by Kanakalatha Mukund in her book on Tamil merchants.[10] The nagarams served as a fulcrum for this continuum as well. Hence, it is not a surprise to see a plethora of nagarams which were functional during the Chola period (and also in the Pandya period) as shown in Figure 4.4.[11]

FIGURE 4.4 Distribution of Nagarams during the Chola and Pandya Period

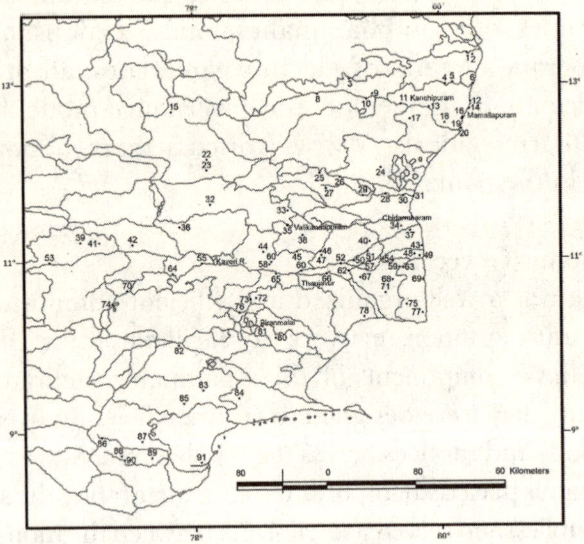

Index

1 Tiruppalaivanam
2 Kattur
3 Melpadi
4 Tirumalisai
5 Puntamalli
6 Mayilappur
7 Takkolam
8 Virinchipuram
9 Kaverippakkam
10 Sakkaramallur
11 Kanchipuram
12 Kovalam
13 Palur
14 Tiruvidandai
15 Hosur
16 Mamallapuram
17 Uttaramerur
18 Tirukkalukunram
19 Saturangappattinam
20 Vayalur
21 Marakkanam
22 Kadagattur
23 Adiyamankottai
24 Vikkiravandi
25 Jambai
26 Kilur (Tirukkoyilur)
27 Rishivandhyam
28 Tiruvadi
29 Tirunamanallur
30 Tiruvendiram
31 Kadalur
32 Salem
33 Aragalur
34 Chidambaram
35 Venganur
36 Tiruchengodu
37 Achchapuram
38 Valikandapuram
39 Annur
40 Gangaikonda-cholapuram
41 Avinasi
42 Vijayamangalam
43 Kavirippum-pattinam
44 Singalantapuram
45 Uttatur
46 Melappaluvur
47 Paluvur
48 Tillaiyadi
49 Tarangampadi
50 Tiruppurambiyam
51 Tribhuvanam
52 Kamarasavalli
53 Perur
54 Konerirajapuram
55 Karur
56 Tiruvellarai
57 Tirunagesvaram
58 Tiruppangili
59 Koyil Tirumalam
60 Anbil
61 Tiruvaiyaru
62 Tirukkarugavur
63 Tirukkannapuram
64 Chinnadharapuram
65 Tiruchirrappalli
66 Thanjavur
67 Kovil Venni
68 Tiruvarur
69 Nagapattinam
70 Dalavaypattinam
71 Kottur
72 Kodumbalur
73 Kovilpatti
74 Kolumam
75 Kalyanapuran-gonda pattina
76 Tuvarankurichi
77 Vedaranyam
78 Adirampattinam
79 Piranmalai
80 Pillaiyarpatti
81 Tiruppattur
82 Vikkiramangalam
83 Aruppukkottai
84 Kamudi
85 Sattur
86 Kuttalam
87 Ukkirankottai
88 Mannarkoil
89 Tirunelveli
90 Kallidaikkurichi
91 Korkai

Source: Adapted from N. Karashima, Y. Subbarayalu and P. Shanmugam, 'Nagaram during the Chola and Pandyan Period: Commerce and Towns in the Tamil Country A.D. 850–1350', *Indian Historical Review*, 35 (1), 2008.

The efficacy of the nagarams as redistributive and logistic hubs, where products ranging from agriculture, cotton goods and artisan products to food items, spices and so on were sold, was mainly due to the alliances that were formed with the land-owning Vellalars (Piranmalai inscriptions). These alliances enabled traders to trade in the naadu's markets with the approval of the Vellalars. This safeguarded the monopoly of the respective nagarams. These alliances also ensured that there was a seamless integration between the agricultural–land owning class and the commercial–trading communities in the region. It is also important to add that most of these alliances were centred on nagarams which were in the hinterland. Most of the pattinams, that is, coastal towns, provided for the merchants and guilds in the coastal areas without the alliances with the Vellalars. In that sense, there was a distinction between the governance structure in the coastal areas and the hinterland due to local needs. In addition to this, there were also managarams which were larger cities located in areas such as Kanchipuram or Mamallapuram.

In this governance structure, a few things stand out. First, the attempt was to create an integrated and inclusive commercial ecosystem among the numerous stakeholders (and the attempt was to benefit all of them). This shows us the wisdom of the Cholas—they understood the importance of the local dynamics (and the need to keep the locals happy) despite having a grand pan-Bharat vision in their minds. Second, it also shows an attempt to decentralize the commercial structures so that the local villages and small nagarams could become the epicentre of commercial activity rather than only the bigger maanagarams and naadus. This was also consistent with the emphasis given by the Cholas to build large and small temples across the empire which, besides serving religious and cultural purposes, also served as decentralized financial institutions that financed the Srenis and facilitated commercial activities. Last, the connecting rods of all these governance principles and structures—inclusivity, decentralization, religiosity, ethics—were derived from Dharmic principles, which we have mentioned earlier. These principles were evident across geographies and time, as we saw in my previous book, *Kautilyanomics for Modern Times*, as well.

Srenis

According to a dissertation by R. Jayasurya:

> It therefore appears that Manigraamam was the name of a merchant guild of southern Bharat like the Valanjiyar and Ayyapolil associations, membership to which have been open to all merchants, as such irrespective of their religion, and whose constitution was almost analogous to that of the Sreni of Ancient India, the assembly of eminent merchants defined as composed of traders and artisans; including men of different jatis but pursuing similar means of livelihood.[12]

An important part of the governance structure of the economy was the presence of Srenis, that is, corporate guilds.[13] These were based on the idea of Sreni Dharma which we mentioned earlier. The principles of Sreni Dharma were the cornerstone of these srenis across Bharat. The Cholas, though they had their own customized versions of the principles, were no different in terms of the philosophical underpinning of the srenis. According to the inscriptions, between the ninth and the thirteenth century, with a geographical distribution spanning Tamil Nadu, Karnataka, Sumatra, Thailand and Myanmar, there were four main srenis which have been mentioned in many places. They were Anjuvannam,

Manigraamam, Ainnuruvar and Naanaadesi (also called Padinen Vishayam and Padinen Bhumi). Anjuvannam is believed to have consisted mainly of foreign residents—Jews, Christians, Persians—who had migrated to the Southwest of Bharat and settled there. Manigraamam was said to have descended from the Vanika Graama of Kaveripoompattinam according to the inscriptions from the ninth century CE. Examples of these inscriptions include those in Kerela, where the Kollam copper plate inscription of Sthanu Ravi records grants of land and labourers in Kollam. A Kochi copper plate of Bhaskara Ravivarman recorded the grant of title and privileges to a Jew named Joseph Rabban. More details are given in Table 4.7 for those who are interested in the granular details of the Sreni inscriptions and its related evidence. If not, please continue the chapter from page 92 onwards.

It is important to note that there were also several smaller and regionalized or decentralized Srenis which served important socioeconomic functions. Based on inscription-based evidence, we will focus on some of these Srenis.

Ainnuruvar stands out as one of the most prominent srenis during the Chola era. They were governed by Sasanas which were considered to be the Dharma of merchants. They were mainly of Yadava lineage and had a close association with Aihole and its kula devata Paramesvari. A summary of their structure and their philosophical underpinnings is as follows:

> Ayyavole five hundred, mentioned in the inscriptions of Aihole of early 8th century, was another important mercantile guild. The Tisaiyayirattu Ainnuruvar meaning the five hundred of the thousand directions had its origin at Aihole and extended its influence over the entire Deccan and outside. They overshadowed the other guilds by the great authority vested in them

to augment the commercial wealth of the country, and to promote cultural unity among the artisans. They were the protectors of Vira-Bananjadharma and the Chitrameli corporation. The mercantile corporation of the eighteen towns existed on either bank of the river Kaveri. The Ainnuruvar, often styled the 500 Svamis of Ayyavolepura (Aihole), was the most celebrated of the southern Bharat merchant guilds. Like the great kings of the age, they had a prasasti of their own which recounted their traditions and achievements. They were the protectors of the Vira-Bananjadharma, i.e., the law of the noble merchants, Bananja being obviously derived from Samskritam Vanija merchant. This Dharma was embodied in five hundred Vira Sasanas edicts of heroes. They had the picture of a bull on their flag and were noted throughout the world for their daring enterprise. Among the countries they visited were Chera, Chola, Pandya, Malaya, Magadha, Kausala, Saurashtra, Kurumba, Kambhoja and Nepala. They traversed land routes and water routes, penetrating all the countries of the six continents. They traded in elephants, pearls, rubies, diamonds, carbuncles, emeralds and other precious articles, cardamom, cloves, sandal, camphor, musk, saffron and other spices and perfumes. They either sold them wholesale or hawked them about on their shoulders. They paid the sunka regularly and filled the royal treasury with jewels and replenished the king's armoury; they bestowed gifts on Pandits and were well versed in the four sangas and six darsanas.

Copper-plate inscriptions of Nellore mention that the organisation of Ayyavola, or Ayyavola-enumbaru-swamigalu, were the protectors of the Vira-Balanja Dharma (aka Vira-Bananja Dharma) and followed

TABLE 4.7 Srenis Appearing in Inscriptions

Name of Sreni	Inscription Evidence	Origins and Constituents	Time Period	Examples
Anjuvannam*		Jews, Christians, Persians	Ninth to thirteenth century	
Manigraamam*	Kollam, Kochi in Kerala, Takua Pa in Southern Thailand	Vanika Graama of Kaveri-poompattinam	Ninth century	Varman Ku (na) … Manthan Naankuurula Yaa(n) Thotta Kulam per Siri Avani Naranam Manikkramatharkkum Sena Muhatarkum Patharkum Adaikalam[14]
Ainnuruvar	Oldest inscription in Kamudi in tenth century, Barus inscription	Chettis, Veerar and a group of people called Gaamudasvaami	Tenth century but peaked in twelfth century	Kamudi says: 'They had been given 500 Veera Saasanam (charters), bore Lakshmi on their chest and descended from Vasudeva, Kandali and Moolabhadra, sons of Paramesvari. They transacted in 18 Pattinams, 32 Velapurams, 64 Kadigai Taavalam (Ghatikaa Sthaanam).' Barus inscription: Ainnuruvar merchants met at Velapuram in Vaarosu (Barus), also called Maatangari Vallava Desi Uyyakonda Pattinam;
Naanaadesi	Pagan (Myanmar) inscription			Naanaadesi Vinnagar (most likely a Vishnu temple built by the Ainnuruvar)

Name of Sreni	Inscription Evidence	Origins and Constituents	Time Period	Examples
Eri Veera Pattinam (Town of Brave Soldiers)				Some have interpreted these as towns of merchants that were protected by soldiers or as midway points between nagarams (inland) and pattinams (coastal towns). This definition of nagarams and pattinams is in line with that mentioned in the *Arthashastra*. In the Chola context, pattinams also referred to important emporia towns of the interior. Such towns were designated as EVP.
	Samuttirapatti		1050	These places were designated as EVP because Veerakkodiyaar (flag-bearing soldiers) protected Ainnuruvar in a fight with other merchants and rescued three important members of the Ainnuruvar guild.
Piranmalai inscription				Pattinam was a place where people sang and danced, spoke three kinds of Tamil (cosmopolitan); where fruits, trees and flowers grew and all religious rites were properly performed.

				Mentions three levels of towns where activities of trade were conducted—pattinams, valarpuram (coastal port towns as well) and taavalam (seasonal centre of trade).
	Viharehinna inscription		1150	Veerar and Naattu Chettiyar reciprocated the honour accorded to them by the merchants of the town (Viharehinna) by relinquishing a share of their income entitlement from the town. Thus, EVPs—where merchants lived together with Veerakkodiyaar—granted privileges to the latter in exchange for deeds of bravery. Inscriptions have Ainnuruvar addressing Veerakkodiyaar/Veerar as 'Nam Makkal' (our children), in a paternalistic, protective way.
	Kovilppatti inscription		1350	Talks about the assembly of five groups of people—Ainnuruvar (Nattu Chettigal and Tala Chettigal), Munai and Munai Veerakkodiyaar (called Nam Makkal), and Chitrameli Periya Naadu (a large assembly of the collection of naadus, likely comprising artisans and those that produced goods for the merchants)—in Acchakkandaka grove in the Vada Daliyoor Siva temple.

Name of Sreni	Inscription Evidence	Origins and Constituents	Time Period	Examples
				A decision was taken to contribute the Pattanam Pagudi to the deity of the temple. This contribution was to be made by the members of the four nagarams (mentioned in the inscription). Thus, a major decision of the Ainnuruvar was to be performed by the members of specific nagarams, indicating a corporate-style hierarchy. (Separate discussion on nagaram–naadu relationship later in the book.) All these inscriptions mention the kind of commodities that form part of the Pattanam Pagudi (pepper, cloth, medicines etc.). The most comprehensive list of the Pattanam Pagudi type comes from Belur (sixty-four commodities) that mentions the regular agricultural commodities, salt, sandal, cotton and cloth and also iron-bar and oil, indicating the level of development of these industries.

	Sarkaar Periya Paalayam inscription		1289	Members of Ainnuruvar and Padinen Vishayam (mentioned earlier), comprising Chettigal, Chetti Veera Puttirargal (against the paternalistic reference to the soldiers), Malai Mandalathu Pala Nagarangal (those from Kerala, as Kovilppatti is close to Kerala) met in the Siva temple, as the Ainnuruvar Peruniravi (big assembly) and the Padinen Vishayam Peruniravi, and along with the Nattu Chettigal and Tala Chettigal (the repeated mention here and in Kovilppatti indicates that these denoted the merchants of that specific naadu and Talam), Arupathu Naangu Munai and Munai Veerakkodiyaar, and contributed Pattanam Pagudi for holding a festival in the Siva temple of Veera Chola Vala Naadu.

*Later, in the twelfth century, both Anjuvannam and Manigraamam became subsidiaries of a larger Sreni called Ainnuruvar which gained prominence in the twelfth century.

the Vira-Balanja-Samaya. According to an inscription dated 1240 CE found at Chintapalli in Guntur district, the Vira-Balanja Samaya (a trade corporation) consisted of Ubhayananadesis, the Kavarais and the Mumuridandas; and they were the recipients of five hundred hero edicts. Of these, the Ubhayananadesis were a unit of merchants derived from all quarters and countries, consisting of Desis, Paradesis and Nanadesis, while the Kavarai derived their name as a body of merchants from an ancient Tamil community which did 'Conch/Shell' Cutting doing Ornaments.[15]

A translation of an original inscription from 1055:

> Famed throughout the world, adorned with many good qualities, truth, purity, good conduct, policy, condescension and prudence; protectors of the Vira-Bananju-Dharma (law of the heroic traders), having 32 veloma, 18 cities, 64 yoga-pithas, and asramas at the four points of the compass; born to be wanderers over many countries, the earth as their sack … the serpent race as the cords, the betel pouch as a secret pocket … by land routes and water routes penetrating into the regions of the six continents, with superior elephants, well-bred horses, large sapphires, moonstones, pearls, rubies, diamonds … cardamoms, cloves, sandal, camphor, musk, saffron and other perfumes and drugs, by selling which wholesale or hawking about on their shoulders, preventing the loss by customs duties, they fill up the emperor's treasury of gold, his treasury of jewels and his armoury of weapons; and from the rest they daily bestow gifts on pundits and munis; white umbrellas as their canopy, the mighty ocean as their moat, Indra as the hand-guard of their swords, Varuna as the standard bearer, Kubera as the treasurer.[16]

It is quite clear that the philosophical moorings of the Ainnuruvar were based on the ideals of Dharma, through the modified version present in the five hundred Vira Sasanas edicts. It is also worthwhile to mention that in the trade mission sent by Rajaraja Chola I to China, almost fifty persons were from Ainnuruvar Sreni. The inscriptions state that they were also a part of the Chola voyages to both Southeast Asia as well as Sri Lanka. They became the most pre-eminent Sreni during the Chola era. Being an integral part of the Chola voyages, they served as trade conduits.

Noted Japanese historian Noboru Karashima says, 'The purpose of the expeditions to the Malay Peninsula conducted by Rajendra I and Virarajendra must have been to gain hegemony over the maritime trade between the West and East.'[17] This indicates the larger geo-economic role played by the Ainnuruvars.

The Ainnuruvars became so big that other guilds such as Anjuvannam, Manigraamam and Nanadesi guilds affiliated to them or merged with them. There are inscriptions from around 1088 in Western Sumatra (Loboe Toewa) in Indonesia which mention in detail about the Ainnuruvar and their prominence in the Southeast Asian region. In the thirteenth century CE, a Vishnu temple was built in Pagan, Myanmar, by the Nanadesi guilds and gifts were made to the temple by merchants from the Malabar coast.[18] Not only does this illustrate the globalized nature of Ainnuruvar, it also reiterates the importance and proximity of this Sreni to the senior-most officials of the Chola empire.

In addition to this, the Ainnuruvar was so encompassing that it did not just consist of merchant groups alone. In the assembly convening some of these Ainnuruvar meetings, there were an assortment of merchant groups including 'chetti (setti), chetti-puttiran (setti-guttaru), kavarai (gavare), nagaram (nagara) and entunadu-padinaruvaru';[19] local organizations of landlords, soldiers and soldier groups which were protecting the merchants in their various business journeys; organization of foreign merchants and other professional groups. Given the scale and importance of Ainnuruvar, it was a much wider movement that impacted the larger socioeconomic and geopolitical dynamics of the rulers of the states of which they were a part.

In all these srenis, it is important to note that the role of the state was minimal. The srenis functioned independently, had their own finances and did trade on their own terms in most cases. While they would have definitely piggy-backed on the progress of the state, that is, the expansion of the Chola empire, to further their commercial enterprise, they were not controlled by the monarch or the state in any significant manner. In addition, there are inscriptions that suggest close proximity of the state's powerful players to some of these srenis in Kerala and Andhra Pradesh[20], but the day-to-day functioning and governance were independent of the state. This was in direct contrast to how such srenis worked in medieval Europe and China during those times. In Europe, the guilds (or similar entities) had 'monopoly rights and state backing … stood for self-organization and autonomy of merchant class' whereas the Chinese guilds were 'powerless against officialdom'.[21] The merchant srenis among the Cholas were fiercely independent, had more freedom compared to the Chinese and had less state backing when compared to the Europeans. In essence, they were entities that were akin to modern-day corporations, governed and regulated by the laws of the land as established by the state where they operated.

Communities

Communities played an important role in the socioeconomic progress of the Chola empire. While the role of jatis was an integral part of the communities being referred to here, there was a much wider definition at play. In earlier sections, we discussed about the governance structure and the role of Srenis—both of them were based on Dharmic philosophies—yet none of them would have thrived without the active participation of the communities at large. They played three distinct roles—to facilitate the movement of goods from the source to nagarams and eventually to export markets, production of goods and services that could be traded and to serve as a bulwark or buffer to resolve disputes and issues related to trade and commercial activities.

Land-owning communities such as Vellalars and Uluvars were considered to be at the top of the hierarchy followed by cowherds, shepherds, artisans, armed men, fisherfolks and so on. In reality though, these hierarchies were quite fluid especially when it came to commerce and trade activities. While jatis did exist during the Chola era, the society seemed quite egalitarian with most of the jati related definitions used for commercial activities rather than anything else. There was also less rigidity than what I had imagined before I started to research the subject. For example, there is a theory that the Ainnuruvar Sreni itself was started by a group of Kannada Brahmins in Ayyavole in Karnataka.[22] This shows that the Vaishya community alone did not participate in trade but the participation was far wider and a larger set of communities participated in trade and srenis.

If there was one common factor that resonated among all the communities, it was their adherence to Dharmic principles and values. This Dharmic connection was exemplified by the central role the temples played in the socioeconomic fabric of the land.[23] This centrality grew much more during the Chola period and continued subsequently thereafter. The temple flourished not just as a religious institution but as a socioeconomic entity, just as important as many commercial and regulatory institutions today. It served as a cultural destination for mass assembly, a storage place where surplus grains were kept and redistributed, and served as a financial institution which supported economic activities, especially trade. It is therefore no surprise that most of the large temples built in ancient Bharat were within reasonable proximity of large ports. Another important reason for the key role of the temple was the universal acceptance of its special and sacred position in being a guiding light for the people. People from all communities believed in its sanctity and revered the temple as a central part of their lives. All the communities mentioned earlier, including the ones active in the Srenis, saw the temple as a collective object of veneration. All this was due to the common thread of Dharmic values connecting the communities. Thus, Dharma played an important role that catalysed the communities to help in socioeconomic activities and function in an ethical, responsible and egalitarian manner.

Earlier, we discussed about the role of governance, Srenis, communities and the Dharmic underpinning of the institutions that served as a bedrock for commerce and trade. So it is natural to ask—What were the economic and commercial activities that took place during the Chola era? What was the role of agriculture in the economy? Did manufacturing play an important role in the Chola economy? What were the trade routes that they used, both to the west and east of Bharat? What was the quantum and impact of trade on other countries and their economies? Most importantly, how did the socioeconomic structure that we mentioned earlier help expand economic activities? Let us try to address all these questions.

Dharmic Ecosystem via Temples

Temples were the core of the Dharmic civilization that was present during the Chola era. The sheer number of temples built across villages in just the Tanjore belt stand testimony today to the resilience and strength of the temple as an institution. However, it is a pity that very few historians have discussed role of this Dharmic ecosystem as a catalyst for economic growth during the Chola era. Let us discuss it in detail.

The Cholas were some of the greatest Dharmic kings that Bharata Desa has ever seen. There is a vast amount of evidence in terms of inscriptions and excavations available on the subject. The temples were considered to be, primarily, religious institutions whose influence was pan-Bharat by all accounts. Even the famous Gangaikonda Cholapuram temple by its very name indicates the sanctity of the Ganges, besides the vast outreach of the Chola empire. Therefore, the religiosity of the rulers was a given fact. However, what is fascinating is that these institutions served as massive economic centres of excellence in terms of construction, organization, redistribution of income, irrigation and, in some cases, financial institutions for the Srenis and trade transactions. I will illustrate some of these themes followed by a classic example of the impressive Brihadisvara temple as a case study to highlight some of these points.

Employment Generators

Most of these temples were large employment generators, mainly through construction and the ancillary activities related to their maintenance. This was perhaps one of their most important non-religious function. The labour supply and labour participation in the temple ecosystem provided employment to thousands of artisans, sculptors, construction workers, labour contractors, craftsmen, cooks, priests, merchants and so on. Given that there was at least one major temple in each village, employment generation was a continuous process, not just during the construction stage of the temple. Thus, temples became the key catalyst for labour participation in the economic growth during the Chola empire, so much so that researchers have argued that 'the position of the temple as an employer providing work and means of livelihood for a large number of people'[24] was critical and played an important role in the socioeconomic functioning[25] of empires such as the Cholas. Here is a description of an inscription during Rajaraja I's reign. No. 66, on the outer side of the Thanjavur Periya Kovil (Brihadisvara temple), mentions:

> This very long inscription, which bears the same date as No. 65 and resembles it in style, records an order of king Rajarajadeva by which he assigned certain produce to a number of men who had to perform various services in connection with the temple, and to four hundred women, evidently dancing-girls, who had been transferred to the establishment of the Rajarajesvara temple from other temples in the Chola country. Each person received one or more shares, each of which consisted of the produce of one veli of land, which was calculated at 100 kalam of paddy. ... The second part of the inscription (paragraphs 403 to 510) consists of a list of male temple servants viz., dancing-masters, musicians, drummers, singers, accountants, parasol-bearers, lamp-lighters, watermen, potters, washermen, barbers, astrologers, tailors, a brazier, carpenters, a goldsmith and others, the reading or meaning of whose designations remains doubtful.[26]

These are clear references to the employment generated and the income provided to a number of professionals across the spectrum for providing services to the temple.

Public–Private–Temple Partnership

In a twelfth-century CE inscription,[27] there is a clear example of a public–private–temple partnership in infrastructure development. The inscription says that the temple had provided some part of the land that it owned as tax-free (i.e., without having to pay land tax) to a private individual as a sort of encouragement or boost for that individual's efforts to help construct a tank in order to irrigate lands. This was an effort by the temple to encourage a private individual via a commercial incentive to contribute to a public activity, in this case, the construction of the tank, for the benefit of the society. The state, on its part, ensured that the regulations were minimized and construction could take place at an effective pace so as to benefit the people. Many such cases, existed where the public–private institutions and the temple cooperated to boost infrastructure projects of different sizes. This was very effective during disasters and natural calamities since this model would be applied to address large issues in a cooperative financing model, rather than the state bearing the complete load of infrastructure expenses.

Capital Formation and Improvement

Another important application of the temple's economic strength was its role in capital formation and improvement. An example of this was its participation in commercial transactions which boosted the capital of the local nagarams. For example,[28] when a piece of land was being sold to a temple by the nagaram, there was an understanding that the nagaram would waive off taxes for the temple after it made the purchase. This provided an incentive for the temple to buy the land. Once the transaction was completed, the capital collected from this sale was used by the nagaram to invest in commercial or productive investments, including infrastructure projects in the nagaram. The profits from these investments compensated for waiving off of the land taxes and were a revenue for the nagarams. This is a good example of a win-win situation where the temple funds were used to accelerate capital formation in the region. Besides, there were also instances of asset improvement where the temple provided improvement in facilities due to its large economies of scale. For instance, let us continue with the example of the land that was purchased by the temple from the nagaram. Subsequently, the temple would lease out this land to cultivators on a profit-sharing basis, with the temple retaining melavaram (major share) and the cultivators having kudivaram (minor share). However, given the investments in irrigation infrastructure made by the temple, both sides gained significantly due to this asset improvement provided by the temple. Needless to say, all of this boosted the local economy.

Financial Institution Such as Bank or Venture Capitalist

The temple served as a financial institution like a bank or a venture capitalist as well. Besides the common people, the rich gave large sums to the temples for their development, and hence the temples had large financial resources. While there was a constraint to use these funds for the purposes mentioned by the donors, the temple was at liberty to loan its funds to both public and private entities. This ensured that there was constant liquidity in the system which could be used for financing public and private projects. In addition, the money would not sit idle in the temple coffers but earn very good interest for the temple as well. Examples include a tenth-century CE inscription[29] during the reign of Parantaka I. The temple loaned some amount of gold gifted by a Chola prince to the residents of a village:

> … who agreed to pay interest once in six months on the deposited amount and to give two meals every day to the man that came to demand the interest thereon. The rate of interest was three manjadi per kalanju per annum (i.e., fifteen per cent).

In another inscription in Tanjore,[30] there is a description that the temple provided funding to a village affected by a natural calamity. It says that 1,011 kalanju of gold and 464 palam of silver was given by the temple in exchange for 8 ¾ veli of land given by the village upon whose produce they would pay interest to the temple. Similar barter transactions took place with private individuals in need of finances on a case-by-case basis. The average interest rates varied generally from 12.5 to 15 per cent a year[31] and they seemed to depend on macro-economic factors. Some researchers like Spencer argue that this interest rate was mostly around 12.5 per cent per annum.[32] There is also evidence of an active credit market, especially for the merchant srenis and private entities (further evidence is provided later in this chapter). It is important to note that the sabhas (village assemblies) were also receiving funds from the temples at agreed rates of interest. The temples would loan out the cash and gold deposits with them to these sabhas at the interest rates mentioned. The interest received served as an important income for the temple and was utilized for some of its daily expenses. These sabhas belonged to various nadus and valanadus within Cholamandalam. Much of the funding or credit lines that the sabhas received were used for the development of the local community and enhancement of infrastructure.

This was in addition to the endowment-led model of infrastructure financing which we will detail in the next few paragraphs.

Endowment-Led Infrastructure Formation

There is reasonable evidence in the inscriptions of the Tirupati Venkateshwara temple to suggest that the endowments from temples were used extensively to build irrigation infrastructure which boosted the local economy.[33] We will discuss this in the chapter on the Vijayanagar empire. However, there are questions whether a similar model existed during the Cholas rule.[34] Some people believe that the endowments were used as much for developmental purposes during the Cholas reign as during other kingdoms.[35] My view is that endowments were used to build infrastructure, but it was not as extensive as it was during the Vijayanagar empire because the irrigation systems were already well established by the ninth century CE in the territories ruled by the Cholas. So the need for the temples to do this to the extent that it was important enough to be mentioned in the inscriptions was lower, as compared to other kingdoms. At the same time, the role of temples in supporting other forms of infrastructure formation should also be observed, including their role in being redistributive centres of resources.

Redistributive Centres to Bridge Inequality

The role of the temples as redistributive centres is presented in the next chapter on the Vijayanagar empire in detail. The Cholas also used the Dharmic ecosystem of the temples to redistribute economic activity so as to ensure various types of inequalities were reduced. This ensured that the temple catalysed money and livestock to higher productivity resulting in more diversified development for the local communities as a whole.[36]

First, there was a redistribution of resources within the Cholamandalam. For example, those in the military, who were not involved in war and were available, were transferred to activities related to the Dharmic ecosystem, which provided employment for them. Similarly, the temples ensured that the extra livestock was shared with the agrarian community to ensure that their productivity improved and there was a resource transfer done, if needed.[37] This ensured that resources were not concentrated all the time in one place. Second, the endowment-led financing model which we mentioned earlier was a form of wealth transfer to support public goods and infrastructure. This ensured that the extra wealth from the rich was given voluntarily for enabling the development of public goods. The Dharmic ecosystem was a facilitator of this process. Third, and most importantly, the temple served as a food bank for large sections of the poor. For people in the lower income strata, for three times a day, free food was guaranteed. This was financed by the endowments received by the temples from royal patrons.

In this manner there was a redistribution of resources and wealth, and the poor were given support through the economy around the Dharmic ecosystem.

Brihadisvara Temple

There are some architectural wonders that fascinate our imagination and there are others that represent a civilizational moment and evoke a spiritual desire. However, there are very few which combine both these facets. The Brihadisvara temple, Rajarajeswaram, as it was called by the Cholas, is one of those architectural wonders. The temple was built by Rajaraja Chola I and was completed in 1010. The sheer complexity, endurance, aura, artistic exquisiteness and imperiousness make it a UNESCO world heritage monument and a jewel for the world. To focus on the topic at hand, we will briefly discuss its economic functions. Here are some interesting facts about it:

- The construction of the temple began around 1003 and was completed in the 25th year of Rajaraja Chola's reign in 1010.
- Gifts to the temple included 41,500 kalanjus of gold, 50,650 kalanjus of silver and jewels valued at almost 10,200 kasus.
- Revenue from land contracts and grants related to the temple amounted to approximately 145,899 kalams of paddy.
- The temple complex was 240.79m east to west and 121.92m north to south. The sanctum sanctorum was built in a basement 5m in height. The imperious srivimana (the main tower) was almost 13 stories tall and crowned by a single block of granite which was 7.77sqm.
- The main Shiva lingam and the huge Nandi were said to weigh a massive 20 tonnes each, with the outer gopuram weighing almost 80 tonnes.
- Remarkably, the temple was designed in such a way that it did not cast a shadow despite its towering height.[38]

Because of all these splendid characteristics, the temple epitomizes all the characteristics of the Dharmic ecosystem.

The economic functions of the temple were boosted by several factors. First, the economies of scale were enhanced significantly since this was a huge temple. It was considered to be one of the most ambitious projects of its times, so the scale and the grandness of activities was unparalleled. The bureaucracy also gave it huge importance. As a result of this, and its central location as the Chola empire's core nucleus, the employment generation capabilities of the temple were vast. This catalysed large economies of scale and amplified some of the economic outcomes (such as employment generation) manifold compared to other events or institutions. For example, there were almost 800 people employed by the temple as full-time employees to cater to the functioning of the temple. As mentioned in the inscriptions referred to in the earlier section on employment generation, the diversity of professionals who served the temple's ecosystem was quite significant.[39]

Second, the temple served a very important financial role as a bank and a supplier of credit for the entire Cholamandalam. The financing from the temple was done at scale and ensured that those who needed funds and were qualified for them were provided with the necessary credit at relevant interest rates. It was not just the sabhas that we mentioned earlier that were provided with this financing. Qualified individuals and private enterprises were also provided with funding. An example of this is mentioned in inscription 24 in the inner gopura to the left of the entrance of the temple.[40] This inscription says that financing was provided to the people in the bazaar in Tanjore, who were involved in production and trade of cardamom seeds, and to private entities who were involved in trading other products. Providing credit in cases such as these ensured that there was no liquidity crunch in the region. The large size of the temple ensured that it was effectively the largest bank in the region.

Incentives were also provided to people who had good repayment and credit history, thus ensuring that there were rewards-based credit transactions for the various stakeholders. Mechanisms were also in place so that there were not too many defaults to avoid nonperforming assets and loans during the Chola era! It is also important to understand that the temple's own funds came from quite diverse sources like land grants, donations, endowments, cash and gold deposits and so on. This ensured that the institution was sustainable and not overly leveraged or dependent on one form of financing.

Third, this temple represented the redistributive mechanisms that I mentioned in the earlier sections. Being the largest temple in the region, it symbolized the redistributive mechanism at scale for all the villages in the region. It is evident that the king, his extended family and the elite in the society donated extensively to the Brihadisvara temple, given its importance to the Cholas.[41] As such, the scale of potential financing was quite large though some argue that this potential wasn't fully utilized.

Key Economic Pillars of the Chola Economy

Let us look at some of the key pillars of the Chola economy.

Agriculture

As in most ancient kingdoms, agriculture was a very important component of the economy and remained central to providing employment to large sections of the people. The Chola empire provided extensive support to agriculture for two main reasons—the first was that most of the employment opportunities were either directly involved with agriculture or were a part of the offshoots of the agricultural production process. The second was that agriculture involved land and irrigation, which were the key pillars of the economy during those times.

Land was both collectively as well as individually owned.[42] Collective or communal ownership was mainly applicable during redistribution of wasteland. Terms such as sabhamanjikkam and urmanjikkam—which are used in some of the inscriptions—highlight the nomenclature of communal ownership. Inscriptions of Sundara Chola provide a description of an auction of a wasteland for communal ownership. Individual owners of land, other than the royalty and people running the state, were also recognized. Common folks could own and inherit land from their family without any interference from the state.

Agriculture produce included a number of vegetables and food products. Estimates suggest that there were two or three crops raised every year in the land growing paddy. While fertile land was aplenty in the region, ancient Tamizh farmers were aware of different soil types, the best crops to grow and the various irrigation systems suitable for any given region. In the five geographical divisions of the Tamil country in Sangam literature, the Marutam region was the most fit for cultivation, as it had the most fertile lands.

Land was classified according to its fertility as Menpulam (fertile land), Pinpulam (dry land), Vanpulam (hard land) and Kalarnilam or Uvarnilam (salty land). Menpulam yielded rich produce of a variety of crops, but Pinpulam was cultivated only with dry crops due to limited irrigation facilities. The yield from Vanpulam was limited, while Kalarnilam was unfit for cultivation.[43] Besides agriculture, cattle and dairy farming was also done extensively in many communities. Most of the focus in the agricultural infrastructure was on the development of irrigation facilities in which the Cholas were masters.

Irrigation networks were central to the flourishing Chola empire. Blessed by the river Kaveri and its tributaries, the Cholas constructed vast irrigation networks and dams to use the water resources for commercial and individual use. Examples of large irrigation tanks include Kallinangaipuram at Solapuram, Vairamega Tataka at Uthiramerur and Cola-varidhi at Sholingur. The main role of the village assemblies was to remove the silt in the tanks before the arrival of the monsoon to ensure optimal storage of rain water in these tanks. The state also provided endowments for maintenance and sustenance of some of these irrigation channels and tanks. There was a clear awareness of the importance and significance of these irrigation networks for agriculture and other aspects of governance including disaster and flood management. An eleventh-century CE inscription mentions a breach in a tank at Tirukkanji in a storm and the repairs made by a local, which included construction of stone revetments on the banks.[44]

Manufacturing

The mass manufacture of artefacts, jewellery, iron and metal objects, influenced by centuries of anglicized thoughts, was not a post industrialization phenomenon, as many people believe. As mentioned earlier, even in the Saraswati–Sindhu civilization, we have seen trends of manufacturing and industrialization at scale. These were continued in the Chola era as well. The Cholas were experts in making artefacts and jewellery of various kinds, besides other goods.

Manufacturing metal goods was an important activity for the Cholas. Besides their use in large temples for artistic and operational purposes, many of the household utensils, especially for the wealthy, were made of exquisite metal casting. Inscriptions in the Tanjore temples are further evidence of a flourishing metal casting industry in ancient Bharat. Given that jewellery symbolized royal wealth and, as an extension, political and societal power, expertise in manufacturing jewellery was encouraged and quite sought-after, especially among the royals. Besides jewellery, the numerous Chola era sculptures[45] which adorn many temples and, unfortunately, foreign museums today, were manufacturing marvels executed hundreds of years ago. Many of the castings of temple deities involved amalgamation of many metals, including copper, zinc, tin, gold and silver. Artefacts such as the famous bronze Chola statues were precisely sculptured and manufactured with attention to minute details which ensured that no defects can be seen even today. Their expertise can be appreciated from the fact that making such sculptures and statues today, even with all the technology at our disposal, is an arduous task.

Tools required for agriculture were also manufactured. These included basic tools needed for ploughing—namely, meli and kalappa—as well as for harvesting crops.

The manufacturing expertise of the Cholas was not limited to just metals but also commodity manufacturing such as salt and agricultural products. Along the sea coast, Kanyakumari, Variyur and Ayutrai were centres of salt manufacturing. These units were provided some government patronage and were also subject to the regulations of the state. Besides these, weavers were also prominent. They wove clothes for traders, merchants and the royalty as well.

There is evidence of exemptions provided to certain industries to boost their growth and also reinforce their importance. For example, the weavers of Kanchipuram were exempted from taxes and royal dues.[46]

Economic Trade and Its Components

The textile industry of both Trichinopoly (or Uraiyur) and Tanjore has been famous from early times. There can be little doubt that some of the finest fabrics that reached the Roman world came from this kingdom of Chola. From this part of India, in the Middle Ages, came those gold-threaded embroideries which were in such demand in the Saracen markets.[47]

Internal Trade

Before we look at international trade, let us understand the internal trade that took place within the Chola kingdom. The production and supply to the local market was important for industries and merchants alike. Evidence of movement of merchants, mercantile corporations and Srenis within the Chola kingdom and within contemporary Bharata Desa is showcased in many ways. For example, 'a merchant from Malai-naadu (Malabar) is seen trading in Tiruvadandai in the Chingleput district (current Chengalpattu), one from Mylapore is found in Tanjore and a man from Ceylon endows a lamp in the temple at Sucindram (South Travancore)'.[48] The movement of people from one place to another was a common phenomenon. But how were goods transported internally?

The presence of roads is evident in many inscriptions in the Chola kingdom and elsewhere. There were two types of roads mentioned, according to K.A. Nilakanta Sastri.[49] One was the vadi, which were suitable only for light traffic and were marginally better than footpaths. The other was the peruvali, which were more robust roads used for transportation internally. Examples of these roads include Thanjavur-peruvali and Konga-peruvali.

Maritime Trade

While there was domestic trade which was taking place in Bharat, the main focus of the Chola empire was to scale up maritime trade across new geographies with a greater variety of products to be traded. The trading routes are shown in Figure 4.5.

FIGURE 4.5 Trading Routes of Cholas

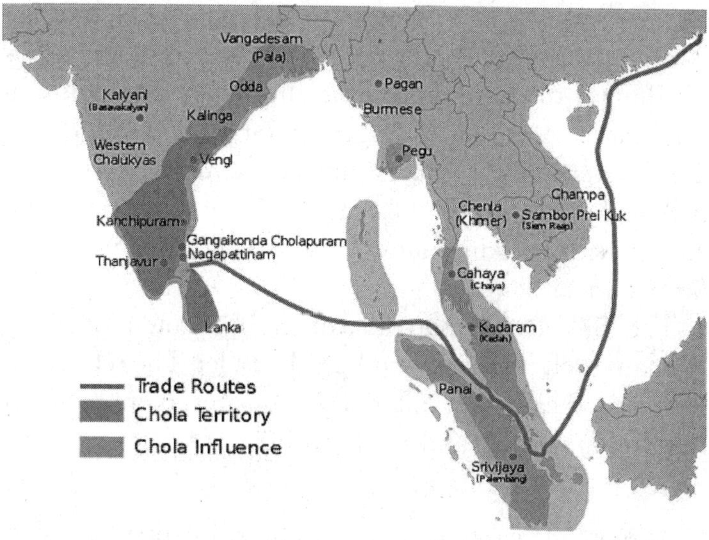

Source: https://commons.wikimedia.org/wiki/File:Chola_empire_map.jpg

Among the maritime trade routes, one of the important ones was the direct sea route between China and Bharat, which gained prominence after the seventh century CE. Chinese embassy notes also indicate the importance given by the Chinese to Rajaraja Chola's entourage and the need to maintain cordial relations with the Cholas. This was further consolidated during the ninth-century CE trade with the Chinese (Song dynasty) and also subsequently by Rajendra Chola's Kadaram expedition. Chinese notes also mention trade missions sent by the Cholas in the tenth and eleventh century CE. Around the tenth century CE, the Chinese started to induce traders to come to their land with incentives such as gold and piece-goods. The Cholas were eager to expand their commercial empire into Chinese lands and make use of these opportunities. There is a possibility that a group of South Indian merchants settled in the port-town of Chuan-choi as per some records.[50]

This was supplemented by the sea routes via the Arabian sea into Persia and the trade routes via Bay of Bengal to Kambuja Desa and other kingdoms in Southeast Asia, including the Srivijaya kingdoms. These were trade routes that were not explored at that scale prior to the Cholas nor were alliances made earlier with the kingdoms to the east of Bharat at such far distances.

The Silk Road map has often been mentioned by Romans such as Strabo and Piny the Elder. The references seem to indicate a very planned trade movement between the Roman empire and southern Bharat.

> A Roman captain named Hippalus first sailed a direct route from Rome to Bharat, using the monsoon winds. His method was later improved upon by merchants who shortened the voyage by sailing due east from the port of Cana or Cape Guardafui, finding that by that route it was possible to go directly from Rome to Tamilakam. Strabo writes that every year, about the time of the summer solstice, a fleet of one hundred and twenty vessels sailed from Myos Hormos, a port of Egypt on the Red Sea, and headed toward Bharat. With assistance from the monsoon, the voyage took forty days to reach the ports of Tamilakam or Ceylon. Pliny writes that if the monsoons were blowing regularly,

> it was a forty-day trip to Muziris from Ocelis located at the entrance to the Red Sea from the south. He writes that the passengers preferred to embark at Bacare (Vaikkarai) in Pandya country, rather than Muziris, which was infested with pirates. The ships returned from Tamilakam carrying rich cargo which was transported in camel trains from the Red Sea to the Nile, then up the river to Alexandria, finally reaching the capital of the Roman empire. Evidence of Tamil trading presence in Egypt is seen in the form of Tamil inscriptions on pottery in Red Sea ports.[51]

Key centres of trade during this time, between ninth and eleventh century CE, included Kaveripoompattinam, Saaliyur, Korkai and Quilon. Besides, lands representing modern-day Sri Lanka, Nicobar, Lakshadweep and Maldives were also important stops for ships during long voyages. Internationally, China, Srivijaya (current Indonesia) and Baghdad served as important trading centres which were used by the Chola kings for their commercial activities.

Import and Export Dynamics

Some of the key imports of southern Bharat during the early part of the Common Era, coinciding with the Chola era, included luxury items such as glassware and even horses from Arabia. Given the wealth and resources of Bharat, it is not surprising that there was a big current account surplus, that is, the exports were more than imports. Exports included a wide variety of products like jewels, especially beryls (vaiduriyam), pearls, spices, condiments, sapphire, diamonds and ivory, among other things. Clothing, food items and jewels were among the top products exported. It is also interesting to note that as the products were being exported, Bharat's culture was also being exported to the rest of the world. Many of the names given to food products in other countries were inspired from Tamizh names. For example, Greek names for rice (oryza), ginger (gingibar) and cinnamon (karpion) are almost similar to their Tamil names—arisi, inchiver and karuvara.

Besides the range of products, it is also important to understand the quantum of trade that Bharat conducted with the rest of the world. Pliny mentions that between India, China and Arabia, the trade value was almost 100 million sesterces per year from Rome and out of this, almost half went to Bharat. This was estimated by Mommsen to be about 550,000 pounds, with the majority of the money going to southern Bharat. These numbers indicate a few important trends that summarize the importance and scale of trade during the Chola era and other earlier kingdoms.

First, the quantum of trade was substantial given the large trade numbers that we are talking about with just one country within a particular year. For example, the impact of trade with the Romans was so central to the Roman economy that there are historical accounts which show that the current account deficit of the Roman empire was mainly due to its trade with Bharat. There was a large shortage of gold and ornaments in the Roman empire since most of them were used to purchase a wide variety of products from Bharat (the peak of this interaction was mostly around the accession of Augustus in 27 BCE till about the beginning of the common era[52]). This is further corroborated by the recent discoveries of large hordes of Roman coins in various cities and towns of Tamil Nadu. The discoveries cover a period of nearly three centuries and includes coins of most, if not all, the Roman emperors, from

Augustus (27 BCE) to Alexander Severus (235 CE) and the quantity of these coins runs into thousands. This was just one country. We can imagine the quantum of trade with all the countries put together, during that time. It is quite clear that there was a very vibrant and large-scale economic activity taking place between the Chola kingdom and the rest of the world.

Second, none of this could have happened without the support infrastructure provided by the state. I have often argued in my previous works, including *Kautilyanomics for Modern Times*, that contrary to the common perception, the presence of a monarchy does not necessarily imply a state which controls the populace and micro-manages their activities, especially related to trade and commerce. Frequently, the evidence is opposite to the perception, as in the case of the Cholas. The Cholas played an important intermediary role in the trading activities. As mentioned earlier about the srenis, who were central to the trading supply chain, the kings were largely hands-off on what, how, whom and when to trade products and services. There was a broad regulatory framework for trade, including taxation and general laws, coupled with infrastructure support for ensuring smooth trade activities. For example, key ports were developed by the Cholas with the necessary lighthouses and warehouses supporting the ports. These included ports like Kaveripoompattinam (i.e., Puhar), Nagapattinam, Marakkanam and Arikamedu, among others on the eastern coast.

This was not specific to the Cholas because the Pandyas and Cheras also built their ports during their reign over Tamizhakam. Evidence from the *Periplus of the Eritrean Sea* and early common era accounts by Phily support this. The ports were provided the required infrastructure to help in trading activities. The state also provided administrative support in terms of having an easy taxation regime and enhancing ease of doing business for the traders, across the board. For example, custom check points (sungachavadi) were instituted to ensure tax compliance and also safe transportation of goods and services throughout the Chola land.

Dharmanomics and Its Role in Economic Policy

The ideas of Dharma and Dharmic values were an important foundational element in the economic policies of the Cholas. Let us assess the extent to which the features of Dharmanomics were present in the economic model that the Cholas pursued.

There are many inscriptions, travelogues and literary works as well as archaeological evidence for several historical occurrences—including the Chola era—but, as in most of the ancient history of Bharat, very little is known in terms of the processes behind them. This is especially true about the interpretation of the political economy. In the Chola era, trends are similar, even though there are so many inscriptions which provide definitive evidence on these subjects. With this background, let us look at correlations of Dharma and the economic policies during the Chola era.

Let us look again at the Chola economic model that we discussed earlier in Figure 4.3. Based on this economic model, I will present some information related to governance, Sreni Dharma and communities and correlate it with the Dharmanomics model that I discussed earlier. In my analysis, I will look through the core prism of ethics, responsibilities and harmony which are central to the KDC model. I will also look at the references to Dharmic ecosystems and Sreni Dharma as well.

Governance

The core themes that I discussed in the earlier sections vis-à-vis governance were the mechanisms of political governance via the Uthiramerur inscriptions, the integral role played by the nagarams in connecting the urs or assemblies to the broader naadu and serving as a commercial connecting rod for the state and the decentralized nature of the governance structure.

There are two kinds of governance which need to be addressed—political governance and economic governance. Let me begin with political governance as seen in the Uthiramerur inscriptions.

The obvious question here is—How were the political governance structures linked to Dharmic values in the way they have been defined in this book? In the three aspects of governance mentioned in these inscriptions—candidate selection, conduct of election and committees—there are clear ethics-based restrictions. For example, a person's conduct had to be good and he/she should not have defaulted (in repayment of loans) in order to run for office. Even if his family members were defaulters, he/she could not stand in the election. In fact, the inscription mentioned earlier—அர்த்த சௌசமும் ஆன்ம சௌசமும் உடையாராய்—refers to 'saucham' in terms of 'artha' as well as 'aanma'. In essence, it refers to the need for the candidate running for office to have utmost economic and individual honesty—a clean individual in a figurative sense. It is important to note that saucham, in a literal sense, refers to cleanliness. This is derived from the Samskritam word 'saucham' which is an important definition of Dharma itself. So we can see a direct linkage (focus on ethics for political governance) and an indirect linkage (through the inscriptions referring to saucham) that indicate a Dharmic underpinning to the structures of political governance.

There is a need in every democratic society to have free and fair elections and to prevent monopolisation of the system. In the pot-ticket system, there were a set of principles that defined the eligibility of candidates. A person who was elected to the assembly once was not repeated the next time. Moreover, the cap of one year on the duration of the position ensured that there was no dominance by any individual or group in the assembly deliberations. The underlying principle behind these rules was to ensure that the society had an electoral structure which was difficult to game or dominate by monopolies. There was a constant churn for newer ideas and for people to deliberate and discuss social issues in the sabhas and mahasabhas. Such a well-thought-out governance model could not be devised without an underlying societal responsibility at play and that is visible throughout in the inscriptions as well.

In economic governance, the obvious questions are—How did the nagarams play the role of liaison for commerce and trade? What were some of the governing principles of the state and its bureaucratic machinery? There is little evidence to suggest how individual bureaucrats viewed governance, but as a collective, it is quite clear that the state administration was a representation of the attributes and aspirations of the monarchy. The Cholas (especially those from the ninth century till the thirteenth century CE) were one of the most pious Hindu Dharmic kings of ancient Bharat. The construction of the marvellous Rajareshwaram, that is, the Periya Kovil, in Thanjavur, is an indicative example. There are hundreds of temples that were built in Thanjavur that remain rock-solid even today, thousands of years later. Besides the construction of temples, the thinking behind Gangaikonda Cholapuram and the reverence for Lord Shiva among most Chola kings clearly shows a pious Dharmic monarchy. Hence it would be obvious to expect the state officials to follow similar values, given the vast control and power that the Cholas exhibited.

Ethics, responsibilities and societal harmony—the three pillars through which we define Dharma in *Kautilyanomics for Modern Times*—is self-evident here. Many inscriptions refer to fines for ethical overreach. In addition, there are several examples where the state administration promoted social responsibilities as part of their governance structure. An example of the devout nature of the monarchy and their affinity towards Dharmic values is shown through the two inscriptions mentioned in Figures 4.6 and 4.7.

FIGURE 4.6 Inscription No. 63

No. 63 on the Outside of the North Enclosure of the Brihadisvara Temple in Thanjavur

From the published portion of No. 63, we learn that this inscription consists of a list of shepherds who had to supply ghee for temple lamps from the milk of a number of cattle, which had been presented to the temple before the 29th year of the reign of Rajarajadeva by the king himself and by others, or bought from the funds of the temple. To each lamp were allotted 96 ewes, or 48 cows, or 16 she-buffaloes. The daily supply for each lamp was one *urakku* of ghee.

FIGURE 4.7 Inscription No. 65

No. 65 on the Outside of the North Enclosure of the Brihadisvara Temple in Thanjavur

This inscription records an order of King Rajarajadeva by which he assigned a daily allowance of paddy to each of forty-eight persons, whom he had appointed before the 29th year of his reign to recite the Tiruppadiyam in the temple, and to two persons who had to accompany the others on drums. This statement is of considerable importance for the history of Tamil literature as an unmistakable proof of the existence of the Saiva hymns which go by the name of padigam or padiyam, and which are collected in the Devaram, in the time of Rajaraja.

Source: https://www.whatisindia.com/inscriptions/south_indian_inscriptions/volume_2/no_63_65_outside_of_north_enclosure.html

In the first inscription, that is, Figure 4.6, we see that there was a systematic effort to ensure that ghee was supplied for lamps in the temple. This clearly shows that the state had made efforts to contribute to and promote the well-being of perhaps the largest social gathering organization—the temple. This is further corroborated in the second inscription, given in Figure 4.7, which mentions the allowances provided to ensure that the recital of tiruppadiyam was continously done at the temple by forty-eight people. This is another indication of the state supporting the main cultural centres of the society through direct grants.

There was also a collective effort to encourage social harmony among all sections of the society. There was definitely a social construct that valued all communities. An example of this is found in the inscriptions in a Vishnu temple in Utkal in Figure 4.8.

FIGURE 4.8 Inscription No. 1

No. 1 on the North Wall of the Shrine

This inscription is dated in the 23rd year of the reign of the ancient Chola king Rajakesarivarman. It records that a certain Brahmadhiraja (ll. 4 and 11) deposited

200 kalanju of gold with the villagers and that the latter pledged themselves to apply the interest of this sum to the feeding of twelve learned Brahmanas.

(Line 1.) Hail! Prosperity! In the twenty-third year (of the reign) of king Rajakesarivarman. The writing of us, the assembly of Sivachulamanimangalam, *alias* Apara[ji]ta-chaturvedimangalam, (*a village*) in Pagur-nadu, (*a subdivision*) of Kaliyur-kottam.

(L. 3.) (*We*) have received two hundred *kalanju* of gold from Tiruvikrama-Bhattar, *alias* Brahmadhirajar, of Sedi [ru]r, (*one*) among the commissioners (*ganattar*) ruling over Uthiramerur-chaturvedimangalam, [2] (*a village*) in its own subdivision (*kuru*) [3] of the same *kottam*.

(L. 5.) From the interest of this gold, twelve Brahmanas who know the Veda, have to be fed daily, before the god (*peruman-adigal*) of the Puvanimanikka-Vishnugriham in our vIllage receives offerings at noon-time.

(L. 7.) We have received these two hundred *kalanju*, in order to supply as long as the moon and the stars exist, to each of these twelve (*brahmanas*), (*one*) *alakku* of ghee, five dishes of curry, five *ulakku* of curds, two areca-nuts, and betel-leaves until they are satisfied, (and) in order to supply everything else to these twelve Brahmans, to the cooks and to those who fetch firewood.

(L. 9.) Those who do not feed (*them*) thus and cause obstruction, shall incur all the sins committed between the Ganga and Kumari.

(L. 10.) If (*any persons*) hinder this, the sacrifices and charitable deeds (*ishtapurta*) which they have performed themselves before, shall devolve on Brahmadhirajan.

(L. 11.) Having agreed thus, we, the assembly, engraved (*this*) on stone. Hail! Prosperity!

Source: https://www.whatisindia.com/inscriptions/south_indian_inscriptions/volume_3/no_1_to_4_ukkal.html

FIGURE 4.9 Inscription No. 2

No. 2 on the North and West Walls of the Shrine

This inscription is dated in the 13th year of the reign of Rajaraja-Kesarivarman. The king receives the epithet who destroyed the ships at Salai, and must be identified accordingly with the great Chola king Rajaraja I., who ascended the throne in A.D. 984-85.

The inscription records that a certain Narayana Rajasimha, a native of the Chola country, purchased 550 *kuli* of land, and made them over to the assembly of the village, under the condition that their produce should be utilized for supplying the god with 4 *nali* of rice daily.

(Line 1.) Hail! Prosperity! In the 13th year (*of the reign*) of king Rajaraja-Kesarivarman, who destroyed the ships (*at*) Salai. The writing of us, the great assembly of Sivachulamanimangalam, *alias* Sri-Vikramabharana-chaturvedimangalam, (*a village*) in its own subdivision of Kaliyur-kottam.

(L. 2.) Kaduvang-udaiyan Narayanan Rajasimhan of Kaduvangudi, (*a village*) in Tiruvindalur-nadu, (*a district*) on the northern bank (*of the Kaveri*) in Sonadu, had purchased from Sattikumara-Kramavittan[9] of Uruppputtur five hundred and fifty *kuli*—(*measured*) by a graduated rod, beginning (*to measure*) from the land (*of the temple*) of Sri-Raghavadevar in the north—of land to the west of the road (*vadi*) to (*the temple of*) Samandarayana (*and*) to the north of the *Tarudamba* channel, and had assigned (*it*) for (*providing*) four *nali* (of rice) for the oblations to be offered at noon-time to (*the god*) Tiruva[y]molidevar in our village.

(L. 5.) Having received the revenue of this land, and having exempted (*it*) from taxes for as long as the moon and the sun exist, we, the assembly, engraved (*this*) on stone.

(L. 6.) Having been present in the assembly and having heard (*their*) order, I, the arbitrator (*madhyastha*) Ayirattirunurruvan, *alias* Brahmagunakaravidyasthana-Mangaladitya-Samanjasapriyan, the son of Nalayiravan, wrote (*this*). Prosperity!

Source: https://www.whatisindia.com/inscriptions/south_indian_inscriptions/volume_3/no_1_to_4_ukkal.html

Figure 4.8 clearly shows the effort made by the people to promote the well-being of learned Brahmins. It is important to note that the Brahmins did not earn much and were not usually wealthy. Their primary role was to promote and propagate Vedic knowledge and provide support and advice to the kings, as needed. Their financial resources were limited. This inscription shows how the interest accrued from a financial transaction was used to benefit the Brahmins. In modern parlance, it used a financial instrument (such as a loan) to redistribute wealth to sections of the society that were not well off.

There is little evidence to suggest that excessive privileges were given to any particular community. For example, according to the copper plate inscriptions, if the names and jatis of state officers were deciphered, it indicated an interesting picture. Almost 70 per cent of the officers were 'muvenda velan' (vellalars)—agriculturalists from the lowest jati. This was followed by the Kshatriya jatis, who were 15 per cent, and Brahmins, who were about 14 per cent.[53] This indicates that the Cholas had a sensitive approach to representation and jati arithmetic in governance.

The Cholas were aware that in a largely agrarian and trade-driven economy, some sections of the people, who were poorer than others, needed higher representation in the administrative setup. Not only was this a socioeconomic need but also a very important political requirement to ensure that the majority of the people were feeling well-represented. In a sense, this would pacify them if there were other issues in governance. On the other hand, there was also a need to be equitable and help, if need be, the less well-off sections of the society. An example of this was shown in the inscriptions mentioned. This was a very delicate balancing act, ensuring Samanya Dharma for people across jatis, thereby ensuring social harmony.

In inscription no. 2 (Figure 4.9), it is mentioned that a native of the Chola country purchased 550 kuli of land and gave it to the assembly of the village under the condition that the produce from this land should be utilized for supplying the god with 4 nali of rice daily. This is clearly indicative of two things—that people were philanthropic and that there was an inherent desire to protect the Dharmic culture. While the donation was meant to be mainly for the deity, it was also a redistributive mechanism for enhancing social harmony and alleviating poverty. The rice for the deity would eventually go to the people as prasad and its continuous availability through philanthropic acts such as these would ensure that the poor would always have some amount of food for their survival.

Looking at the state machinery, a question crops up—Who were the other stakeholders who were responsible for the nagaram to serve as a primary commercial centre connecting commerce from the village to the ports? It is quite obvious that the Srenis were central to the success of the nagarams being commercial liaisons. It wouldn't be amiss to say that they played a bigger role than the state machinery itself since the latter was mainly taking care of law and order and regulations.

Sreni Dharma

The Srenis played an important role in enhancing trade, both domestic and outside Bharat. As mentioned earlier, most of the Srenis, including the largest one, Ainnuruvar, followed the principles of Dharma in their organizational structure. The type of Dharma they followed varied—some of them followed the Vira Bananjadhara or Panchasata Virasasnam, whereas others followed the Samanya Dharma and some others had their own individual Sreni Dharma; but the principles behind all the Dharmic norms were similar. Let us look again at some of the components of Dharma that we discussed earlier, including the role of ethics, responsibility and societal harmony.

On ethics, there was a clear understanding among the Srenis that the business environment had to be as corruption-free as possible. The conceptualization and application of Dharmic principles for governing the Srenis communicated the message of moral probity and high ethical values. There are references to the importance of probity both in public as well as private lives of people. The administration at large—the monarch and the officials—were extremely pious and in most cases wanted to do the right thing. This reduced the propensity for corruption.

The Dharmic values of philanthropy through the prism of social responsibility and sustainability through the prism of protection of wildlife and environment were exhibited by the srenis through numerous examples. One such example,[54] according to an inscription in 981 CE, was of a member of the Ainnuruvar who gifted land to temples. There were other instances where Anjuvannam, along with other srenis, also donated to local temples through tax gifts. There were also instances where individual merchants, independent of the srenis contributed to the temples and promoted their development. An example of this is in inscription no. 89 in Figure 4.10.

FIGURE 4.10 Inscription No. 89

No. 89 on a Niche of the West Enclosure

This inscription records the gift of two ornaments to the shrine of Pillaiyar Ganapatiyar by a merchant living in one of the suburbs of Tanjore. The gift was made in the 29th year (of Rajarajadeva).

Translation:
Hail! Prosperity! The jewels presented until the twenty-ninth year (of the king's reign) of this (shrine of) Ganapatiyar by Narayanan Kamappai-setti, a merchant living in the suburban *madigai* of Thanjavur in Thanjavur-kurram, were engraved (*i.e.,* recorded) on stone after (they) had been weighed by the stone called (after) Dakshinameru-Vitankan and after the gold had been weighed by the stone called (after) Adavallan.
2. One *karkandu* filled with a conch "weighing, inclusive of the two crystals fastened on (it) and of the handle made of gold, four *karanju*," valued at one *kasu* and a quarter.
3. One string of round beads, (consisting) of nine *karanju* and three *manjadi* of gold.

In terms of adhering to the principles of Vasudaiva Kutumbakam and ensuring communal harmony, the Cholas stood out among the other kings. Despite fighting so many wars, there was a consistent increase in economic outcomes and trade for the people of Dakshin Bharat.

One of the main reasons for this was the emphasis on communal harmony and focus on sustainable growth and welfare. These two factors were evident in many of the inscriptions. The Cholas went out of their way to ensure that a cohesive society could sustain and that was the key reason for the longevity of their reign. Furthermore, the emphasis on sustainability—both environment and wildlife protection—through the enforcement of responsibilities and duties, is also an example of how Dharma and its values were the cornerstone of their governance structure.

Thus, it is quite evident that the Srenis were run on Dharmic principles as prescribed in the Sreni Dharma. They were the foundation of the nagaram, besides the state's administrative machinery. In that sense, the continuity of Dharmic principles—from the Srenis to the nagarams to the monarchy—indicate a governance model which was run on the principles of Dharma. Explicit mentions of this in terms of inscriptions are not many, but the implicit meaning of all the activities mentioned in the inscriptions and the stakeholders mentioned in the governance system clearly indicate Dharmic underpinning to an objective researcher.

Communities

Another important component of the economic philosophy of the Cholas was the role of communities and different jatis in the promotion of trade and commerce in the kingdom. Let us look at the connection between communities and Dharmanomics.

The role of communities in enhancing social capital is important even in contemporary Bharat.[55] I believe that 70–75 per cent of the informal economy in contemporary Bharat is driven by the informal community-based economic interactions in terms of lending, asset amortization, liquidity supply and entrepreneurial networks. Hence, the role of communities is a very important construct in the Dharmic frameworks even today, centuries after the Chola era.

During the Chola era, as mentioned earlier, in the hierarchy of communities, Vellalars and Uluvars were considered to be on the top, followed by cowherds, shepherds, artisans, armed men, fisherfolks and so on. We also saw how this functioned and the seamless assimilation of communities, especially in the operationalization of the trading srenis. The foundations of the communities were the pillars of KDC—ethics, responsibilities and social harmony—and the Dharmic ecosystem.

On ethics, it is quite clear that during the Chola era the communities placed a high premium on ethics as a foundation of their social and economic life. For example, the Chola kings were so transparent that they wanted all their contributions to be recorded for the public to be able to see them at that time, as well as thousands of years later. The plethora of inscriptions in the Brihadisvara temple (the pinnacle of Chola architectural and socioeconomic symbolism) are almost an accountancy exercise and highlight the inflows and outflows related to the temple. The high premium placed on transparency in transactions is reflected through the insistence on making these inscriptions by the Cholas. This obviously extended to the communities as well. In their trade/commerce and dealings with the state, they had to be ethically beyond doubt to be respected and admired in any measure.

On responsibilities, it is quite self-evident how communities were the bedrock of socioeconomic progress in the regions administered by the Cholas. Even today, there is evidence of communities backing other communities in terms of commercial business transactions in the private sector. Examples include the

Chettairs, Gounders and Vellalar, among others. There are several other examples given in this book. Commercial finance and loans between small traders were (and is still) motivated by factors such as trust, family and the cogent environment around them.

On social harmony, the egalitarian nature of the Srenis and the composition of various communities across religions highlight the inherent social harmony of the communities during the Chola era.

Dharmic Ecosystem via Temples

It is quite clear from the discussions on the Dharmic ecosystem that it was an intrinsic part of Dharmanomics. Much of the economies of scale, economic heft and strength that a temple had was a result of its primary role as a custodian of the Dharma and its role as a religious institution. A temple without its anushthana is a mere building. Its anushthana, rituals, practices and traditions, along with the Dharmic way of life, create a sacred environment that is built into a large institution.

The employment generated by a temple was largely a result of the activities related to the Dharmic way of life within the temple. The employment for the activities in the temple for craftsmen, artists, singers, construction workers, cooks and various others were the result of these activities.

The endowment-driven infrastructure and capital formation in the temples came from an innate sense of Dharma to utilize resources for the broader good of the society while ensuring that the temple also benefited from them. The emphasis was not just on the monetary returns from these commercial transactions but on the larger Dharmic good. Without this positive intent, the role of the temple would have been diminished, but driven with the intent, the role was magnified manifold.

The same applies to the role of the Dharmic ecosystem in financial institutions and banks today. A combination of broader intent for Dharmic good along with commercial acumen creates a beneficial situation for all stakeholders in the economic ecosystem. Considering that we still grapple with some of these issues in finance even today, it is amazing that thousands of years ago, Bharatiyas had very complex yet very rewarding financial instruments which provided a substantive yield to all stakeholders involved.

The Dharmic way of life drove the Dharmic ecosystem which empowered and enabled the temples to remain a central part of the economic fabric of the Cholas empire.

Concluding Thoughts and Summary Table

As I summarize the ideas mentioned in this chapter, it is important to acknowledge the findings by some researchers which might not completely align with my view. I respect these alternate views. For instance, Spencer says that the observations and inscriptions are limited to a few rulers and broader generalizations should not be made.[56] How many of the sabhas utilized these resources for sustainable investment is also a question. He also says that there is an implication of the transfer of wealth from the military to the agrarian sector through this redistribution. Burton Stein makes an argument that the military activity of the Cholas was meant to compensate for the resource constraints in the agrarian sector.[57]

However, both these scholars exhibit a lack of understanding of the Dharmic economy. This could be due to their lack of exposure to the Dharmic way of life and their prejudiced views on some of these subjects, given their background in history without much understanding of Bharatiya economic thought. Their assessment is not multi-dimensional in nature. A complex empire such as the Cholas needs to be viewed through multiple angles—socioeconomic factors, cultural factors, economic variables, secondary accounts from other sources, first-hand travelogues, anecdotal evidences and so on—and a more multi-dimensional analysis needs to be undertaken.

The evidence I have presented in this chapter tries to portray this multi-dimensionality through the foundation of Dharma in formulation of economic policies. The evidence I provide in this book substantiates that these inscriptions were not exceptions or anomalies.

Table 4.8 summarizes the centrality of Dharmanomics to the Chola economic model. It provides a brief overview of the points discussed in the chapter and links the economic model with components of Dharmanomics.

TABLE 4.8 Dharmanomics and Chola Economics

		Governance	Srenis	Communities
KDC	Ethics	– Candidate selection: requirement of honesty and high ethical standards – Conduct of elections and committees: avoiding monopolies and ensuring that there was a one year limit on terms of office	Need for businesses to not be corrupt and have high ethical standards	Enforced the role of ethical behaviour at the local/village/district level through assemblies (sabhas and mahasabhas)
	Responsibilities	– Collective effort to have an honest electoral system (societal responsibilities) – Discussion of societal issues in sabhas and mahasabhas (societal participation)	Srenis were very generous philanthropies (e.g., their gifts to temples and people)	Collective responsibility to ensure that justice was done to people within the community
	Harmony	Collective well-being and societal cohesion	Societal upliftment initiatives	Social cohesion by enabling upliftment of poor
Dharmic Ecosystem		Development of large temples and an ecosystem around them	Propagation of Sreni Dharma	Development and protection of local, community-owned temples
Sreni Dharma		Samanya Dharma, which was a subset of Sreni Dharma	Sreni Dharma was the core guide for Srenis from social, economic and legal angles	Samanya Dharma, which was a subset of Sreni Dharma

Source: Author's analysis

5

Pallavas, Pandyas and Vijayanagar Empire

Pallavas

The Pallavas were considered to be the fiercest rivals of the Cholas and one of the most dominant kingdoms in southern Bharat besides the Cholas themselves. They ruled for many years in southern Bharat prior to the Cholas and then again after the rule of the Cholas ended.

History of the Pallavas

The Pallavas ruled mainly from the mid-third century CE, with Kanchipuram as their capital, until about the eighth century CE. At their peak, they ruled over the southern part of Andhra Pradesh, Bellary district and the northern part of Tamil Nadu. There is evidence to suggest that they were not around the Sangam period which was approximately from 5 CE to 300 CE. The rise of the Pallavas coincided with the development of post Sangam literature (after 300 CE)—*Silapadikaram*, *Manimekalai* and *Thirukkural*—and also the Bhakti movement, both of which started around the fifth century CE. Most of the leaders of the Pallava empire were devout Hindus who believed in the need to promote and protect Bharatiya culture. This is seen through the scholarship of their kings, the construction and maintenance of some of the most beautiful temples in southern Bharat and their efforts to build this heritage through inscriptions, promotion of arts and keeping Dharma at the forefront of governance frameworks.

The early copper plates indicate that the early Pallava language was some form of Prakrit.

There are different theories about their origin. Based on an inscription in Pahladpur near the Ganges, one theory states that they were from North India and similar to the Pahlava tribe.[1] Another theory suggests that they had deep connections with the Deccan region and that they were the original rulers of the Deccan. This is substantiated by the copper plate inscriptions, features of their governments and institutions and their matrimonial alliances with the royal family of Deccan—according to tradition, the first king of Chalukyas, based in Deccan, married a Pallava princess.[2] There is another theory which suggests that the first Pallava king was born after the marriage of Ashwatthama (son of Drona in the Mahabharata) and a Nagin princess.[3]

Besides their origin, the interesting part of the Pallavas was their association with other countries and societies. A prime example was their linkage with Kambuja Desa (Cambodia) whose Dharmic lineages will be discussed in the next chapter. Inscriptions in Kambuja Desa clearly indicate that a Vedic Brahmin by the name of Kaudinya (of the Pallava clan) had travelled to Kambuja Desa for trade. He fell in love with Soma, queen of Cambodia, and subsequently established a Hindu kingdom there.[4]

A very interesting connection of the Pallavas with the Southeast Asian kingdoms was the coronation of Nandivarman II as the king in 732 CE. The previous king, Parmeswaran II, had no children and there were no descendants to succeed him when he was killed during a war with the Chalukyas. A search team went looking for a Pallava lineage successor to many states and eventually landed in Kambuja Desa.[5] The team discovered that about 140 years earlier, the then Pallava king's brother,

Bhimavarman, had migrated to Kambuja Desa. They met local king, King Hiranyavarman, who was a descendant of Bhimavarman, in Champa (present-day Vietnam). It is important to note here that at this time, the ruler of Champa was Vikrantavarman II, whose lineage was from the Khmer empire (based on an inscription from the time of his father's rule in 657 CE) in the neighbouring Kambuja Desa[6]. This shows the cultural connection (and perhaps rivalry at times) between neighbouring empires which we will discuss in subsequent chapters. Though some sources indicate the search team went to Kambuja Desa, it could very well have been Champa, which was part of the Khmer kingdom at that time.

The Pallava search team presented its credentials and informed the purpose of their visit—to offer one of Hiranyavarman's sons the throne of Kanchipuram, given their Pallava lineage. The king agreed to their request but his eldest three sons were not interested in the offer. His fourth son was interested and thus the 13-year-old boy was anointed Nandivarman II, the king of Kanchipuram. Nandivarman II went on to create history by building the famous Vaikunta Perumal temple and was considered as one of the most successful rulers of the Pallava dynasty.

There are several inscriptions about the reign of Nandivarman II and his grandson Nandivarman III in Kanchipuram. Here is an extract from K.N. Sastri's paper which explains a Tamizh inscription in Tachi-Pua in Siam:

> The inscription is of incredible historical importance and belongs to the time of one of the later Pallava kings Nandivarman III who ruled at Kanchipuram and whose exploits form the subject of the laudatory poem 'Nandikkalambakam' in the Tamil language. In this poem the king is repeatedly called Avani-naranan (vv. 14, 18, 22, and 66) and the village of Kaverippakkam about twenty

> miles north of Kanchipuram bears in its inscriptions the name Avani-narayana-caturvedimangalam. Naranan is the common Tamil variant of the fuller Samskritam form 'Narayana', and the title with this form is also found in the Tamil poem in some verses (e.g., v. 64). This poem also describes him as the unrivalled master of the four oceans—Narkadarkoru-navakan (v. 26), and our inscription is important as the solitary piece of concrete evidence in support of this tall claim made on behalf of Nandivarman III by his court-poet.

These inscriptions further reinforce some of the points mentioned earlier with regard to the Pallavas interactions and connections with Southeast Asia as well as the accounts of travellers and researchers.

The early Pallava kings are listed in Table 5.1.

TABLE 5.1 Early Pallava Kings

Period (in CE)	**King's Name**
275–300	Simhavarman
Unknown	Shivskandvarman
Unknown	Skandavarman
Unknown	Vijayskandavarman
350–355	Vishnugopa I
350–370	Kumaravishnu I
370–385	Skandavarman II
385–400	Viravarman
400–436	Skandavarman III
436–460	Simhavarman II
460–480	Skandavarman IV
480–510	Nandivarman I
510–530	Kumaravishnu II
530–540	Buddhavarman
540–550	Kumaravishnu III
550–560	Simhavarman III

Source: K.A. Nilakanta Sastri, *The History of South India* (Oxford University Press, 1966)

The later era Pallavas are listed in Table 5.2.

TABLE 5.2 Later Pallava Kings

Period (in CE)	**King's Name**
575–600	Simhavishnu
600–630	Mahendravarman I
630–668	Narasimhavarman I (Mamalla)
668–672	Mahendravarman II
670–695	Paramesvaravarman I
695–722	Narasimhavarman II (Raja Simha)
705–710	Paramesvaravarman II
732–796	Nandivarman II (Pallavamalla) son of Hiranyavarman of Kadavakula
795–846	Dantivarman
846–869	Nandivarman III
879–897	Aparajitavarman

Source: K.A. Nilakanta Sastri, *The History of South India* (Oxford University Press, 1966)

FIGURE 5.1 Pallava Era Coin During the Reign of Narasimhavarman I (630–668 CE)

Source: https://en.wikipedia.org/wiki/Pallava_dynasty#/media/File: Pallavas_of_Coromandel.jpg

Economic Policies of the Pallavas

The broad contours of the economic policies of the Pallavas were similar to what the Cholas had. Agriculture, trade and manufacturing were key to economy. However, there were some distinct differences in how they approached economic policy compared to the Cholas. In this section, we will look at some of the broad economic trends and highlight some of the differences.

Agriculture and Land

Land Surveys

Though the Cholas were considered to be the pioneers of the system of land surveys, much of the foundational work on surveys had already been done during the Pallava period. In the Pallava system, there were a considerable number of features that were quite distinct in their own right. The Pallavas had a method of accurately defining and measuring assets, including land. The surveys were monitored by key government officials at the local and district levels. This also indicates that land surveys were important. The Uruvappali inscription gives the level of detail in the surveys:

> In this village there are two hundred Nivartanas. The limits of those Nivartanas are: on the west, the boundaries of the village of Kanduküra are the limit; on the south the river Suprayogä is the limit; on the east, the same is the limit; to the north by south of the cast there is a rock on the side of the great road; proceeding thence to the north, there is a tamarind tree; proceeding thence to the north, there is a rock on the road to the village of Karupüra, and to the village of Kandukura; proceeding thence to the north, there is a heap of rocks; proceeding thence to the north, there is a rock on the limit of the cultivated field of the Brahmans in the village of Karupura; on the north the limit is a large tamarind tree surrounded by a heap of

Lord Brahma, Kbal Spean, Cambodia

One thousand Shiva lingams across the stream in various places, Kbal Spean, Cambodia

Lord Ranganatha, Kbal Spean, Cambodia

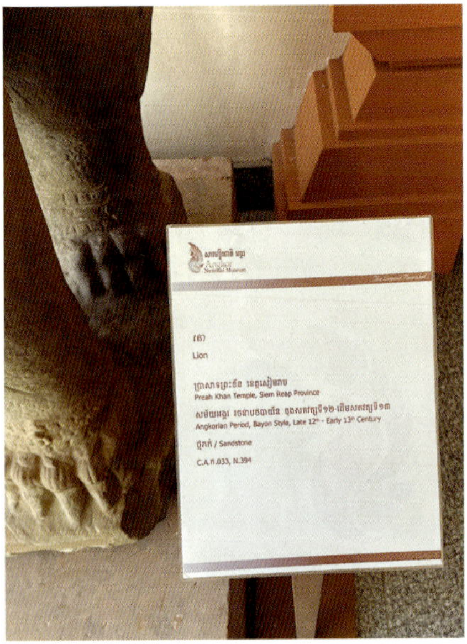

One of the Bayon-style sculptures from the Preah Khan temple in Siem Reap displayed at the Angkor National Museum. The time period is 12–13 centuries CE. This was likely commissioned during Jayavarman VII's time, possibly when temple architecture was transitioning to sandstone (see section on iron production, pp. 199–200).

In and around the Bayon temple in Siem Reap. Photograph on the top right is of a Shiva Linga in the temple premises. Thousands of such lingas can be seen across temples and villages in Kambuja Desa. The exterior structures of the temples bear striking similarities to the temple styles in Bharat.

In and around the Preah Khan temple in Siem Reap. Depictions of scenes from the Mahabharata war in Kurukshetra are common, as in the photograph at the bottom, where a charioteer can be seen in action. Other inscriptions have also been found in this temple related to Bharatiya traditions (see Chapter 6).

The exterior of the majestic 12th-century Angkor Wat temple complex. The temple is surrounded by a lake, which was part of the sophisticated irrigation system built during that time. In a sense, this is meant to be a floating temple in an island when it gets flooded. The photograph at the bottom right was taken from inside an erstwhile library in the interior courtyard of the Angkor Wat – the main temple can be seen in the background.

Photographs from the inner structures of the main Angkor Wat temple. (*Top left*) A Maha-Vishnu statue with eight hands stretching out; subsequent to Buddhist invasions, the head was replaced with the Buddha's head. (*Top right*) Depiction of a scene from the Ramayana on the interior walls of Angkor Wat. (*Middle*) View of the temple from the innermost compound. One has to climb steep stairs to enter the inner sanctorum in the gopuram of the innermost compound.

The imperious Brihadisvara temple. The size, grandeur and the architectural marvel continue to inspire awe even after a thousand years. The temple survived many earthquakes, rulers and socioeconomic changes, yet its authenticity and endurance seem everlasting. The longevity of such monuments is testament to the Dharmic economic models which provided one of the foundations for its construction and endurance.

Inscriptions carved into the lower half of the temple in all directions. These inscriptions, which I have quoted and used extensively in this book, provide key details about the Cholas during this era. Rajaraja Chola and other rulers had the foresight to inscribe all of this in stone. Their transparency in governance is also showcased by how they inscribed even the most mundane of contributions to the temple in this form.

I made it a point to go to Gangaikonda Cholapuram, a replica of the Brihadisvara temple built by Rajendra Chola. While the replica was equally fascinating, it was deliberately kept low-key so as not to overshadow the original's glory. This temple and the surrounding area remained the capital during Rajendra Chola's reign too and the name denotes Rajendra Chola's conquests north of the Vindhyas – Gangaikonda Cholan literally means 'the Chola king who conquered the (plains of) River Ganga'.

> rocks; proceeding thence to the west, the limit is the edge of the boundaries of the village Kondamuruvudu.

This gives a description of a survey in a particular area. This is not one-off; such descriptions are present in other inscriptions at Pattamangalam and Udayendiram plates as well.[7]

Among a variety of taxes that were imposed on many products, it is possible that agricultural output was also taxed. This is not surprising since Kautilya himself had proposed this many centuries ago. It was called 'eccoru', a word made from 'el' (a day of two–four hours) and 'soru' (boiled rice).[8] Land that belonged to the royalty and was under the king's jurisdiction was exempt from taxes.

Land Ownership

Contrary to popular perception, the presence of a monarchy does not always imply that it will completely usurp the land that is available in the kingdom. Similar to Kautilya's times, there is ample evidence to show that the Pallava kings were merely the guardians of the land and not necessarily the owners. There are inscriptions which describe several types of land owners. According to the Gudimallam inscriptions,[9] there were private land owners who owned land either through inheritance or commercial transactions. There was eripatti, which was private land used for construction and maintenance of tanks, bunds, land slices and so on. There was also land owned by temples, which were mainly Hindu, though there were Jain temples too which were called 'pallicandam'. Besides these, there was land called 'devadena' and 'brahmadaya', which was land given as a gift by the royalty as an act of philanthropy or as a reward to Brahmins for their efforts, respectively. There were reasonably detailed procedures laid out for tenants in state-owned and private-owned farms. These procedures included revenue sharing formulae, tax exemptions and, if need be, the geography of the land as per the land surveys, as well as the tenure of the rental, as a part of the agreement with tenants.

Thus, land ownership was not a simple, unilateral exercise but a reasonably sophisticated structure which was cognizant of the economic and financial implications of land ownership. We should note that some of these principles of governance were akin to those of the Sreni Dharma as discussed in previous chapters. The principles of Sreni Dharma were considered to be the foundational base for governance.

Agriculture

Agriculture was obviously a key component of the economy during the Pallava era. While a variety of crops were grown, by far the most important crop was rice. Rice was a key source of food for the local population as well as an important item for export. An inscription around the seventh century states that rice was sent all the way to China,[10] among other countries. Several varieties of rice were grown. They included reddish paddy (sennel), paddy for cultivation (narnel) and paddy used for food (irainel), according to the Kampavaraman and Nandivarman III inscriptions.[11]

Other crops included coconut, palmyra palms, areca palms and oil seeds.[12] Several medicinal plants such as Sengodiveli, Karusarangani, Damanagam and Kuvalai were also cultivated. This also suggests the active presence or usage of Ayurvedic techniques during those times to cure diseases. Cotton was another important crop that was grown quite extensively in Kanchipuram during the Pallava rule.

In terms of the infrastructure related to agriculture, there were very good irrigation systems that facilitated agricultural activities. Examples of large tanks include Tenneri (mentioned as Tirayaneri in inscriptions), Mahendra Tataka in Mahendravadi, Citramega Tataka in Mamandur, and Parameswara Tataka and Vairamega Tataka in Uthiramerur.[13] These tanks were supported by an extensive infrastructure of wells and canals. Canals were seen as the prime way to irrigate lands and they were called 'arrukkal'. They carried the water from the rivers to feed tanks, which were the key sources of water for the cities. In the context of Uthiramerur, whose inscriptions were mentioned earlier, the Ganapati and Sridhara Vaykkal were branch-canals constructed as offshoots of the Vairamega Tataka to feed the tanks which, in turn, irrigated the fields in the Uthiramerur area. Irrigation maintenance was taken care by the sabhas at the village level. There were also tank maintenance committees called 'Erivariya perumakkal' according to the Uthiramerur inscriptions mentioned earlier. Here is a sample quotation from one of the inscriptions:

> No. 90 of 1898: In the 15th year of Kampavarman's reign, the Uttiramerür sabha received from Devandai Kalukkunran, 100 kalañjus of gold and 28 kadis of irai paddy, to be utilised for dredging the Vairamegha tank. This inscription records that the sabha of Uttiramerür should let the money on interest at 10% and receive an interest of 3 kadis of paddy for the year on the 28 kadis. These 10 kalañjus of gold and the 3 kadis of paddy should suffice to meet the cost of labour for dredging the tank for two months every year from Vaikäsi.
>
> No. 65 of 1898: In the 18th year of Kampavarman, the Uttiramerur sabha received 100 kalañjus of Ürkkar semmai gold rom Manni Päkkilan of Terkkilangädi and also 20 manais. The sabhä entrusted the gift to the tank committee, which agreed to invest the money on

> a reasonable rate of 15% and utilise the income both from the gold and the land for dredging the Vairamegha Tataka.[14]

Despite the administrative control of the water supply for irrigation, the state was more than willing to encourage private donors and non-state entities to take an active role in the construction and maintenance of irrigation systems. Some of them were also provided with support infrastructure to build these systems, especially when the state's capacity seemed limited for these activities. This facet of governance is an important point to understand. It shows that the discrimination against private entities, which is assumed to be true by default in a monarchy, was largely absent. What was vital was the capability of the state to implement the projects and whether it was efficient and effective in doing so. If not, the state was open to letting non-state entities do the job. In such cases, the state played the role of an enabler to ensure effective outcomes. This was akin to a public–private partnership—more than a thousand years ago!

Trade and Commerce

The Pallavas had a reputation for being avid travellers. The trading ecosystem of the Pallavas needs to be seen through three areas—infrastructure, types of products and the role of the state in facilitating trade and commerce.

In infrastructure, port infrastructure was vital for trading activities. Mamallapuram served as the largest port in the Pallava kingdom. It had a continuous array of trade-related expeditions, given how busy the port was. Nagapattinam was considered to be the major port of the Cholas, and it was also functioning during the Pallavas reign, though on a much smaller scale compared to Mamallapuram. The traders operated across many centres internally within southern Bharat and in countries of Southeast Asia as well. In addition to the external infrastructure, the internal trading mechanisms were also well developed. Within every village, there were markets set up for trading, which were similar to the combination of bazaars and mandis that operate today.

The products traded included oil, ghee, coconuts, sugar and various types of vegetables and flowers.[15] Similar to today's markets around temples, a plethora of shops operated around the temples even then. These shops were required to have a licence to operate, something similar to the trade licence required for commercial activities today. Inscriptions in the Ulagalantha Perumal temple state that there was a trade licence provided to commercial vendors in the town of Kudaraicerri to open shops near the temple area.

This shows that there was a system in place for commerce within the Pallava kingdom where internal trade and commerce was promoted, with certain regulations, to ensure order and governance.

Dharmic Influences on the Economy

The economic frameworks and structures of the Pallavas were similar to the Cholas. Their reliance on agriculture, emphasis on trade and commerce and their actions to ensure the welfare of their people are all evident in their economic policies. Let us explore how the components of Dharmanomics were applicable to their rule.

With respect to the KDC model, the Pallavas had their foundations based on ethics, responsibilities and harmony. We have seen some of the examples that reflect the definitions of Dharma that were incorporated in their economic activities. The outcomes of KDC—a rule-enforcing yet non-intrusive state, a globalized approach via trade and sustainable growth—are also apparent in their economic policies. For example, the example given earlier about how the public–private partnerships worked during the Pallava era, where the private players were encouraged to build infrastructure such as irrigation systems if they were competent, signifies a system which was rule-enforcing (in terms of regulations and rule of law) but not necessarily prescriptive nor state-oriented in nature all the time. Another example is that of the trade guilds which went as far as Champa (Vietnam) to trade in a variety of products regularly, which indicates an institutional interest in engaging with the rest of the world for commerce and trade. The traders were travelling at ease to these countries, so much so that they travelled all the way to Kambuja Desa and Champa to find a successor to the throne in Nandivarman II! Such was the level of trust and ease with which business and commerce was taking place across the borders. This is indicative of a state which was open to engaging with the rest of the world.

On sustainable growth, we have seen references to the idea of societal responsibilities being fostered, especially at the village or gram panchayat levels. These included the instances where the village committees pooled resources through philanthropic grants, which were then invested to get a good return on investment. This income was used to maintain local tanks and irrigation facilities.

With respect to the Dharmic ecosystem, there is no doubt that the temples played a very important role in the socioeconomic fabric of the Pallavas. However, unlike Kambuja Desa, which we will discuss later, researchers have not systematically looked at this aspect. Something as obvious as this should have been researched more.

The temples played a very important role in economic activity and social harmony. There were also other parts of the economy which were equally prosperous, including agriculture and trade, but Dharmic philosophy was central to the economic model and its functioning.

On the Sreni Dharma, there is little research during the reign of the Pallavas as compared to the Cholas and other kingdoms. We should also note that there was a lot of continuity between the Pallava era and the Chola era, especially in the later Pallava era. For example, in the Uthiramerur inscriptions, there are references to Pallava rule as well, though the inscriptions were primarily written during the Chola era.

A case can definitely be made about the continuity of systems and processes at the level of governance after the Cholas took over. It is possible that Sreni Dharma and the governance structures of the srenis were far more refined and sophisticated during the Chola era as compared to the Pallava era. Here I am not referring to the extent or quantum of trade (that is a different story) but the level of governance and the inscriptional evidence available on the principles of Sreni Dharma. There are undercurrents of Sreni Dharma in the way the Pallava guilds functioned, but inscriptional evidence regarding this is scanty.

Overall, the history of Pallava era has a substantial correlation with the KDC model, reasonable correlation with the Dharmic ecosystem and offers implicit assumptions vis-à-vis the Sreni Dharma. As such, the influence of Dharmic principles and, more importantly, Dharmanomics is evident during the Pallava rule.

Pandyas

The Pandyas were considered to be the foremost rulers of southern Bharat, along with the Cholas and Pallavas. Much of their territory was in the southern part of Tamil Nadu and their capital was in Madurai for many years. In this chapter, I will describe the historical contours of the Pandya empire, their rule and economic models.

History of the Pandya Empire

The historical lineage of the empire is shown in Table 5.3 for those who are interested. Most of the information is definitive, but it is important to note that by some accounts, Pandya kingdom originated in around 200 BCE.[16] The information about the earlier kings is uncertain. In this book, I refer to the Pandya kings in the post-Sangam era (1–300 CE).[17]

TABLE 5.3 Pallava Kings

Kings	**Reign**	**Comments**
Early Pandya Rulers		
Pudap Pandyan	NA	NA
Mudukudumi Paruvaludhi	NA	NA
Nedunjeliyan I	270 BCE	Valorous Pandya king who was a contemporary of Chera King Senguttuvan; his name is mentioned in the Silappadikaram.
Nedunjeliyan II	210 CE	He defeated the confederacy of the Cholas and Cheras at Talaiyalanganam near Tiruvarur and conquered most of the Tamil region. His era has been described in detail in the Maduraikkanci.
Nan Maran	NA	NA
Nedunjeliyan III	NA	NA
Maran Valudi	NA	NA
Kadalan Valuthi	NA	NA
Musiri Mutriya Cheliyan	NA	NA
Ukkirap Peruvaludi	NA	NA

Kings	Reign	Comments
Medieval, Imperial and Tenkasi Pandya Rulers		
Kadungon	590–620	Referred as 'Pandyadhiraja' and was known to have ended the Kalabhra rule, starting a new era in the Tamil speaking region.
Maravarman Avani Culamani	620–645	Took the title of 'Maravarman'.
Jayantavarman	645–670	Also known as 'Seliyan Sendan'.
Arikesari Maravarman	670–710	Also known as 'Arikesari Parankusa'.
Kochadaiyan Ranadhiran	710–740	Established Pandyas' superiority over the Cheras and Cholas in the city of Mangalapuram, the modern-day Mangaluru.
Maravarman Rajasimha I	740–765	He was the son and successor of Kochadaiyan Ranadhiran.
Jatila Parantaka	765–815	Also known as 'Varaguna maharaja'; he performed the consecration of the Vishnu temple built by Marangari in Annamalai in 770.
Srimara Srivallabha	815–862	Constructed many tanks, canals and water reservoirs.
Varagunavarman II	862–880	Contemporary of the great Saivite saint and author Manikavasagar, who wrote the epoch-making book *Thiruvasagam*.

Kings	**Reign**	**Comments**
Parantaka Viranarayana	880–900	Ascended the throne after the battle of Purambiyam.
Maravarman Rajasimha III	900–920	He opposed the Chola king of Thanjavur at Kodumbalur and plundered the Chera capital at Vanchi in Kongu Nadu. After successive defeats, he fled to modern-day Sri Lanka but did not get shelter. Then he went to Kerala, as he was a descendant (partially) of a Chera king. He spent the rest of his days there, keeping a low profile. Around 950, Vira Pandya I fought with the Chola king Sundara parantaka and was killed by Aditya Karikala. In 1020, Rajendra Chola invaded and conquered the Pandya kingdom.
Maravarman Srivallabha	1132–1161	
Parakrama I	1161–1162	
Kulasekara III		Civil war between Kulasekara III and Parakrama.
Vira Pandya III		Civil war between Vikram Pandya (son of Kulasekara) and Vira Pandya (son of Parakrama). The latter won the battle.
Jatavarman Srivallabha	1175–1180	
Jatavarman Kulasekara I	1190–1216	
Marvarman Sundara Pandya I	1216–1238	

Kings	Reign	Comments
Marvarman Sundara Pandya II	1238–1251	
Jayavarman Sundara Pandya	1251–1268	
Maravarman Kulasekara I	1268–1310	There were many sub-kings or sub-coordinate kings during his rule. He conquered the current-day Sri Lanka in 1284.
Sundara Pandya IV	1310–1327	Malik Kafur's invasion of Madura took place in 1310; establishment of the Sultanate of Madura in 1329–30.
Vira Pandya IV	1309–1345	
Jatavarman Vikrama Pandya	1401-1422	
Arikesari Parakrama Manabarana	1422–1429	
Kulasekara alias SriVallabha	1429–1435	
Arikesvara	1435–1443	
Maravarman Vira Pandya II	1443–1473	
Vira Pandya	1473–1479	
Parakrama alias Kulasekhara	1479–1531	
Maravarman Sundara Pandya (III)	153–-1534	
Jatavarman Srivallabha	1534–1543	
Kulasekara Parakrama	1543–1551	
Tirunelveliperumal Kulasekara	1551–1563	
Ativirarama Srivallabha	1563–1588	
Varatungarama	1588–1615	

Source: Author's analysis using K.A. Nilakanta Sastri's *The Pandya Kingdom*, https://archive.org/details/ThePandyaKingdom/page/n51/mode/2up and https://www.jagranjosh.com/general-knowledge/list-of-pandya-rulers-and-their-contributions-1509450706-1

There are several anecdotal references to the Pandyas from various travellers and travelogues over the centuries. These include references to the early as well as later-day Pandyas. There are both internal as well as external sources for this.

Some of the internal sources include references in several ancient Tamizh texts. A few examples are:

> The Purananuru and Agananuru collections contain poems sung in praise of various Pandya rulers and also poems that were claimed to be composed by the rulers themselves. Besides the poems, king Peruvaludi is also mentioned in later copper-plate grant (8th–9th century CE). In the work Mathuraikkanci, the author Mankudi Maruthanar refers to his patron, Talaihalanganum Nedunjeliyan, as the Lord of Korkai and the Warlord of the Southern Parathavar People (then Parathavar poryere). It contains a full-length description of Madurai and the Pandya country under the rule of Nedunjeliyan. In the famous battle of Talaiyalanganam (in east Tanjore), the Pandya is said to have defeated his enemies (which included the Chera and the Chola). He is also praised for his victory of Mizhalai and Mutturu, two 'vel' centres along the ocean (in Pudukkottai). The Netunalvatai (in the collection of Pattupattu) by Nakkirar contains a description of king Nedunjeliyan's palace.[18]

Some examples of the external sources include:

- In around 140 CE, Ptolemy mentions about the Pandyas and refers to them as 'Pandya Medeiterranea' and 'Modura Pandionis'.
- The Roman Emperor Julion received an embassy note from the Pandyas in around 361 CE.[19]

- The Chinese historian Yu Huan, in his 3rd century CE text, *Weilüe*, mentions that the Pandyan kingdom was several thousand miles southeast of North India and its inhabitants were small in size. The Chinese traveller Xuanzang says, 'A kingdom further south from Kanchipuram, a kingdom named Malakutta, identified with Madurai, described by his Buddhist friends at Kanchipuram.'
- Marco Polo's travels took him to the Pandya kingdom (between 1288 and 1293) and he provides important descriptions based on his observations.
- Strabo mentions about an ancient Indian king by the name Pandyan who sent Augustus Caesar 'presents and gifts' and another ambassador of a similar king was sent to meet Caesar around 13 CE.[20]

Economic Philosophy and Structure of the Pandya Empire

Economic Philosophy

The economic philosophy of the Pandyas seems to have been quite similar to both the Pallavas and Cholas but with some structural variations. First, the role of Dharma being central to their socioeconomic functioning seems to be quite evident. Besides a plethora of inscriptions referring to the promotion of Dharmic principles, the role of Dharma was so central that even inscriptions of other kingdoms mention it. For example, there is an inscription by the Mauryan king Ashoka:

> The conquest by Dharma has been won here, on the borders, and even six hundred yojanas (5,400–9,600 km) away, where the Greek king Antiochos rules, beyond there where the four kings named Ptolemy, Antigonos, Magas and Alexander rule, likewise in the south among the Cholas, the Pandyas, and as far as Tamraparni river.[21]

While Ashoka clearly refers to the early Pandyas before the Common Era, it shows that even then the philosophy of Dharma was not just a common reference point but an integral part of how the Pandya kingdoms functioned.

Second, the state seems to have been facilitating economic potential rather than micro-managing economic activity. The functioning of the Srenis and their central role in economic trade and activity is visible in both inscriptions as well as anecdotal evidence. Last, the philosophy of protecting the needy and empowering them also seems to have been a key part of the Pandya legacy.

In terms of differences in the economic policies of the Pandyas with the Cholas and Pallavas, I believe most of them were due to the geographical regions which they ruled. For example, agriculture was more predominant in the Chola empire as compared to the Pandyas because of the Kaveri delta and its surrounding influences. On the other hand, many of the commodities that were traded were sourced from mineral-rich Pandya territory and hence bilateral trade with countries in the West was far more important for the Pandyas. This difference increased due to the manufacturing potential of some key products using, for example, iron and copper, which were extensively available in the commodity-rich Pandya regions.

Economic Structure

The economic structure of the Pandya empire was an amalgamation of the structures of other empires that we have discussed thus far. The topography of the territory and the fact that they controlled different geographical pockets at different times makes us wonder if their economic policy was specialized or not. There were various gradations of influence even within the earlier and later Pandya periods in terms of economic structure and the role of different stakeholders in the economic system. The main sectors of the economy included agriculture, trade and manufacturing, as mentioned earlier.

Coinage/Currency during Pandya Rule

Like other rulers, the Pandyas had their own currency in the form of distinctive coins which were used by the traders and the general society. These coins represented either the heritage of the Pandyas—coins with fish as a sign; or their king's identity—for example, during Sundara Pandya's rule the coins had a 'Su' abbreviation on them; or their diverse metallic traditions—there were silver, copper and gold coins available.[22]

Agriculture during the Pandya Rule

Agriculture was an important component of all ancient economies and the Pandyas were no exception. The focus on agriculture and agricultural produce was an important component of economic policy of the Pandyas. Besides taxes—agriculture was taxed in those times unlike today—the employment that agriculture generated was very crucial to the proper functioning of the labour markets. The type of agriculture produce was similar to the Cholas but the quantum and scale of agriculture was limited compared to the Cholas given the latter's proximity to the fertile Kaveri delta region. On the other hand, the Vaigai and Tamira Bharani rivers provided the much needed fertile soil for agricultural activities in the region.

Trade during the Pandya Rule

Trade was an important and thriving component of the Pandya economy. The *Arthashastra* refers to the textiles and fabrics that were traded in Madurai during the reign of the Pandya rulers.[23] While the Cholas and Pallavas were also active in trading, given the location of their ports, the

Pandyas mainly had terminal trade whereas the Cholas used their ports for transit trade. That is, most of the goods traded by the Pandyas were consumed in their kingdom itself. It was a bilateral trade between the source (say Romans) and the Pandyas.[24] On the other hand, the Cholas, besides the goods needed for their own consumption, used their ports also as transit points for other destinations. The goods transiting their ports went not just to Southeast Asia but eventually reached China as well. Thus their ports played a key role in the trade between the Middle East/ Europe and China. It is also interesting to note that most of the natural resources required for commodities were available in the Pandya and Chera regions rather than in the Chola region. The Cholas had exceptional agricultural potential (due to the Kaveri river) but their resources to produce commodities were limited. Yet their ability to expand port networks and ensure most products went through their major ports were admirable.[25]

Trade in commodities was a fairly regular phenomenon in the Pandya rule. As we have seen in the earlier sections, a wide range of products and commodities were traded in ancient Bharat. So it is not a surprise to see the diversity of products traded, and this inscription in Kovilpatti presents a unique basket of products that were being traded:

> Agil (aloe), arisi (rice), avarai (beans), erudu (bull), erumai (buffalo), kadugu (mustard), kampi (iron), kana mdlai (garlands?), karpuram (camphor), karu alai mdlai (garlands?), kasturi (musk), kidii (cattle), kudirai (horse), mayir (hair), milaku (pepper), nel (paddy), ouai (camel), pacu (cow), pdkku (areca-nuts), pudavai (saree/ long cloth), pul (grass), puli (tamarind), sdmai (millet), sandanam (sandal), sangu (conch), tantam (ivory), tuvarai (dhal), ulandu-putavai (woollen cloth), uppu (salt) and varagu (millet).[26]

Goods imported by Bharat included a variety of products, including the ones mentioned above as well as other products such as coins, coral, clothes, copper, tin, lead and even wine.[27] Horses were imported from Arab countries, and the *Madurakkana* makes references to this as well.

Jewellery was an important item of export from the Pandya territory, along with pearls, which were called 'muthu' in Tamizh. Pearls from those times have been found in parts of Southeast Asia, Middle East and even Rome.[28] Spices were another important item and were exported to the rest of the world. They included pepper (which was mainly off the Chera coast but the Pandyas still produced it) and cardamom (which was found in Madurai, Tirunelveli and Dindugal area).[29]

Manufacturing during the Pandya Rule

There were certain key industries that were important to export goods and services to the rest of the world. These included textiles, spinning and weaving, copper and iron production. Most of these units were reasonably scaled up, but their impact on overall employment in the region cannot be determined with the information currently available.

Dharmic Influences on the Economy

Much like the other kingdoms, understanding the influence of Dharmanomics on the role of economic policy is key to the research presented in this book. It is important to note that information about the Pandya economy, in concrete terms, is not as easy to analyse compared to the other kingdoms. Much of the evidence is poetry based, and there is a general lack of coherent literature on the subject.

In terms of KDC, as mentioned in the earlier section on the Pallavas, the Pandyas were definitely open to engaging with the world vis-à-vis trade and commerce and also believed in the principles of sustainable growth and social responsibilities. The other key factor in KDC is the role of the state, which should enable commerce and allow freedom to pursue economic activities to all the stakeholders. Scholars say that it is difficult to judge the role of the state. In some cases, kings have been praised for promoting commerce through state support for economic activities. In other cases, the state's actions on other geopolitical issues have been questioned. An example of this is the Sangam poetry about Pandya king Neduncheliyan, which deals with both these points.[30] My interpretation is that purely from an economic viewpoint, the role of the state was supportive—similar to the Cholas and Pallavas—especially in the context of enabling the Srenis to accelerate economic activity and also to enable the Dharmic ecosystem to flourish, providing economic benefits in the process. However, there are some instances where the state's intervention for political and strategic reasons could have been significant. While there are some examples of the state providing support for economic activities and trade, there is very little (negligible) evidence to suggest they impeded commerce or trade in any way. Overall, I believe that the state played a positive role in enabling economic activities, not an intrusive one.

Srenis and the role of Sreni Dharma was, again, quite prominent during the Pandya era, much like the Chola period. As mentioned at the end of the S–S chapter earlier, there were references to vēḷir (a Sreni specializing in casting and alloy metal work in Purananur) which indicated prominence of some of these Srenis in the Pandya rule as well. There were Srenis which were mentioned in the list in Chapter 4 as well as newer ones. These were central to the functioning of the economy and their Dharma-based principles were used for governance and functioning.

The Dharmic ecosystem was an important factor in the economic activity of the Pandya rule. The temple economy flourished along the same lines as mentioned in the Chola and the Pallava chapters. Most of the parameters of the Dharmic ecosystem remained applicable to the Pandyas as well. There were some variations in the extent of the temple ecosystem, but the operating parameters appeared quite similar.

As in other periods, the temples served religious as well as redistributive functions. The role of temples and village assemblies as financial institutions was an important catalyst for economic activities. The village assemblies served as public trustees and local banks. For example, in a ninth century Ambasamudram inscription[31], during the rule of the Pandya ruler Varaguna, there is a mention about the unspent interest payments from the corpus of the village assemblies being used for community purposes.

It is quite evident from anecdotal and inscription-based sources that Dharmanomics was quite relevant in the Pandya empire as well—similar to the southern Bharat kingdoms that I have discussed in this book.

Vijayanagar Empire

The Vijayanagar empire was one of the most important kingdoms south of the Vindhyas and existed from the thirteenth century CE until almost the seventeenth century CE. Considered to be one of the most important civilizations of southern Bharat, it was seen as a civilizational bulwark that resisted the onslaught of the Mughals south of the Vindhyas. There can be many books written on them, but to remain within the subject matter of this book, I will discuss their rule briefly and the economic philosophies they followed.

History of the Vijayanagar Empire

Unlike other rulers in Bharat including the Cholas, the Vijayanagar rulers were not portrayed as larger-than-life. The Vijayanagar rulers were divided into four dynasties—Sangama, Saluva, Tulluva and Aravidu dynasties. All the rulers have been listed in Table 5.4.

Table 5.4 shows a continuous reign of rulers through three dynasties, all under the umbrella of the Vijayanagar empire almost uninterrupted throughout. All these rulers had their own unique characteristics, but since we are focused on economic history in this book, we will go straight to the economy of Vijayanagar empire.

Economic Characteristics of the Vijayanagar Empire

Krishnadevaraya, in his sixteenth century CE poem 'Amuktamalyada' says:

> The extent of the state is not the cause of its prosperity. When a state is small in extent then both virtue (Dharma) and prosperity (artha) will increase only when tanks and irrigation canals are constructed and favour is shown to the poor cultivators in the matter of taxation and services.

Similar to other kingdoms that I have reviewed thus far, key sectors of growth in the Vijayanagar empire were in agriculture, trade and manufacturing. Let me show how Dharma implicitly played an important role and Dharmanomics played a more explicit role in the economic policies of the empire.

Monetary and Fiscal Policies of the State

On the fiscal side, there was a general attempt at fiscal prudence primarily because of Dharmic values which did

latter was generally used for commercial transactions, taxation and other administrative purposes.

This meant that there were several coins in circulation within the economy, similar to the circulation of currency today. It also meant that the rulers were cognizant of the challenges of having too much or too little liquidity, that is coins, in the system. We had seen even during Kautilya's time,[39] almost a thousand years earlier, there were mentions of officers stationed in villages who monitored the prices of products. There was probably a system to monitor prices across the Vijayanagar empire, too. Furthermore, the relevance of maintaining prices under control was an important feature of the governance of the empire.

Dharmic Ecosystem via Temples

The temple ecosystem played a very important structural role in the economic activities of the Vijayanagar empire. The geographical construct of the empire was such that the requirement for plenty of water for 'wet' agriculture could be met by rains throughout the year, supported by river canals and tanks all over the kingdom. In some parts, there was 'dry' agriculture depending on the type of soil, water supply and rainfall. These areas produced crops such as millets, sorghum, oilseeds and cotton, with most places producing one crop per year.[40]

One of the most useful ways to integrate the agricultural regions was through the construction and investment in large temples. These temples served as not just religious institutions and financial centres (as we have seen earlier) but also as key facilitators for irrigation and agriculture. For example, large areas of land were controlled by temples and through public and private investments, excellent irrigation facilities were developed, especially in the dry regions of the Vijayanagar empire. The decision making on agricultural matters was highly decentralized around the tenth century CE, with smaller irrigation networks being controlled by local groups and individuals. These networks evolved and grew over time with the involvement of temples in agricultural production. This was done with the help of Nayaka rulers from the Pandya empire, enlisted by the Vijayanagar empire through greater local ties by investments and alliances with local religious centres.[41] Thus, the agricultural ecosystem—its production, infrastructure and its sustenance, especially in drier areas—was primarily driven by the temple ecosystem. So the agricultural activity correlated with the prosperity of the temples.

This involvement of temples was not just restricted to their immediate neighbourhood. The temples used their endowments for building infrastructure and for public activities based on their own choice and not on the directions of the state. For example, an inscription from around 1510 in the Kalahasti temple says:

> We, the supervisors of the Treasury of the God at Kalahasti ... agree to arrange for offerings of sweet rice cakes on eleven occasions. Virappannar Ayyan deposited with us for the purpose 1,306 pan which was to be invested in the new settlements of Mallayammansamudram ... with a view to bring the lands under cultivation [and] Lakkusettipuram. ... The lands of the latter settlement were to be irrigated and brought under the plow with the help of the waters of Virasamudram lake [which] will be repaired and maintained by investing 1,006 pan of the amount deposited.[42]

Therefore, it is quite clear that the temple ecosystem was central to the economic system and was a catalyst for the economic activities in the villages, cities and the region as a whole.

The situation for trade was similar to what we saw in the earlier chapters on other kingdoms. The temples served as financial institutions for traders, especially in the coastal belt of Karnataka and some parts of Kerala. There were a plethora of ports in the kingdom—almost 300 of them by some estimates, on both sides of the coast[43]—and all of them would have needed some level of financial intermediation, given the large number of guilds present. There are several implicit and explicit examples of this. For example, in an inscription in Sevalur dated around 1503, during the reign of Danmayara Maharaya, there was a recorded sale of land in Tenur to the local Bhumisvaramudaiya Nayanar temple for 300 sakkaram-panam. This was supposed to have been borrowed earlier from the temple treasury to pay the monarch's dues.[44] This is evidence that the temple was serving the role of a local bank and facilitating commercial transactions.

Redistribution was an important function attributed to the temples during the Vijayanagar empire. Theoretically, we could attribute this to any temple in any era, but I believe that there was an attempt at triggering redistribution by the Vijayanagar state—a sort of a fourteenth century CE nudge. The basic concept was that the temple received funds as donations and endowments essentially from people who were rich or in the upper echelons of the society. These funds were used for temple rituals and activities which included providing prasadam (food with divine blessing) to thousands of people who came to pray at these temples. As a result of this, people received free food. I see it as the main redistributive process that was reducing inequality through wealth transfers from the rich (endowments) to the poorer devotees.

Tirupati Tirumala
Sri Venkateshwara Temple: Key Facts

– It is the world's most visited and richest temple by many estimates, with average daily collections of ₹22.5 million.[45]

– It is one of the largest annaprasadam centres in the world, providing food to more than one lakh people per day, three times a day. The laddu prasadam has a GI (Geographical Indication) tag![46]

– The main temple is spread over 16.2 acres.[47] It has five deities in the garbhagriha. It is a part of seven hills and is considered to be one of the holiest shrines in the country.

– It has several stone inscriptions about past rulers. They are 1,180 in total and belong to the ruling period of Kondoi Veedu, King Krishna Deva Rayar, Sadasiva Rayar, Achchuthan Rayar, Chalukya kings and some Chola kings.[48]

– The temple holds a special significance to Hindus as it is one of the Vishnu Swayambhu Kshetras and is mentioned in several scriptures. The emerald that Lord Balaji is wearing is said to be one of the largest emeralds in the world.[49] As per folklore, the divine lamp of the temple in front of the garba griha has been there since time immemorial.

My own experiences with the divine Lord Balaji have been numerous. I am in awe every time I visit the temple. There is no doubt in my mind that everything, including this book, is surrendered at his feet and subject to his grace.

It is important to note that this redistributive process was not necessarily state driven but rather a voluntary exercise, which was nudged by the state in some cases. Researchers draw a distinction between the consequences of the support of the state and its entities for the temple and the motives for which the support was given.[50] There was also a clear reference that priority was to be given first to temple rituals and sustenance protection and then to other social concerns.[51] The main purpose or motive of the state was to support Hindu institutions and their rituals, temples and their Dharmic responsibilities. For instance, an inscription states that Krishnadevaraya saved about 10,000 varahas for some Shiva and Vishnu temples by waiving off certain usurious taxes.[52] As a result of this support, if the temple flourished and decided to support land development, provide loans to commercial firms or support irrigation activities, then it was a welcome consequence. However, the main motive of the state, in this case, in giving the tax concession was not for the developmental support by the temple but for supporting it as a religious institution. It is important to understand this in the context of how the rulers dealt with temples as an institution.

The temple was primarily a revered divine institution towards which the rulers had great devotion; most of the benefits from the temple's resources like infrastructure building or poverty alleviation were not a systemic, state driven agenda. Of course, in some cases, the state did provide additional support on technical matters and manpower for projects. It provided a sort of 'Dharmic nudge'[53] to ensure greater efficiency in some of the temple-driven projects since that would eventually benefit the people at large. However, the state did not believe that the primary purpose of the temple was to take care of the commercial needs of the society.

Sreni Dharma

The role of Srenis and their associated Dharma has been discussed in detail earlier in the section on the Cholas. The Vijayanagar empire adopted a similar approach for the guilds but with some differences in terms of their scale, regional ambitions beyond the seas and political influences, which were all much greater during the Chola period. However, the primary role of the Srenis as a driver of economic activity remained the same, along with the foundational principles. This was quite unique because most of the Srenis in the Vijayanagar period were present during the Chola time as well but performed their roles quite differently due to geopolitical differences.

Srenis played an important role in facilitating trade internally and externally in the Vijayanagar empire. External trade routes from the western coast were driven by the sea ports. The ports were located in three belts—the Konkan, Tulunadu and Malabar belts. On the eastern side, the belts containing the ports were Coromandel and Telangana. For internal trade, the key highways included those connecting present-day Goa with Bankapur, Srirangam via Sivasasmudram and Dhanushkoti via Chandragiri, Tirupati, Kanchi, Chidambaram, Madurai and Rameswaram.[54] Through all these routes, a variety of products such as pepper, cinnamon, precious stones, pearls, cotton, porcelain (mainly to West Asian countries), iron and steel were traded externally and internally. Most of the exports were related to commodities, spices and other items that were unique to Bharat. All these trading transactions were facilitated and handled by the Srenis.

We had mentioned many guilds earlier, including Ainnuruvar, Naandaanese, Virabanajigas and Nakaramu. Some of them, though with different names, also continued to be present during the Vijayanagar empire. For example, Ainnuruvar was sometimes called 'Pekandru' which means 'many'. This guild was famous for trade in places like Tirupurantakam, Warangal and much of the current Andhra Pradesh. The Virabanajigas Sreni was another important Sreni. We had discussed earlier in the chapter on Cholas that Vira-Bananjadharma was a pivotal governance foundation for the guilds of Ainnuruvar. We can draw a similar conclusion as to how these Srenis governed themselves in the Vijayanagar empire. Besides these, the Settis and their Srenis were also influential operators in the western ghats of Karnataka.[55]

All of these Srenis had very similar organizational structure as those mentioned in the Cholas chapter. They were all governed by a broader 'Samanya Dharma' for their own Srenis, or they had a specific regional identity-based Dharmic structure like Viraja-Bananjadharma or they had certain jati based identities which were also intertwined with Dharmic values. Overall, the governance and operational excellence of these Srenis were mainly due to their strong organizational structures, for which Sreni Dharma was the central edifice.

6

Kambuja Desa

Overview of Kambuja Desa

Introduction

KAMBUJA DESA IS THE ancient name for contemporary Cambodia and the Indic kingdoms that dominated that landscape from 1 CE till about the tenth to eleventh century. These kingdoms, referred as the 'Khmer', were prosperous Hindu kingdoms which had an advanced level of social development and captured the imagination of large sections of the populace, so much so that many of the large temples and infrastructure that they built remain popular even today. In this chapter, we will explore the history and cultural context of Kambuja Desa, the evolution of the Khmer and Saivite kingdoms in Kambuja Desa, development of marvels such as the Angkor Wat temple and the connections of all these to the idea of Dharmic capitalism and its role in developing a coherent and sustainable economic model in this part of the world.

Historically, the Cambodian people have been a part of some of the world's most successful civilizational movements. The presence of Dharmic civilizations and their remnants even today signify the longevity of the imprints of the past. Throughout my travels in Siem Reap (the city that hosts Angkor Wat) and other Cambodian cities, this sentiment was very evident—its illustrious glory was self-evident for anyone visiting the country. The economic power that the country had was a direct offshoot of the social and cultural development of the Dharmic civilizations in the country.

To understand their economic prosperity, it is important to get a perspective of the historical evolution and lineage of the Kambuja empire. While summarizing it, I hope to retain the indigenous essence of the civilizational ethos of the land. I will focus first on the historical lineage of the kings of Kambuja Desa and their core societal constructs based on the philosophy of Dharma, followed by their economic models and their correlation with Dharmic capitalism as we have discussed earlier.

Ancient Times

Prior to the establishment of Kambuja Desa, the land was essentially a collection of small states ruled by different tribal communities. The populace was mainly dominated by the Mon–Khmers and Tibetan–Myanmarese (current-day Myanmar and erstwhile Burma), who were believed to have migrated in from Bharat and Mongolia respectively. The Mon-Khmers were mainly two tribes—Mon and Khmers—and their linguistic origins are considered to be from the Munda and Khasi tribes in Bharat and the Semai and Sekang from the Malay peninsula. There is some evidence to suggest that the Khmers owe their heritage to Kamarupa which is modern-day Assam in Northeastern Bharat.[1] They could have arrived in Cambodia through the land route via China and the Dangrek mountains (beyond Northern Cambodia in today's Laos) or through the sea routes used for trading. The latter is definitely a possibility since traveller accounts such as the *Periplus of the Erythraean Sea* mention that maritime travel from Bharat to Southeast Asia was quite common in the first century CE itself.

Funan

Among the various small kingdoms mentioned in ancient books, the most prominent one in the first century was Funan. Its territory is likely to have encompassed modern-day Vietnam, central Mekong, Menam valley and the Malay peninsula.[2] The inscriptions in Champa (657 CE) and traveller accounts of the Chinese traveller K'ang T'ai state that the first king of Funan was a Vedic Brahmin named Kaudinya from Kanchipuram (erstwhile Pallava kingdom) in southern Bharat. Folklore says that he obtained a spear from Drona's son Ashwatthama and had a divine calling

FIGURE 6.1 Map of Southeast Asia c. 900 CE

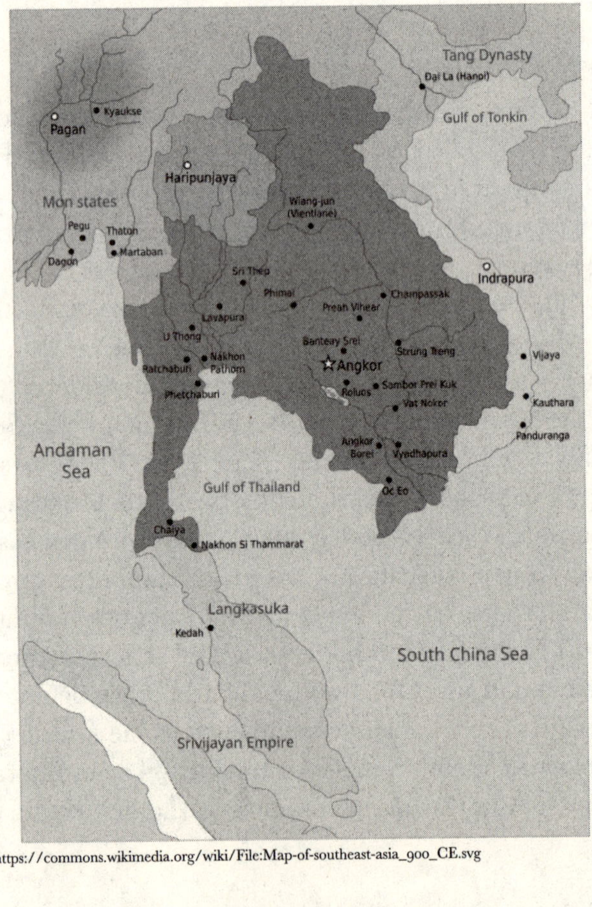

Source: https://commons.wikimedia.org/wiki/File:Map-of-southeast-asia_900_CE.svg

to travel across the sea on the eastern trade routes. In the process of passing through Cambodia, he fell in love with a local queen there named Soma and their marriage led to the beginning of the Hindu civilization in Cambodia. Secondary evidence—of the commemoration of this union in a thirteenth century CE inscription in Angkor Wat and a similar one celebrated by the Pallava kings of Kanchi—seems to confirm the veracity of this story.[3] Another folklore is that the origin of some of the kings of Funan was from the lineage of Kambu Svayambhuva, the king of Aryadesa and his descendants. Sruthavaraman and Shrestavarman were the first kings of this lineage.

In essence, it appears that there were two royal dynasties that were in place—one from the Kaudinyan lineage and the other from the Kambu lineage. While the first seems to have acknowledged the suzerainty of Funan[4], yet seems to have achieved its independence, it was the second dynasty that appears to have transcended Funan to conquer a much wider region around the fifth or sixth century and sowed the seeds of the Kambuja empire.

Kambuja Desa

'Kambuja Desa' has many connotations, but in this book, for the sake of authenticity, convenience and uniformity, we will stay with the definition given by Prof. R.C. Majumdar in his book *Kambuja Desa.* In simple terms, Kambuja Desa refers to the land from sixth century CE onwards in the post-Funan period, until about the thirteenth century. The lineage of the kings of Kambuja Desa begins mostly from 1 CE, at the advent of the Funan dynasty. Historical records indicate that the evolution of Kambuja Desa was a continuous process.

Conventional classification by historians is that the first to the eighth century CE was the pre-Angkorian period, ninth to the thirteenth century was the

Angkorian period and after the fourteenth century was the post-Angkorian period.[5] There are several theories, both inscription based and folklore based, about the origins of Kambuja Desa, and I will try to summarize the principal ones as succinctly as possible. Subsequently, we will also look at a summary of the rulers of Kambuja Desa as we did of the Chola rulers. Table 6.1 summarizes the lineage of the rulers for the post-Funan period.

TABLE 6.1 Lineage of the Rulers of Kambuja Desa

Era (CE)	**Rulers**	**Key Events and Characteristics**
514	Kaudinya Jayavarman	Beginning of the end of the Funan period that had started from Kaudinya I
514–550	Rudravarman	Sent six ambassadors to China during 517–539
598	Bhavavarman	Founded the new capital Bhavapura and seemed to be connected to the royal families of Funan and Kambuja
Beginning around 600	Chitrasena Mahendravarman	Expanded Kambuja's area of control
616–635	Isanavarman I	Expanded Kambuja's area of control
639	Bhavavarman II	Expanded Kambuja's area of control
657–681	Jayavarman I	Was ruling almost all of Kambuja and was one of the last rulers till the uncertainty that started around Javanese rule in the country
713	Jayadevi	Uncertain times during Javanese occupation; Jayadevi was one of the earliest female rulers of the region
716[6]	Pushkaraksha	Uncertain times during Javanese occupation

Era (CE)	Rulers	Key Events and Characteristics
802–850	Jayavarman II	Established the new capital Harihalayala in the Angkor region; he is also thought to have ruled from Mahendraparvata, which was recently discovered to be an urban metropolis with an advanced water management system, among other modern features[7]
850–873	Jayavarman III	
877–889	Indravarman	
889–900	Yasovarman	One of the famous kings of the Kambuja lineage; he produced numerous inscriptions (no. 60–77A)[8] and established a new capital Yashodarapura which included Angkor Thom and Phnom Bakheng, which was a hill just outside the city
900–922	Harshavarman	
925	Isanavarman II	
928–942	Jayavarman IV	Moved the capital to Koh Kher, about fifty miles northeast of Angkor
942–944	Harshavarman II	
944–968	Rajendravarman	Brought the capital back to Angkor
968–1001	Jayavarman V.	During the reign from 877–1011, Kambuja's territory was said to have extended to China and current Myanmar in the north; after Jayavarman's demise, civil war erupted till Suryavarman I took power
1001	Udayadityavarman I	
1002–1050	Suryavarman I	Conquered the whole of Thailand and extended the territorial conquest to Lower Myanmar; instituted a system of 'oath of fealty' to be taken by royal officials to ensure that loyalty to the sovereign is supreme, which is still followed in in Cambodia

Era (CE)	**Rulers**	**Key Events and Characteristics**
1050–1066	Udayadityavarman II	
1066–1080	Harshavarman III	
1080–1107	Jayavarman VI	Set up an independent kingdom and was succeeded by his elder brother
1107–1113	Dharanindravarman I	Ousted by his sister's daughter's son, Suryavarman II
1113 to after 1145	Suryavarman II	One of the most powerful reigns; he built the world-famous Angkor Wat; Chinese accounts note that his reign extended from Champa (Vietnam) to Lower Myanmar till the northern part of the Malay peninsula
1160	Dharanindravarman II	Was followed by Yasovarman II and Thribuvanadityavarman, but there are no records to back this; due to internal rebellion, these kings were defeated by Jayavarman VII
1181–1220	Jayavarman VII	Conquered Champa and Lower Myanmar; considered to be the last valorous king of Kambuja kula; built the capital city of Angkor Thom; set up almost 102 hospitals and 102 vahnigrha (Dharma sabha) for the people's welfare; Ta Prohm inscriptions suggest that the raja-vihara, adjacent to the temple, had 439 professors and 970 scholars, besides employing thousands of people[9]
1220–1243	Indravarman II	
1243–1295	Jayavarman VIII	
1295–1327	Srindravarman	
1307–1327	Srindrajayavarman	
1327–	Avarmadiparamesvara	Era ends with the Thai and Annamite closing in to take over Kambuja Desa

Source: G. Coedes, *Indianized States of Southeast Asia*

As seen from Table 6.1, from the fifth century CE onwards, until almost the thirteenth century (except the period from Jayavarman I to Jayavarman II, that is, 681 to 802, which was shrouded in uncertainty[10]), there was a continuity of rulers of Kambuja Desa who were all predominantly Hindu, with the exception of a few, who were Buddhist. There is no doubt that all of them were under the broader umbrella of Dharma-based religions of the contemporary world. They were also prosperous for a variety of reasons.

First, they served as the central hub for trade from South Asia to China and vice-versa. Much like the modern port-city–state–country of Singapore, which serves as a gateway to East Asia for trade with the rest of the world, cities along the Cambodian and Thai coast served as important trading ports for movement of goods and services to East Asia. The movement of goods via sea was very important for China's commercial interactions with the rest of the world, given that the land routes were arduous and time consuming, with challenging terrains. Besides this, there is also more recent research that suggests that Angkor was one of the earliest urban complexes of the pre-industrial world.[11] It had an extensive hydraulic and water management system that was far ahead of its times.

Second, during this period, that is, approximately fifth to the thirteenth century, some of the world's most stunning architecture was built in this region. This included the world's largest Hindu temple, Angkor Wat, and a variety of other temples, most of which are non-functional today. Even amid the ruins, they look spectacular, as my travels in the Siem Reap region showed. We should not view them just through a religious prism, instead, we should consider what defined economic and political power during those times. At that time, a culture's dominance was viewed through trade and the ability to build large architectural marvels. The Angkor Wat structures were huge, extremely intricately designed and have lasted more than a thousand years. Such intricate craftsmanship and grandeur are a symbol of the prosperity of Kambuja Desa.

Last, in comparison, if we look at the Western world just after 1 CE, civilization barely existed there at that time. Forget about complex civil engineering spectacles such as the world's largest temple structure, they were not even able to do basic things that were needed to sustain a civilization. On a comparative level, the economic structures and outcomes from Kambuja Desa were far superior to most of the world during the early common era period. This is also seen from the anecdotal evidence from people who travelled to these lands during those times.

It is quite clear that much of this prosperity spanned from the fifth to the thirteenth century. It is also a fact that it was not a mere coincidence that the prosperous kingdoms were Dharmic kingdoms. Given that Kambuja Desa was not the source where these Dharmic systems emanated, it is interesting to see the cultural depth, longevity and continuous prosperity of these kingdoms over the years. This made me wonder—what was the deeper philosophical and socioeconomic underpinning that ensured such continuity, especially in a distant land, far away from where the philosophy originated? I hope to answer the question in the subsequent part of this chapter.

Philosophical Underpinnings of the Economy of Kambuja Desa

What was the secret to the success of Kambuja Desa?

This is a simple question but the answer, as for most questions on economy of the ancient times, is not so simple. This question can have several answers and, for the most part, they are often interpretative, contextual and involve assumptions, unlike answers on contemporary economics. Nevertheless, I will uncover them as far as practically possible.

Before I delve into the intricacies of economic activities, it is necessary to understand the philosophical and civilizational underpinnings of economic prosperity, similar to what we had witnessed during this period in other lands. So, what were the philosophies that were foundational to this prosperity? How did they influence the economy?

To answer these questions, we need to look at them through the lens of the nomenclature or language and the books or research material used by travellers and historians, and the contextual references made by them on this subject. We also need to look at some of the outcomes of the economic structures and policy to derive the philosophies behind them. This is a sort of a reverse engineering, but it needs to be performed since we only have patchy evidence based on inscriptions which are hundreds of years old. This shortcoming could be overcome if we could identify consistent, broad themes—rather than minute details—of the economic policies in Kambuja Desa and then derive the relevant philosophical underpinnings. Not only would this be logical but it would also cross-check our theories based on outcomes of actual activities that had taken place in Kambuja Desa.

Language, Nomenclature and Titles

From the nomenclature and the inscriptional texts, it is quite clear that most, if not all, of them are in Samskritam or a form of Samskritam or Prakrit that was used in ancient Bharat. In addition, we should note that the dominance of Indic languages, mainly Samskritam, was at its peak during the period. The language was so prevalent that Jayavarman VII used Samskritam in almost all the inscriptions, including political, administrative and social ones. In addition to this, there are also inscriptions which suggest that Panini was studied in depth and commentaries on *Mahabhasya* were written by King Yasovarman.[12] King Yasovarman has given references of scholars such as Vatsyayana, Visalaksa, Pravarasena, Mayura, Gunadya and Susrutha (ancient scholar on surgeries).

Thus, it would be reasonable to state that Samskritam, along with Khmer, was the main language of governance during the reigns of most of the Kambuja kings. There are many instances where the nomenclature used for governance and the titles given to people originated from Samskritam or Prakrit. This also happened when the nomenclature of governance—both in prose and poetry—was Dharmic in nature. For example, as shown in Table 6.2, in an eighth century inscription, there is a reference to the merchant chief as 'vanijam adhipa'. 'Vanijam' and 'vanigam' in Samskritam and Tamil mean 'merchant' (i.e., related to finance) and 'adhipa' means 'head'. Other examples include words such as 'vyavahari' which means 'merchant'.

TABLE 6.2 Samskritam or Prakrit Roots

Inscription	**Province**	CE	**Merchant**	**Comment**
K. 259S (IV) (Sk text)	Siem Reap	8th c.	*vaṇijām adhipaḥ* (merchant chief)	Individual given title by King Nṛpāditya
K. 263B	Siem Reap	984	*travaṅ vanik* (trapeang vanik)	Location: refers to limits of land
K. 221N	Battambang	1011	*vanik* (merchant)	Gift of 1 *tai*

Inscription	Province	CE	Merchant	Comment
K. 221S	Battambang	1011	*khloñ jnvāl vanik* (merchant chief)	Participant in sale of rice field
K. 221S	Battambang	1011	*khloñ vanik* (merchant chief *jnvāl*)	Title of the *kaṃsteṅ*, principal donor
K. 220S	Battambang	1012	*khloñ jnvāl vanik* (merchant chief *jnvāl*)	Donor of 2 *tai* via *kaṃsteṅ*
K. 843B	Siem Reap	1025	*vanik* (merchant)	Legal: Objects claimed from a trader
K. 249	Siem Reap	1109	*mūla tamrvac vyavahāri* (merchant inspector)	Amongst those who prepared list of property

Source: E. Lusting, *Power and Pragmaticism in the Political Economy of Angkor* (University of Sydney, 2009)

The usage of Samskritam terms such as varna, varga and kula were quite common even in casual conversations in Kambuja Desa. Research also suggests that kings such as Jayavarman V integrated the elites and the kulas into varna and temple communities,[13] and until about the tenth century, they were integrated into the state structure in terms of varnas, vargas and religions institutions.[14] The proxy of varna as jati was largely not applicable here and varna was considered to be non-hereditary, by and large. However, that is a wider discussion and beyond our scope here. My limited point is that at every stage of nomenclature, poetry and prose of governance, the usage of Indic and Samskritam based terms was not only the most prominent but also inherently helped to develop an ecosystem that was sustained for more than five hundred years thereafter.

Linkages to Direct and Indirect References to Dharma

Figure 6.2 contains a quotation from a Prah Ko inscription of Indravarman I.

FIGURE 6.2 Quotation from a Prah Ko Inscription

नवरन्ध्राद्रिराज्यस्थस् सोभवन् कम्बुजेश्वरः ।
श्रीन्द्रवर्म्मा त्रिवर्ग्गेण वर्द्धयन हर्षयन् प्रजाः ॥३

3. He, Indra-varmmā, the lord of Kambuja, who became king in the year 799, increased the prosperity of his people by following the three rules of conduct (*dharma, artha, kāma*).

Source: R.C. Majumdar, *Inscriptions of Kambuja*, Inscription No. 55, p. 65

Another inscription in the Four Bassett temple, from around 958 CE, shows that it was a regular practice to have people well-versed in the Dharmasastras to be integral to the monarch and the governance of the kingdom.

> Ins. C, written in Khmer, records that in 964 Saka dignitary named Śrikaṇṭḥa Paṇḍita of the country of Phalapriya bathed the god Śri Jayakṣetra and offered various objects whose weight is specified. Having installed the image of the god and organised its worship, he purchased some lands in exchange of objects of previous metal whose weight is specified, and also of an elephant, some clothes and some quantities of pepper and cardamum. The persons who sold the land are named, and they took a solemn oath never to reclaim the lands sold. A number of high dignitaries fixed the boundaries and the grand priest Śri Mahendra Paṇḍita recited the Dharmaṣāstra.[15]

The following inscription,[16] from 667 CE, around the time of Jayavarman I, indicates a casual conversation where two brothers referring to Ashwini devatas are comparing the two purusharthas—Dharma and artha.

तस्य तौ मन्त्रिणौ आस्तां सम्मतौ कृतवेदिनौ ।
धर्मशास्त्रार्थशास्त्रज्ञौ धर्मार्थौ इव रूपिणौ ॥

These are clear indications of the direct references from the scriptures on both the idea of Dharma and its contemporaneous analogies.

Linkages to Kautilya's Arthashastra *and a Prior Era of Bharatiya Civilization*

Since we have dealt with nomenclature and language, the next natural step is to look at books or ancient texts that were used by the kings of Kambuja Desa for governance. We do not need to look any further than the inscriptions in Kambuja Desa which are visible today. The eminent historian R.C. Majumdar writes in his brilliant book that:

> The Hindu colonists in Kambuja set up an administrative system on the Bharat model. The study of the *Arthashastra* is specifically mentioned in an inscription and most probably Kautilya's *Arthashastra* or some text of this type was actually followed in practice. Interesting evidence of this is supplied by a passing reference in Ins No. 8. The last verse of this inscription says about the donor, a royal official, that he was a favorite of the king (antarangatvam-asthitah) as he was sarvopadha-suddha. Berth, who edited this inscription, failed to realise the meaning and recognize its importance. The term is, however, used in Kautilya's *Arthashastra* (I.10) in connection with the testing of the conduct of royal officials by four kinds of allurements, which are technically known as upadhas. One who does not fall a prey to any of these allurements, to which he is tempted by royal spies, and thereby successfully passes all the tests, is known as sarvopadhasuddha, and Kautilya recommends that he should be appointed a minister. The occurrence of this

> word in connection with a royal servant therefore indicates that probably the method recommended by Kautilya was followed by Kambuja kings in the appointment of ministers.[17]

In addition to this, there are also other inscriptions which indicate the presence of the *Arthashastra* in Kambuja Desa. Majumdar mentions that an inscription made during the rule of Jayavarman I (667 CE) mentions about an installation of a lingam and a temple endowment dedicated to Lord Siva in the town of Adyapura by Simhadatta. There is a direct reference to the study of the *Arthashastra* in this inscription.

In another reference, in his book *Hindu Colonies in the Far East*, Majumdar says:

> The Hindu colonists of Kambuja set up a highly organised system of administration based on the Indian model. The *Arthasästras* or Samskritam texts on political science, like those of Kautilya, were regularly studied and mostly followed in practice.[18]

There is a very interesting phrase mentioned by Jayavarman VII which has a surprising similarity to what Kautilya had prescribed in the third century BCE:

> देहिनां देहरोगो यन्-मनोरोगो रुजत्तराम् ।
> राष्ट्र-दुःखं हि भर्तृणां दुःखं दुःखं तु नात्मनः॥[19]
>
> The bodily pain of the diseased became in him (King Jayavarman VII) a mental agony more tormenting than the former. For the real pain of a king is the pain of his subjects, not that of his own (body).[20]

Kautilya says in *Arthashastra*:

> प्रजासुखे सुखं राज्ञः प्रजानां च हिते हितम् ।
> नात्मप्रियं प्रियं राज्ञः प्रजानां तु प्रियं प्रियम्॥ ॥
> (Arthaśāstra 0.1.19.34)
> A king's happiness lies in the happiness of his subjects, and his welfare in the welfare of his subjects; a king's welfare consists not in what pleases him but in what pleases his subjects.[21]

This is a very important inscription and was a pivotal input in my research on the subject. Inscriptions are rarely found to be in proper condition, especially in foreign lands, given the passage of time and the influence of other cultures in subsequent eras. The clarity of this inscription is a welcome change. It also indicates that there could have been many more such inscriptions which may have been lost due to a variety of reasons. It is in this context that we need to view the quotation and the subsequent reference to the inscription by R.C. Majumdar.

The Kambuja era began around the sixth century CE. Kautilya's *Arthashastra* was written in the third century BCE. Kautilya acknowledged that many of the ideas in the *Arthashastra* were inspired or taken from earlier scriptures such as the *Rig Veda*, Mahabharata and Ramayana. He also acknowledged the efforts of scholars such as Brihaspathi and Shukracharya in the preface of the *Arthashastra*. So, at the minimum, there was a gap of 900–1,000 years between the inscriptions of Kambuja Desa and the original concepts.

Added to this is the fascinating fact that the *Arthashastra* itself was discovered in Bharat by Shamasastry only in 1915. For many centuries, the *Arthashastra* text was missing and most of the knowledge transfer of the text took place through word of mouth. There is also a possibility that the text was discovered earlier and then lost again, but we cannot say that definitely due to lack of evidence. Yet despite all this, amazingly, this inscription in Kambuja Desa tells us that the template and terminology of the *Arthashastra* were used philosophically and practically as a governance manual for governing Kambuja Desa. This is not only interesting for the reader but also an indicator of the durability of the message in the *Arthashastra* and its teachings.

Kambuja Desa's Economic Structure

The exact economic structure of Kambuja Desa is difficult to ascertain given the lack of definite data, as happens in most subjects related to economics history. However, there are certain thematic inferences which can help us get a basic picture. Since we discussed the nomenclature of governance and the philosophical underpinnings of Kambuja Desa, it is natural to link them to our discussion. It is also useful to understand the literature on the subject, which is mainly derived from a Western perspective.

Currency

We have seen in the earlier chapters that there was an extensive usage of coins in the Saraswati–Sindhu civilization as well as by the Cholas and other South Indian kingdoms. We also discussed about the large presence of Roman coins in South India, second only to European countries. Many countries around the world including Southeast Asia and Bharat, used coinage or currency as payment for commercial transactions. So the obvious question is—Did Kambuja Desa have a single currency or coinage for its transactions? It is unlikely to have had a particular coinage, but there isn't a definite answer to that. Researchers have mentioned that most of the inscriptions related to Kambuja Desa talk about transactions that took place between traders in exchange for commodities such as rice, paddy, silver or gold.[22] The concept of 'unit of account' does not seem to be mentioned in the inscriptions, as far as my knowledge goes. While this is plausible, it is difficult to believe that a civilization, which was one of the earliest pre-modern industrial civilizations, did not have a currency of its own.

Some reasons that have been proposed for the lack of coinage of its own in Kambuja Desa are lack of mineral resources, a centralized state which wanted to control the economy and lack of zeal for trade[23]—all these are not convincing enough. There is also a theory that since the system of barter trade of commodities was working smoothly, there was no need for bringing a new common currency into the system.

There is ample evidence that the Khmers were in contact with the Chinese, Bharatiyas (from the south to the north) and other kingdoms in Southeast Asia including the Javans and Champas, all of whom had a variety of coins and coinage which they used for trading purposes. This means that it was not a lack of knowledge of coins or currency that prevented them from having their own coinage, but it could be something else.

My view is that it would have been a conscious decision to avoid currency since the system was working well without it or it could well be that archaeological finds have not discovered it yet. Either way, the lack of a currency in circulation remains a mystery and should be an area for future research.

Economic Model of Kambuja Desa

There are several types of growth frameworks for ancient economies that have been discussed by scholars. Karl

Polanyi, the famous Austrian economist, in his book *The Great Transformation* says that ancient societies did not have a proper understanding of the markets and price-setting mechanisms.[24] He argues that ancient societies worked on reciprocity and redistribution, both of which were done to ensure that the elites and their socioeconomic and familial relationships or alliances were sustained. His views have been contested many times by other scholars[25] For the Khmer and the Angkoran empire, there have been specific frameworks that have been also proposed. These include[26] Asiatic Mode of Production; Core–Periphery and World Systems; Loosely Integrated States Networks; Territorial–Hegemonic; Processual and Temple Hierarchy. Most of these frameworks are based on the three factors of political, economic and ideological means of control, and the variations in the political economies over a sustained period of time.

The two frameworks that have been proposed specifically for Angkor, which I am extrapolating to Kambuja Desa, are the Kulke and Hall frameworks, that is, the Processual and Temple Hierarchy frameworks. Both these scholars have written on this subject for many decades. Kulke says:

> From the 7th century, most Indian states emerged through agrarian expansion and political integration in a process connecting three concentric geographical areas (nuclear, peripheral and beyond) and three chronologically distinct stages of state development (chiefdom, early kingdom and imperial kingdom).[27]

These three stages of development form a linear progression of chiefdom, followed by political control through a developed bureaucracy, an imperial kingdom with many occupied areas and a continuous process of integration.

Hall proposes that the temples and the associated units of the temples played a central role in the economic functioning of Kambuja Desa. He says that temples were central to the economic system, especially in the Angkoran age—seventh century until about the thirteenth century.[28]

Before I explain further, we need to understand the context in which the temples were built and preserved. Temples were considered to contain supreme spiritual wealth and were revered by almost all the kings of Cambodia. A temple embodied a spiritual and divine sanctum beyond the ordinary, which received both the patronage as well as the support of the royals. The temples (or the deity of the temple) were given vast tracts of land as donations or gifts or the lands were acquired by the temples from their wealth. As a result of their presence in vast areas of land, they were seen as an important instrument for the royalty to assume control over people in an indirect manner. The temples also served as a source for decentralized governance as they had an oversight over the governance at the village or local level. The peak of the process of building and maintenance of temples—along with, perhaps, its overall prosperity—was mainly during the rule of Indravarman I (877–889), Yasovarman I (889–900), Rajendravarman II (944–968), Suryavarman I (1002–1050), along with the reigns of Udayadityavarman II (1050–1066), Suryavarman II (1113–1150) and Jayavarman VII (1181–1220).

The temples served multiple needs besides their religious role and were often central to the governance of the local villages. After the seventh century, according to Hall, the Angkor region's agrarian sector grew well, with the use of hydraulic technology playing an important part in boosting output. First, the temples served as investment hubs or like modern-day banks and were a source of capital. Not only was the wealth of the temples used for the temples themselves, but it was also used for a variety of developmental activities and served the political needs or affiliations in the area. (Readers who are familiar with the current Bharatiya context might rush to accuse the author of supporting or condoning the state control of temples—that clearly is not the case!) However, the priority always was to maintain the sanctity and prosperity of the temple before anything else. Second, the temples were important overseers of labour since many labourers were used for activities on the temple lands. The temples also served as an important feedback and monitoring facility for the movement of labour in that area or region. Last, they were also large centres of knowledge and held vast amount of information across a wide range of sectors.

In addition to this, Hall also proposes the theory of regional temple networks and how these temple networks were created. He says:

> The concentration in temples of the authority to manage local resources had a significant impact on the process of local political integration. The implication of such centralization for the economic control system is reflected in epigraphic references to the 'joining together for the enjoyment of the gods', whereby a single or several landholders shifted a share of the income (goods and services) destined to one god or temple to that of another or amalgamated the administration of one temple's lands with that of another. This joining together or joint usufruct is termed saṃparibhoga or miśrabhoga. Through these actions, a pattern of subordination of one local deity to another as well as one local temple to another

> began to emerge in Khmer society. Regional temple networks came to be sustained and controlled by a secular, landed elite who transferred income from their lands or donated material goods and services to temples in the network.

An example of how this hierarchy played out practically is shown in Figure 6.3.

FIGURE 6.3 Temple Network and Hierarchy

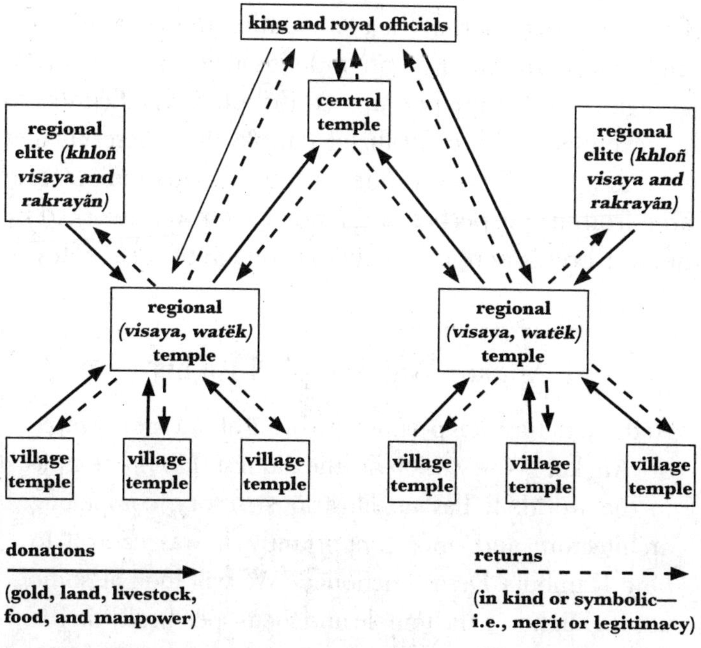

Source: https://scholarspace.manoa.hawaii.edu/server/api/core/bitstreams/04159870-42f8-4dc6-8789-54c0b79496b0/content

There were local temples in the villages which were either family owned or village owned. These local village temples contributed a particular amount from their earnings to the regional (visay, watek) temples. Regional elites contributed further to these regional temples in terms of donations. Subsequently, these regional temples contributed to the central temple which was a sort of a main temple in that state. The dotted lines represent the reverse cycle—the central temple provided people with prasadam, merit or legitimacy to people in power. It provided these benefits from the income from all the rituals done at the temples, besides financial arbitrage. Thus the capital flows into the temple ecosystem were returned to the society through capital outflows, serving a redistributive function.

An important point to note is that redistribution was not a major burden for the local temples. There is considerable evidence to suggest that the contribution made by the local temples was minimal at an individual level[29], but at an aggregate level, they perhaps contributed significantly to the revenue of the centralized temple that these villages were assigned. The revenue of the central temple also came from its properties and lands which were worked by kñuṁ or bondsmen, under the patronage of local elites.

Angkor Wat Temple Insights

At this juncture, it is pertinent to bring about the example of Angkor Wat, which is the largest Hindu temple in the world. It has an illustrious history, compelling architecture and, most importantly, it was central to how Kambuja Desa functioned. We will look at some key highlights of the temple and focus specifically on the economic impact in the region and the country at large.

Key features of the temple include the following:[30]

- It is the world's largest Hindu temple. It was constructed by Suryavarman II in the early twelfth century, dedicated to Lord Vishnu and is currently a UNESCO world heritage site.[31]
- It is located about 5.5 kilometres north of Siem Reap in modern-day Cambodia.

- It combines Khmer and southern Bharat's architecture and represents the Hindu god Mount Meru symbolically.
- It has a moat 200 feet wide and 13 feet deep and 3.6 kilometres in length.
- To build it, 1.5 million cubic metres of sand and silt were moved, with thousands of workers involved in the construction. A series of canals were used to transport sandstone blocks from a quarry 30 km north of Angkor Wat.[32]
- According to researchers, the central tower had a steep staircase and was considered to be the symbolic centre of the nation. It epitomized the confluence of sacred and secular forces.[33]
- The inner walls of the outer galleries depict scenes from the Ramayana and Mahabharata in a very detailed and artistically exquisite manner. The scenes include battle scenes between Rama and Ravana in Ramayana, the Kurukshetra war from the Mahabharata and the famous churning of the sea of milk (Samudra Manthan). The fascinating story telling is linear, along a full stretch and was considered by some scholars as the 'greatest linear arrangement of stone carving'.[34]
- Angkor Wat also has several depictions of devatas and apsaras respectively, with the former almost amounting to 1,796 depictions.
- It is a major international destination and had almost 2.8 million visitors in 2018,[35] though the pandemic led to a huge drop. In 2023, there were well over 40,000 visitors by mid-July which was higher than the previous year.[36]

The features mentioned earlier vis-à-vis the temple economic model applies to Angkor Wat as well. In fact, Angkor Wat, given its centrality and its vastness, leading to large economies of scale, was a very important replica of the temple economic model. Most of the agricultural, trade and manufacturing policies present in Kambuja Desa existed in Angkor Wat as well. Perhaps the scale was smaller, compared to the broader Kambuja Desa story, but the conceptual underpinnings remained the same. Thus the economics around Angkor Wat were a microcosm of the broader Kambuja Desa economic story which we have highlighted in this chapter.

Therefore a practical analysis of the economics of Kambuja Desa could give us a more refined position on the subject. I will base my argument on three key economic parameters—land, labour and capital—and summarize it subsequently.

Sectoral Composition of the Economy

The main sectors in Kambuja Desa's economy were agriculture, trade and commerce. These sectors were present in every ancient economy—though their relative proportions may have differed—and were similar to the Cholas or even the earlier period of the Mauryas. The key differentiators were the role of geography and the role of rulers and their preferential treatment of particular sectors, and its impact on economic growth. While there are many common parameters with other civilizations, we should recognize the key trends and themes that were recurring through many kingdoms.

Agriculture

Land was an important component of the economy because agriculture was a key factor. There were three distinct entities that affected agriculture—the role of the temples, the vast networks of hydraulic systems and the large amounts of certain commodities produced, such as rice, which were important for economic growth.

As mentioned earlier, there is considerable research available to suggest that the temples were central to the output from agriculture in Kambuja Desa from the ninth to the thirteenth century and this extended, in general, to Khmer communities at large.[37] It should be noted that these temples were mostly community temples which were much smaller and disaggregated compared to the larger temples, which were not as many in number. The structure of these temples used to consist of an 'elevated rectilinear area of civic ceremonial buildings, often surrounded by a moat, and associated residential areas and hydraulic farming infrastructure'.[38] Both inputs and outputs, along with the irrigation infrastructure, were also a part of the package. The inputs required for agriculture were available in the temple ecosystem, the output of commodities was also used for the local temples (and then perhaps exported to other areas) and the irrigation infrastructure was maintained and nurtured due to the temple's vast socioeconomic, multi-utility role.

Irrigation networks were the hallmark of the infrastructure of Kambuja Desa after the ninth century. If there was only one thing that the people were experts in, it was designing irrigation networks. Angkor was considered to be the 'hydraulic city' and between the ninth and twelfth century, there were a plethora of reservoirs, channels, water embankments and dams built all over the area.[39] The majestic Angkor Wat temple was surrounded by well-designed waterways. Besides providing irrigation for agriculture, they also served as transportation routes for inland trade. The Mekong River, whose name was supposedly inspired from Maa-Ganga in Bharat, which cuts through five contemporary countries (Cambodia, Thailand, Laos, Myanmar, China and Vietnam) and is almost 5,000 miles long, served as the central river of Kambuja Desa. Not only were these irrigation networks of a pioneering nature at that time, they were enduring and withstood changes for a long period of time and had a high reliability. The West Baray reservoir, which was about 8 km long and 2 km wide, with approximately 50 million cubic cm of water, was one of the largest structures created till the nineteenth century in Cambodia.[40] An outline of the hydraulic systems is shown through an example in Figure 6.4.

FIGURE 6.4 Irrigation Networks in Angkor Region

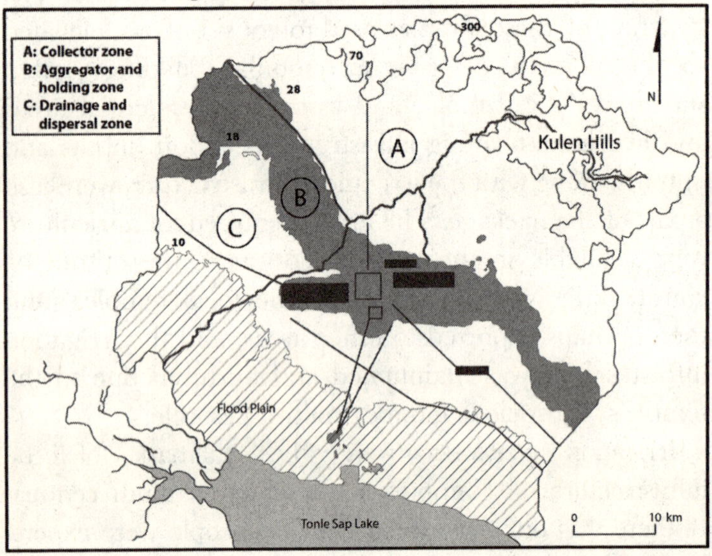

Source: Adapted from https://cdn.angkordatabase.asia/libs/docs/publications/water-management-in angkor/The_water_management_network_of_Angkor_C.pdf.

In Figure 6.4, Zone A refers to the source of the main waterways between the hills and barays where embankments were built to spread the water across the landscape southwards. Zone B consists of a major baray and temple moats which were considered to be large water storage or holding units. Perhaps the purpose of these was to also ensure that they retained the water in this central zone where most of the agricultural and irrigation activities were taking place. Zone C had numerous distribution channels taking the water southwards and eastwards, away from the central zone, into the ocean if needed. The gradients across the planes were likely to be shallow and there was constant monitoring of flow rates and water levels to ensure that the optimal level of water was supplied for various activities.

All this indicates a reasonable level of sophistication in ensuring that water management was done properly. While there were many purposes to this, including rainwater management, the main purpose was to have a constant water supply for agricultural activities since they were an important component of the economy. There is more recent evidence which indicates that these hydraulic systems were used for multi-cropping during the time period mentioned.[41]

A variety of crops were produced but the production of rice was by far the most important for a variety of reasons. It was the staple food in the region.[42] It was also the principal commodity supplied to temples, both for rituals and to prepare food for people who visited these temples. Substantial evidence of rice production and supply to temples is provided in the inscriptions. No other commodity was given as much inscription space and visibility.

Given that the role of a national currency or coinage is still being debated, rice was extensively used for barter trade among merchants and Srenis in Kambuja Desa. There are accounts of Chinese envoys which state that barter trade with rice was being done extensively in Funan. The affinity with rice production was not necessarily a phenomenon in Kambuja Desa, but was a regional phenomenon as Java, Champa and Siam regions had extensive rice surpluses according to some Chinese accounts.

Trade

Ancient maritime trading routes were important for many countries. Kambuja Desa was no exception to this, despite the fact that the Angkor region was inland. There were many historical events in the region which were impacted by trade. If not for trade, Kaudinya himself would not have travelled all the way from Bharat to come to the Khmer land to set up Funan and lay the foundation of Kambuja Desa. There is no doubt that there was a thriving trade taking place through this route between South Asia and China and the Champa region. Despite the inland location of the key cities of Kambuja Desa, sea trade played an important role in economic activity in the country.

Trading of Diverse Products

Research has shown that from the seventh century (or even earlier) onwards until about the twelfth or thirteenth century, there were products being imported and exported at will from Kambuja Desa. Table 6.3 shows the variety of products being traded, with examples from inscriptions.

TABLE 6.3 Products Traded in Kambuja Desa

CE Date	Source	Commodity	Material	Origin
7th century	KS. 407 Vat Maheyang	*cïnadhv(aj) (banner of Chinese fabric)*		China
894 (?)	K. 947 Lolei	*1 dramvaṅ* (tree, object in form of flower) *1 dramvaṅ* (tree, object in form of flower) *1 nü parivära* (cover, accessory, container) *1 tanlap* (box, small box) *1 tanlap dramvaṅ* (box with dramvaṅ) *1 tanlap kralyak* (box for type of offering) *1 tanlvat* (unknown ritual object) *1 vodi* (pitcher, jug, vase)	hanira silver hanira hanira hanira silver silver	China China China China China China China Javä
972	K. 669 (Prasat Komphus)	*1 ãdarśaṇa cïna* (mirror) *1 tanläp deśa* (box) *1 van deśa* (cup with feet?)		China India/ foreign India/ foreign
984	K. 662; K. 663 (Vat Prah Einkosei)	*3 noṅ cïna* (gourd-shaped utensils?) *3 noṅ cïna* (gourd-shaped utensils?)		China China
1026	K. 618 (Sek Ta Tuy)	*canlyak deśa* (garments) *phnäṅ deśa* (hangings)	cotton cotton	India/ foreign India/ foreign

CE Date	Source	Commodity	Material	Origin
1186-91	K. 208 (Prah Khan)	*520 cïna samudga* (boxes) *323 maśakärtha cïnamśuka* (mosquito nets) *patä cïnämśuka* (superior silk)	 silk silk	China China China
1186	K. 273 (Ta Prohm)	*20 cïnaśayyä* (beds, couches) *20 amśuka cïnapaṭa* (cloth) *500 cïna samudga* (boxes)		China China China
1200	K. 485 (Phimanakas)	*100 dhvaj cïnapaṭṭa* (cloth for banner) *1 dhvaj cïnäṃśuka* (banner)	silk	China China

Epigraphic references to imports

Source: E. Lusting, *Power and Pragmaticism in the Political Economy of Angkor*

As seen in Table 6.3, diverse kinds of products were being traded. We see flower boxes, accessories, container vessels, vase, ritual products (could be agarbatti), mirrors, garments, couches, cloth, banners—almost all household items—being imported. This shows that trading was not just an activity reserved for the elites but even common folks had access to the imported products.

Traveller accounts have also verified some of the trading activities in the country. Zhou Daguan, a Chinese diplomat who was travelling to Cambodia as part of an official diplomatic mission sent by the second emperor of the Yuan dynasty in China in 1296, mentioned:

> The people of Cambodia value items made of fine double-threaded silk in various colours. They also value such things as pewter ware from Zenzhou, lacquerware dishes from Wenzhou and celadon ware from Quanzhou. Beans and wheat are particularly sought after, but they cannot be taken there.[43]

Geographical Competition for Trade

The trading routes connecting mainland Angkor and the coastal regions of Champa are an important illustration about the importance of trade. They are shown in Figure 6.5.

FIGURE 6.5 Trading Routes

Source: E. Lusting, *Power and Pragmaticism in the Political Economy of Angkor*, University of Sydney, 2009

As shown in Figure 6.5, several trading routes were possibly being used. These are routes based on the known Khmer roads. These routes went from Angkor to Vat Phu to Amaravati, Angkor to Vat Phu to Vijaya and a further detour to Nha Trang. Another possible route from Sambor could have been through the southern tip of the Mekong river. These possible routes have been suggested by researchers, yet the reader might ask if there was really any need for all these alternate routes. The answer lies in the politics of the region. From the ninth century, there was a continuous battle for dominance between the Khmers and the Champas for regional control. Rajendravarman I, Suryavarman I, Suryavarman II and Jayavarman VI, all had battles with

FIGURE 6.6 Ta Prohm Inscription of Jayavarman VII in 1108

प्राग्राश्चतुस्‌सहस्राणि ग्रामादिभ्यश्च तण्डुलाः ।
खारिका नवतिस्तिस्रो द्रोणो द्वौ कुदुवावपि ॥ ५३

खार्य्यश् शतं त्रयोशीतिर्द्रोणौ प्रस्थाश्च षट् तिलाः ।
मुद्गा द्रोणौ दश प्रस्था द्वौ च खार्य्यश् शते दश ॥ ५४

चतुश्‌शतानि घटिका नव प्रस्था घृतं दधि ।
सप्त प्रस्थास्तथा सप्त घट्यः पञ्च शतानि च ॥ ५५

प्रस्थोऽशीतिष् षट् च घट्यः पयः पञ्च शतानि च ।
मधु पञ्च शतान्यष्टात्रिंशच्च प्रस्थपञ्चकम् ॥ ५६

चतुश्‌शतानि घटिका गुडोऽशीत्युत्तराणि च ।
अथ त्रयोदश प्रस्थास्तैलन्तत्परिमाणकम् ॥ ५७

Source: R.C. Majumdar, *Inscriptions of Kambuja*, No. 177, p. 459

Champa leaders for gaining control of the region. Why did all these leaders compete for the same region? Their objective was to capture the coastal territories, as shown in Figure 6.5, to expand their trade with China and the rest of the world through the eastern ports of Champa. If trade was a very marginal activity, would these kings have made so many attempts to capture Champa? It is quite apparent that there was an intense geopolitical competition for trade since it was an integral part of the envisioned economic prosperity and also enabled the monarchs to expand their territorial dominance in the region. In addition to all this, there was also a possibility of expanding trade in the north via the Silk Road routes as well.

There is also some inscriptional evidence about the levies that traders and farmers had to pay. Figure 6.6 shows a Ta Prohm inscription of Jayavarman VII in 1108.

Manufacturing Industries

In the earlier chapters, we had touched upon the role of manufacturing and industries in the kingdoms of Bharat. Similarly, Kambuja Desa had a fairly thriving industrial sector. The industries that did well were based on indigenous minerals which could be extracted locally. There is evidence to suggest the presence of scalable industrial production in Kambuja Desa.

According to researchers from the Industries for Angkor Project (INDAP),[44] there was an iron ore production facility at Preak Khan of Kompong Sway (Preah Khan). Using a combination of excavations, radar surveys and slag concentration analysis, the researchers were able to find metallurgical waste from a furnace. The place was used as a primary occupation from the eleventh to the thirteenth century, and until the fifteenth century, before the collapse of Kambuja Desa.

There have also been other inferences made on the usage of iron produced from these facilities. For instance, there is evidence which suggests the use of iron in the changing temple architecture between the eleventh and thirteenth centuries.[45] There was possibly a correspondence between the permanent shift to sandstone and the increased usage of iron in the Phnom Dek region, which has the largest source of iron in Cambodia. Incidentally, this is also an example of the temple centred economic system and its impact on manufacturing, among other industries.

In addition to iron manufacturing, traditional arts and crafts, especially stoneware production, were also an important component of manufacturing in Kambuja Desa. An example of this was the huge facility in Cheung Ek which produced both stoneware and earthenware. According to researchers, ceramic stoneware was used both for household as well as ritualistic purposes.[46] Since there is little evidence of this stoneware being exported, most of the uses could be ritualistic, that is, in the temples. Similar production facilities have been found to the immediate east of the Angkoran capital Bangkong, Tani, Thnal Mrech and Torp Chey. These discoveries also indicate that large stoneware and earthenware facilities were not a one-off phenomenon and that there could have been many such facilities in the region.

Dharmanomics and Kambuja's Economic Prosperity

Thus far in this chapter, we have looked at the historical evolution of Kambuja Desa, the philosophical underpinnings of Kambuja Desa's economy, the currency and the frameworks and sectors of the economy. All this gives us a clear indication of what constituted the economy of Kambuja Desa. In this section, I will try to summarize my views on some of the key trends and demonstrate the role played by Dharmanomics in the economy.

Economic Philosophy

In terms of economic philosophy, there are several correlations with the Dharmic philosophies and the KDC model discussed earlier. First, earlier in this chapter, we saw the direct and indirect references to *Arthashastra* in many inscriptions as well as references to Dharma related literature. The tenets were also used in day-to-day governance. For example, there was a requirement of a person learned in the Dharmasastras in some of the governance deliberations to provide people with clarity on the subject. In the inscriptions from the rule of Bhavavarman I and Jayavarman VII, there are direct references about the need to study the ancient texts. The rulers themselves had commented on new bhasyas on a variety of Dharmic texts as well. Even the principles of governance seem similar, for example, emphasizing on the welfare of the people, which was central to the KDC model. On the other hand, references to other non-Dharmic texts during this period are either negligible or not even present. The evidence on the influence of Dharmic philosophical underpinnings of both societal and economic policy, especially from the ninth to the thirteenth century, are quite clear and robust. This also shows a similar conceptual correlation with the KDC model.

Economic Model

I will now summarize my arguments on the economic model through the prism of land, labour and capital, since they are integral to the understanding of any economy. The temple-based economic model and recognition of the Dharmic ecosystem in which the economics of the temple operated is a central component of the discussion. To avoid repetition, I have avoided mentioning the Dharmic ecosystem in every other line.

First, let us start with land. I had mentioned earlier that substantial sections of the land in Kambuja Desa were owned or affiliated with the temples in some form or the other. While the monarchy did have an oversight and control over these lands, the area of the land directly owned by it was perhaps lesser than the temples. In addition, there was a continuous increase in ownership of land by the temples. For example, many private landowners kept giving their land to the temples for religious reasons but rarely took them back once the objectives were met. Besides the temples, there were many private landowners whose families and kith and kin owned large sections of the land. Collectively, as a block, perhaps the temples could have owned the largest amount of land in Kambuja Desa. This is a very important point since land ownership or control is critical for political power as well as economic power even in today's times. Not only the ownership of land, but the geographical vicinity of the temple land was also important. I mentioned earlier how agriculture production was largely a by-product of the local community temples. The strategic positioning of many of these temple lands also made them more valuable than others.

Second, I mentioned earlier that labour was mainly used in activities related to the monarchy, commercial activities such as trade and in the temple lands. Much of the labour was probably concentrated either on monarchy-related activities or in temple lands because, unlike the Cholas and other Bharatiya kingdoms, the influence of trade on Angkor kingdoms may have been lower. Some researchers feel that because of the location of the Angkor kingdom, the influence or importance of maritime trade was fairly limited. There are opposing views, but we shall address all this in subsequent discussions.

On the monarchy-related activities, unless there was a war or some battle, most of the activities were similar to those in the temple lands. What this basically means is that the control of labour—quantity, type and quality—was in the hands of the owners of the lands, in this case the people who were running the temples since the temples owned a major part of the land. The number of people involved with the temples can be an important indication of this. An inscription in Tahm Prohm temple during Jayavarman VII's reign says that almost 12,640 people lived within the walls of the temple compound.[47] A twelfth century inscription of Jayavarman VII[48] in the Prah Khan temple says that there were about 306,372 subjects in about 13,500 villages and as per one calculation, almost 38,000,000 kg of hulled rice was cooked annually for 20,000 gods.[49] We can get an indication of the possible number of people involved as labour in temple-related activities from a similar inscription which mentions that the temple's stores had a 'set of golden dishes weighing more than 500 kg, approximately 40,620 pearls, 876 Chinese veils, etc.',[50] among other things. All these references indicate that the activities of the temples and their control over substantial amounts of land made them a key power that controlled land and labour supply in Kambuja Desa. Hence temples were central in any economic discourse.

Last, we come to capital. The idea of temples being a bank or a financial institution of sorts is not something new. I had mentioned this in the earlier chapters related to the Saraswati–Sindhu civilization and also the Cholas. There is also evidence to suggest that similar financial networks existed even in the Javanese region and other Southeast Asian countries. This was a mere extension of how Dharmic communities functioned in those times, and hence it is not a surprise that the same was followed in Kambuja Desa.

A large part of the income of the temples was received through donations and gifts from families and rich people in the area. There were also endowments—a pool of donor wealth—which served to mobilize capital and labour in the district, village and region. In a sense, this reinforces the proposition that temples provided venture capital funds to businesses for a variety of activities. The temples also served as a safe and secure storage facility for large amounts of ornaments and wealth. The huge wealth discovered at the Padmanabaswamy temple in Kerala, for example, is an indication of how the temple also worked as a safe vault.

The capital used for development and commerce was from what was left over after serving the temple's needs. It is important to emphasize that the temple's needs came first. In many inscriptions, there are references which state that the temple's divine sanctity and its needs—rituals and maintenance—were of utmost importance, before anything else. The other sources of capital, besides donations, were from the state itself, whose major share of revenue was from taxes and the income generated from productive activities that it sponsored. There were foreign traders who were in Kambuja Desa (as detailed earlier) but there is little evidence to suggest that they made investments in land. While its neighbouring Champa region had extensive ports, the major role of the Kambuja ports was merely as a segue to China and East Asia. In modern parlance, there seemed to be a reasonable amount of trade but very little foreign direct investment (FDI) or foreign institutional investors (FIIs) in Kambuja Desa.

Thus, we have analysed the economic pillars of Kambuja Desa through the lens of land, labour and capital. In each of these descriptions, it is quite clear that the role of the temple as a socioeconomic and financial institution was central to Kambuja Desa's economic policies. The temples played an integral role in the economic activities of Kambuja Desa in a variety of ways, including political, statecraft and strategic. To that extent, I am in agreement with researchers such as Hall who proposed the temple hierarchy model. However, to conclude that the mere presence of the temple was the driving force behind the economic activity in Kambuja Desa is not just naïve but also not logical. An entity such as a temple does not gain its power or potency merely by its presence but because of the underlying philosophical and spiritual construct that underpins its foundation. It was the philosophical underpinnings of Dharma with the temple and its ecosystem that was the driving force behind the economic prosperity of Kambuja Desa. In essence, it was the Dharmic ecosystem which was the driver of the economic growth. More than the temple driven economic model, it was an economic model driven by the Dharmic ecosystem with the temple at its centre. Naturally, the influence of this Dharmic ecosystem driven model would feed into all the sectors of the economy as well.

Sectoral Composition of the Economy

In the sectoral composition, we discussed earlier the roles played by agriculture, trade and industry in Kambuja Desa. Let us consider the role played by the components of Dharmanomics in each of these sectors.

In agriculture, we have seen how the community temple was central to the production and distribution of rice and other commodities. The centrality of the temple was not because there was a physical structure present there but because a Dharmic and Vedic temple was operating there. In other words, there was a flourishing Dharmic ecosystem, that is, a Dharmic way of life thriving at this place, which led to an economic ecosystem which was self-sustainable and prosperous. The needs for daily rituals, sustainable practices inculcated in the Dharmic way of life, supply of food to devotees, the requirement of various employees to maintain the temple and the plethora of catalytic economic activities in the surrounding area triggered the agricultural cycle there. For example, the large amount of rice produced in the agricultural lands was used for the rituals and the food needs of the temple, besides being used for barter trade and the needs of the people at large.

Without an operational Dharmic values–based institution such as the temple, the agricultural ecosystem could not have sustained. The numerous kings who ruled from the ninth century to the fourteenth century perhaps realized this intuitively. While some would have been pious and had extensive faith in Hinduism, others would have realized that the sustenance of the Dharmic way of life was central to the economic prosperity of the region. Hence they focused a lot of resources and time to sustain and grow this Dharmic ecosystem, The inability to protect this ecosystem by later kings could have been one of the reasons for the eventual decline of Kambuja Desa after the fourteenth century.

We discussed earlier the importance of trade to Kambuja Desa despite the inland positioning of Angkor and an absence of coastal cities. This was indicated by the diversity of products that were being traded and the intense geopolitical competition to ensure that trading ports were secured. This would also mean the Srenis were operating in Kambuja Desa to ensure that these products (mentioned in Table 6.3) were delivered to the people who needed them. We definitely know that the products coming from Bharat were through the southern and eastern coastal empires such as the Cholas—all of whom had extensive Srenis which followed their own Sreni Dharma. As a result, the operational relevance of Sreni Dharma would still be quite high given the necessity to trade with the Bharatiya kingdoms. Also, given the rich Dharmic ecosystem model that governed Kambuja Desa, there would have been an inherent appreciation of the Sreni Dharma while trading with the Srenis.

From the evidence and the anecdotal observations available, maritime trade negotiations and operational lingo were also linked to the principles of Sreni Dharma in some form or the other.

Summary

Table 6.4 summarizes what I have discussed in this chapter.

TABLE 6.4 Summary of the Economy Systems of Kambuja Desa

	Economic Philosophy	**Economic models**	**Economic Sectoral Composition**
KDC Model	–References to *Arthashastra* in inscriptions and also the Dharmic values. Clear indication of practical elements that were aligned with the structure of the KDC model.	–Not a 1:1 fit but the principles of Dharma broadly apply to the temple-based economic model.	-
Dharmic Ecosystem	–Not a 1:1 fit but the Dharmic principles in the Dharmic ecosystem are a philosophical foundation.	–Central to the economic model of Kambuja Desa. The temple-based economic model served as the foundation for their economic prosperity.	–Agricultural production, demand and supply were all driven by the Dharmic ecosystem.
Sreni Dharma	-	-	Trade was mainly driven by the principles of Sreni Dharma. This could be more out of necessity than structural innovation.

Source: Author's own analysis

I covered a wide range of topics in this chapter. First, I looked at the history of Kambuja Desa—from Funan to Kambuja Desa—and its associated perspectives and theories. Subsequently, I looked at the philosophical underpinnings of Kambuja Desa, with references to Kautilya's *Arthashastra* and other Dharmic inspirations, followed by the economic structure of Kambuja Desa's economy. This included looking at their currency (or the lack of it), different types of economic models and the structure of the economy. I also looked at the influence of Dharmanomics on the economic philosophy and economic models with reference to the temple driven economy—using the analogy of land, labour and capital—and the economic sectors.

Therefore, in my view, the relevance of Dharmanomics to Kambuja is quite pertinent to say the least.

7

Other Dharmic Southeast Asian Kingdoms

BESIDES KAMBUJA DESA, THERE were other Southeast Asian kingdoms which followed Dharmanomics. These included kingdoms in Champa (Vietnam), Java (Indonesia), Kedar (Malaysia) and some parts of Siam (Thailand). While the extent—duration and continuity—of Dharmic leadership is a point of contention, there is no denial of its everlasting influence on their way of life, which can be seen even today. In this chapter, I will briefly examine each of these kingdoms. I will try to capture the essence of their economic policies and their distinct differences with Kambuja Desa and other kingdoms that I have discussed so far.

Champa (Vietnam)

Champa is mentioned in the Kambuja Desa chapter quite a few times. Let us quickly look at their geo strategic importance, economic structures and the influence of Dharmic leaders in their land during the Kambuja Desa period.

Historical Overview

The people of the Cham kingdom (Champa) were historically considered to be the descendants of San

Hyunh (Malaysian origin), who were trying to establish trade with China, Malaysia and Annimates (Vietnamese highlands) around 1000 BCE.[1] The first recorded king was Sri Mara (second century) and a number of kings ruled until about the fourteenth century. Most of these kings followed Hinduism, had the added surname 'Varman', much like the kings of southern Bharat and Kambuja Desa, built large temples and named their cities using Dharmic names such as Panduranga (present-day Phn-rang), Vijaya (present-day Binh-dinh), Simhapura, Amaravati and Indrapura (present-day Trah-kieu). Popular kings during this period included Bhadravarman, Bhadravarman III, Indravarman III, Harivarman II. The Cham kingdom was under constant threat from the north where the Dai Viets held power in the area that is called Northern Vietnam today. Eventually, the Chams were overthrown by Dai Viet after the fourteenth century. The map in Figure 7.1 provides an overview of the coastal cities and the geographical position of the region.

FIGURE 7.1 Map of Champa Kingdom

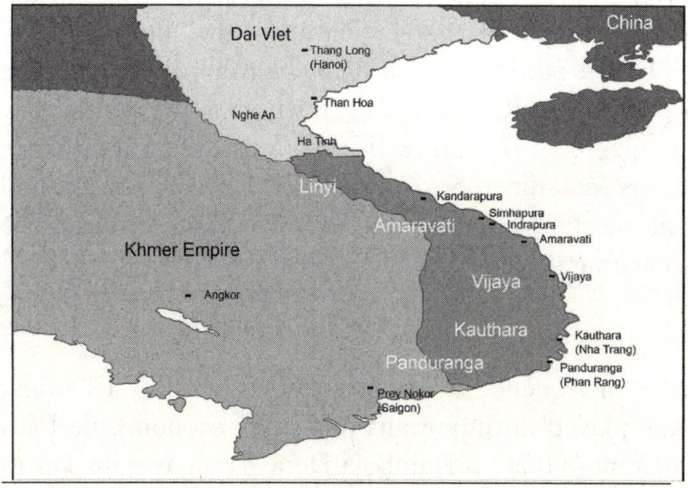

Source: Adapted from https://www.opindia.com/2020/09/kingdom-of-champa-and-the-chams-hinduism-in-vietnam/

Geostrategic Importance and Alliances

The region of Champa had a very long coastline along the South-China sea and was near China, a global powerhouse in those times. This strategic location made Champa a very attractive geopolitical asset for many countries. Some countries tried to maintain friendly relations with it as allies. Others attempted to conquer it through military interventions. The Khmer rulers attacked it many times. There is an interesting theory about how the Cholas became close allies of the Champas. The Cholas conquered Srivijaya in 1025 and Kadaram in around 1070 and were exploring options to expand trade with China through intermediaries. The theory proposed[2] is that in order to counter the northern insurgency and reclaim the land from the Dai Viet army (basically the people who occupied Northern Vietnam), the southern kingdoms, including Panduranga, Kauthara and Vijaya, might have asked for military help from the Cholas, given their linguistic and cultural proximity to them. I have not seen any evidence to contradict this possibility. Not only did the actions of the Cholas help to protect their fellow Tamizh lineage brethren, they also provided them with a geostrategic partner to pursue trade with China.

On the other hand, the Cholas were also said to be close to the Kambuja kings who were continuously threatening to overthrow the Champas to get their share of the coastline. Such examples of geopolitical and strategic statesmanship, that is, Chanakyaniti, makes it a fascinating subject of further research.

Commercial Trade

As a consequence of the strategic location of Champa, trade played an important role in its economy, perhaps much more than in Kambuja Desa. Trade was the key to their progress, especially from the tenth century onwards until about the fourteenth century. When the Song dynasty (1127–1279) made efforts to boost maritime trade, the Champa region became a major beneficiary since it became an important trading point between China and the rest of Asia and the world. A large number of cities along the coast of Champa were buzzing with activity during that time. Since the Champa people were connected to Hinduism and Tamils, they were also seen as friendly allies for the Cholas and other kingdoms of southern Bharat. According to a Vietnamese source, An Nam Chí Lược 安南志略 [Abbreviated Historical Records of An Nam/Vietnam], in an inscription dated in the thirteenth century, the ports of Champa were considered to be the first stopping point for Chinese ships to get fresh water and firewood until the fourteenth century.[3] It is also important to note that unlike other wet-rice cultivation societies in Southeast Asia, Champa did not have extensive hinterland with agrarian development and there were no vast plains like those in the north of the Mekong river. Hence they looked at trade as an alternate source for their revenue.[4]

Dharmic Connections to Both the Economy and Statecraft

Similar to Kambuja Desa, the Champas had very spiritual and Dharma-oriented rulers for a long time. The large number of temples, nomenclature of the cities, architecture and the inscriptions detailing the governance of the kings, all allude to this fact.

Temple-Linked Economic Model

Champa adopted a model similar to Kambuja Desa, with the temple being central to their socioeconomic functioning. However, unlike Kambuja Desa, much remains to be explored in this region since it has remained isolated for many years. An example of the temple linked model was the sixth century Mỹ Sơn temple built for Lord Shiva, where a Shivalinga was recently discovered by Archaeological Society of India (ASI). This temple is considered to be one of the oldest temple sites discovered in Southeast Asia. There is a reasonable amount of evidence to suggest that temples were an integral part of economic activities in Champa. Wet-rice cultivation was common, which was similar to what we saw in Kambuja Desa economy. Earlier, we saw how the local temple and the Dharmic way of life was central to the agricultural input and output dynamics. There is no reason to believe that was not the case in Champa—they had the same topography, geographical location, similar reliance on wet-rice cultivation and, of course, the Dharmic ecosystem as well. There is a theory that the riverine-system model of governance—usage of rivers as central to economic prosperity—could be a better way of representing the economy of Champa.[5]

Administration

Prof. R.C. Majumdar's description of the Champa administration in *Hindu Colonies of Southeast Asia* is an important source of information about the administrative activities of Champa kingdom. The governance and judicial system were based on ideals of Manu and the Dharmasastras, according to Prof. Majumdar. There is also evidence to suggest that the Champa kings were well versed in ancient Vedic scriptures. The administrative setup was divided into three provinces—Amaravati, Vijaya and Panduranga—which were further divided into thirty-two districts during the reign of Harivarman II in 1080, according to Chinese sources. Two officials—the governor and the senapati—were considered to be the key functionaries at the district level. There was an emphasis on clean and honest governance, especially in the successful kingdoms. Given the backdrop of the governance philosophies and the administrative set up, it is quite obvious that Dharmic influence in governance played an important role in structuring and implementing policies for the people.

Architecture

There was a great deal of similarity in the architecture of the Champa temples and monuments with what is seen in southern Bharat. The type of stone used and the common design of the temples[6]—alan (main temple), gopura (gate tower), mandapa (exterior hall), secondary shrines and kosagrha (fire-tower) and enclosures—are indicative of the influence of Dharmic systems from southern Bharat in Champa architecture. There have also been references made to similarities of many of the Chola temples in southern Bharat with those seen in Champa, including the ancient sixth century temple that we mentioned earlier. In line with our earlier discussion on the geopolitical compulsions of the Champa–Chola relationship vis-à-vis trade, it is not a surprise that the cultural fabric of the Cholas also spread to the Champa empire.

Java, Bali and Sumatra (Indonesia)

Anyone who visits Indonesia today will be fascinated by the historical marvels in Bali and the Javanese provinces. Such is the exquisite religiosity and embrace of Dharmic culture that it is hard not to get captivated. During the Angkor period, there was a thriving civilization in Java which had significant Dharmic influences.

Historical Overview

The country was segmented into east, west and central Java. For many years, Hindu kingdoms held control over these regions, but then they were overcome by the

Shailanderas, who were followers of Buddhism. There were many subsequent ups and downs in the monarchy, with several rulers taking power.

Philosophical Inspirations

The people were exposed to a wide range of ancient Indian scriptures and writings, including the *Arthashastra*. There are several references about this. In addition, indigenous Javanese also created their own philosophical texts. Some of these include *Kamandaka*, *Indraloka* and *Nitipraya*. For example, the *Kamandaka*, authored by Bhagavan Kamandaka, explains to students the duties of a king through illustrations from Mahabharata, Ramayana and other texts.

Dharmic Influences on Economy and Governance

There are many Dharma-based influences that we see in the erstwhile Java and Sumatra regions which are now in Indonesia. There are many monuments and temples there which represent the vast civilizational connect with Dharmic ideas. There are also philosophical inspirations from the Dharmic texts in use in these regions even today. The amount of material available would be a full book (or several books) by itself. I will try to be as brief as possible and cover some of the thematic areas of the economy and governance that can be deduced from the inscriptions and textual evidence available.

Governance

The king was the head and held political and social control. There was very little variation in that over the years.[7] He was venerated as a divine incarnation and saviour as per the *Manu Samhita*. This was quite different from the Kautilyan and Kambuja Desa situation where the king served for the welfare of the people. From an administrative sense, the contours of governance seemed to follow a Bharatiya model.

First, the nomenclature of governance positions remained Dharmic in nature. This seemed to have continued during the periods when Hindu kingdoms were in power as well as when they were not. For example, the chief judicial officer was called 'Dharmadikarana' and so were the superintendents of Saiva and Buddhist institutions. Moreover, 'mantri' was the minister and 'senapati' was the head of the army. These indicate that Dharmic terminologies were ingrained in the administration.

Second, the decentralized nature of governance in other kingdoms that we have seen—Cholas and Kambuja Desa, for example—seems to be present even here. The kingdom was divided into smaller parts, with districts and villages being the smallest units. These were overseen by governors and other officials nominated by the head of the state. Most of the units were left, by and large, to govern themselves, with just a few overarching rules and law and order regulations.

Temples and the Economy

Unlike for states such as Kambuja Desa and Champa, substantial evidence is not available (to my knowledge) to suggest that this was a temple-driven economy. There are plenty of temples and Hindu monuments throughout Java (more so in Bali), but their historical correlation with economic activities has not been established as yet. The temple ecosystem could have been an important contributor to the economy and a key resource mobilizer in terms of employment and so on, but its centrality in the economic activities remains to be confirmed. I have spent less time studying this region (compared to others), and I look forward to newer evidence on this.

Srenis and Economic Trade

The presence of Srenis from southern Bharat, whose origins and Dharmic linkages we discussed in earlier chapters, was a very important economic factor for the Java and Sumatra regions. There are several examples available regarding the role of the Srenis. For example, at the time of the Srivijaya empire in around 10–11 century, a major conflict was created due to the restraints put on Srenis from Bharat. This led the Cholas to conquer this region as mentioned earlier in the Cholas chapter. The following commentary on an inscription highlights the formation of guilds and their presence:

> One of these trade guilds is found in Barus, Sumatra (Indonesia) is particularly useful and it has been studied by Y. Subbarayalu. Subbarayalu points out that Ainnuruvar did not only play a dominant role but it also had control of port towns. The inscription refers to Barus as Varoca in Tamil and records the arrangement made by the trade guild in AD 1088–89, for a regular income or gift in gold to the local chief of merchants to be paid by South Indian merchants who came to that port. The role of Ainnuruvar in the overseas trade is also attested by the long lists of expensive imported commodities which has been mentioned in the Shikarpur inscription (Shimoga district, Karnataka) and the Piranmalai inscription (Ramnathapuram district, Tamil Nadu). The Shikarpur inscription provides a long list of commodities traded, e.g., well-bred horses, superior elephants, large sapphires, moonstones, pearls, rubies, diamonds, lapis lazuli, onyx, topaz, carbuncles, bdellium, sandal, camphor, musk, saffron etc.[8]

There are also instances of interactions with kingdoms which pursued Dharma-based economic models as we have mentioned earlier. These include the Cholas, Pallavas, Pandyas kingdoms from southern Bharat, among others. Obviously, the interactions and relationships were not always homogenous and there were ups and downs depending on the geopolitical environment. However, the philosophical underpinnings of the Javanese were complemented and, in some cases, rejuvenated by the influence of the Dharmic kingdoms of southern Bharat. This was further bolstered by the extensive trade between these kingdoms as described below:

- One of the earliest inscriptions, belonging to 883 CE, is from Kalirungan in Kedu in Central Java in 883. This inscription has a list of foreign traders and includes people from Kling (Kalinga), Aryya (Aryapura/Ayyavole), Pandikira (Karnataka) and perhaps Singhala (Sri Lanka).
- The Palebhuan charter of ninth century lists a group of foreigners and foreign traders whose names were similar to the 883 CE inscription suggesting a level of continuity in this regard.
- These seem to indicate that the Indians who came to Java were mainly from southern states such as Tamil Nadu, Andhra Pradesh and Orissa and from the coastal Konkan region on the western side. Inscriptions and other evidence suggest that this was quite prevalent during the ninth to the fourteenth centuries.
- The Kalinga region, in particular, was an important source of cotton textiles for the Javanese. Such dominance in the textiles imports of Java by Kalinga resulted in all South Asians being called by the nickname 'Kling'.
- Post the tenth century and the subsequent rise of the Cholas in southern Bharat, there was a shift in trade

from being west India centric to south India centric. This also resulted in greater product diversification in terms of goods and services. There was an increase in the exports of iron, nuts, commodities and cotton textiles, among others.

– There is an interesting similarity between the patterns of cotton textiles in southern Bharat and Java belonging to the 10–11 centuries. This could be further evidence of the large exports of these textiles from southern Bharat to Java during this period.[9]

Thus we see that there was a reasonable amount of influence on the economy by the Srenis and Dharmic kingdoms. The KDC also appears to have been quite important in the Java and Sumatra economy, given the constant presence of international trade through the centuries, focus on sustainable growth with emphasis on protecting the environment and the role of the state, which was complementary rather than constraining. There was a moderate amount of influence of the Dharmic ecosystem, as described earlier.

Siam (Thailand)

I was initially hesitant to include this section on Siam (Thailand). My original intention was to cover only Champa and Java in this chapter. In a spontaneous conversation, my wife, Lakshmi, mentioned that the Ayutthaya kingdom, inspired by Ayodhya in Bharat, was said to have been a prosperous Dharmic kingdom in the thirteenth century until about seventeenth century or so. This section reflects my subsequent research on the subject. Like other topics in this book, there is a lot of material available to explore, but given the space constraints, I will try to be as brief as possible. I will primarily focus on the Ayutthaya kingdom of Siam and try to present some of its economic models.

Siam played an important role in ancient Bharatiya history mainly because of its geographical location. Given that it was the first large country to the east of Andaman and Nicobar Islands and the fact that cutting across Siam would lead to China much faster for any trading outfit, made it a very strategic country for Bharatiya traders. While the Straits of Malacca are the key maritime route from Bharat to China today, in those days the route through Siam was also considered more suitable, taking into account all the risks involved.

Dharmic Influences on Ayutthaya

The Ayutthaya kingdom, established around 1350, is considered to be one of the most important kingdoms of Siam. The name is derived from Ayodhya, the birthplace of Lord Ram. Even though these two cities were almost 3,500 km apart, the Siamese believed in the tradition of Lord Ram and named their city after him.[10] It is believed that King Ramathibodi named the city. This indicates the strong links between Siam and Bharat through the Ramayana (called 'Ramakien' in Siam). There were other sociocultural linkages as well. These linkages highlight the philosophical underpinnings of a Dharmic civilization, given that the kingdom was named after someone who was almost 3,500 km away. The language of communication was a hybrid of Samskritam and Khmer, which was similar to what we saw in Kambuja Desa.[11] Such was the inherent civilizational connect between Bharat and the Siamese region that it permeated into their way of life, irrespective of what the dominating religion in the country was. This is seen even today as we land at the Bangkok international airport, which is called 'Suvarnabhumi', while the country boasts many monuments connected to Dharmic beliefs. It is clear that the concept of Dharma was intrinsically built in their way of life and Dharma-based economic models were a natural extension of this fact.

Temple-based Economic Activities

In Kambuja Desa, economic activity was based on the temple and the Dharmic ecosystem. In Ayutthaya, it was similar but not as extensive as in Kambuja Desa. There is evidence of the kingdom's desire to build temples. Building temples was both an economic as well as a social prestige project for many of the rulers just as it was in the neighbouring countries. This shows that the temple-based ecosystem played an important role in economic activities. However, more research needs to be conducted in this area.

Economic Trade

From the beginning, Ayutthaya's advantage was due to its geographical location, which was ideal for a flourishing trading environment. Its geographical proximity to the basin of Chao Phraya river and its ability to control the lower and upper Chao Phraya as well as the seaports offered important geostrategic advantages. The kingdom was equidistant from Bharat and China, well protected from the attacks of the Arab and European powers and gained from the power vacuum left by the decline of Angkor.[12]

The vast expanse of its trading connections extended from as far as the Red Sea in the west to Japan in the east, and everything in between was a part of its trade network.[13] Products that were traded included cotton, textiles, saffron, spices and copper, among others. The trading activities were so extensive that the kingdom was considered as one of the leading commercial centres of the world, akin to China and the Vijayanagar empire in Bharat.[14] They traded extensively with many regions and countries including Coromandel (Bharat), China, Laos and other Southeast Asian and middle-eastern countries. While they traded with the Srenis from southern Bharat, trading with the Chinese was of foremost importance. According to the *Suma Oriental*, the Siam area and the Ayutthaya kingdom had 'plenteous with many peoples and cities, with many lands and many foreign merchants, and most of these foreigners are Chinese, because Siam does a great deal of trade with China'.[15]

Other Countries in Southeast Asia and East Asia with Dharmic Influences

There is evidence to suggest that Dharmic frameworks existed in some form or the other in most, if not all, Southeast Asian countries and extended to some parts of East Asia as well. An example of this was the presence of Dharmic kingdoms from around the ninth to the fifteenth century in Philippines. They were a combination of Hindu–Malayan kingdoms which had Buddhist leanings as well.[16] There were similar kingdoms in smaller countries in the region during this time. Most of them followed similar economic models based on Dharma, but influenced by their own geography and socioeconomic and cultural confluences.

The research related to Dharmic economies in these Southeast Asian countries are at an initial stage. Each country has a narrative and an economic philosophy that prevailed in the early Common Era based on Dharma that is yet to be explored and discerned through dedicated research. The research areas could include exploring such frameworks in other Asian countries such as Japan[17], which could have had similar Dharmic frameworks.

8

Dharmanomics through 5,000 Years

DHARMANOMICS IS A CONCEPT that has survived for more than 5000 years (including the S–S period and at least 2000 years if one excludes the S–S period).[1] In this book thus far, we have traversed a vast ocean of knowledge, right from the Saraswati–Sindhu civilization, all the way till the Vijayanagar empire. The various theories and concepts I have articulated are in the backdrop of one of the most prosperous periods in the history of Bharat. The amount of information I have presented is extensive. It is not easy to absorb all of it in one go, primarily because of the historicity and intensity of the information and the numerous kingdoms that have been covered. Nevertheless, despite the effort required, I think there is a definite need to study it. Unless we make a concerted effort to create a qualitative time-series of Dharma-based economic models, it is impossible to make a scholarly case for the continuous importance of Dharma in economic theories.

In this chapter, I will provide in brief some of the anecdotal evidence that we find on the interactions between the various kingdoms mentioned in this book and the philosophical commonalities between them. This is in addition to the references that I have provided earlier in the text which were integrated with the narrative. I will also summarize all the pointers that I have mentioned to highlight the extent of Dharmanomics in these kingdoms and illustrate its continuity for sustainable economic prosperity.

Anecdotal Evidence on Dharmanomics

Philosophical Commonality across Kingdoms

This is perhaps an obvious fact but sometimes even the obvious needs to be spelt out for better appreciation. To get a clearer sense and perspective of both the magnitude and continuity of Dharmic civilizations, let us look at the chronology of the kings of all these kingdoms.

It is very clear that during the period from Saraswati–Sindhu to Kautilya and to Table 8.1 (from 600 CE till about 1300 CE) there was a continuous Dharmic civilizational construct in these regions. The extent and the quantum of Dharmanomics in these civilizations might have varied, but their underpinning philosophy with Dharma as a central construct remained a very important constant. This could well be because of the eternal nature of Dharmic principles.

Books and Texts Written on the Subject by Travellers

In all the references that we have made in this book, one intriguing and key set of references is from the travelogues and books written by the travellers and diplomats. *Periplus of the Erythraean Sea*, which was written by a traveller from the Middle East in the first century, or the accounts by the Chinese diplomat Zhou Daguan titled *The Customs of Cambodia*, or the Roman travel accounts, or the travel accounts of the Greek traveller Megasthenes, or even the numerous local Puranic tales related to these kingdoms—all these showcase a civilizational resurgence in these kingdoms, economically and socially, during the period covered in this book. Of course, the quantum and scale might vary across the kingdoms, but all these references seem to indicate a prosperous society to which much of the Western world was looking up to in those times. Much of the literature seems to indicate that the economies of the Bharatiya-inspired civilizations were all reasonably prosperous and were pioneers in engineering, science and commerce of that era.

Linkages between the Dharmic Kingdoms

Anecdotal evidence clearly suggests that there were cross-sectional linkages between the kingdoms that we have discussed in the book. To get a better sense of the anecdotal stories about these kingdoms, it is important to get an overview of the rulers in these countries during that time. Once the chronology is studied, it becomes easy to highlight some of the examples. These are, again, evidence to suggest the transfer of knowledge and exchange of information and ideas between different kingdoms.

Let us now consider the evidence which indicates cross-sectional knowledge transfer and communication between these kingdoms.

Rajendra Chola I (Cholas) and Suryavarman I (Kambuja Desa)

According to some theories, one of the main reasons for the expedition of Rajendra Chola I into Southeast Asia was due to a geopolitical conflict between the Kambuja Desa king and the Srivijaya and Tambralinga kingdoms. Suryavarman I had apparently requested the Cholas to help them in this conflict. Besides this, there were also simmering tensions with the Srivijaya empire about the way the Srenis from the Chola empire were treated. The Cholas won the battles against these kingdoms. The fact that the Cholas did not stay on and govern these places clearly indicates that their war was mainly for geopolitical reasons besides economic reasons—the Srenis and their ease-of-doing-business in those parts. In addition to this, the

TABLE 8.1 Chronology of the Kings of the Region

Years/ Kingdoms	**Pallavas**	**Cholas**	**Kambuja Desa**	**Champa**
600–700	Mahendravarman I Narasimhavarman I (Mamalla) Mahendravarman II Paramesvaravarman I Narasimhavarman II (Raja Simha)		Chitrasena Mahendravarman Isanavarman I Bhavavarman II Jayavarman I	Kandarpadharmavarman Prabhasadharma Bhadresvaravarman Vikrantavarman I Naravahanavarman Vikrantavarman II
700–800	Paramesvaravarman II Nandivarman II (Pallavamalla) son of Hiranyavarman of Kadavakula Dantivarman		Jayadevi Pushkaraksha	Prithindravarman Satyavarman Indravarman I
800–900	Nandivarman III Aparajitavarman	Vijayalaya Chola Aditya I	Jayavarman II Jayavarman III Indra[illegible] Yasovarm[illegible]	Harivarman I Vikrantavarman III Indravarman II Jaya Simhavarman I

Years/ Kingdoms	Pallavas	Cholas	Kambuja Desa	Champa
900–1000		Parantaka Chola I Gandaraditya Chola Arinjaya Chola Sundara Chola Uttama Chola Rajaraja Chola I	Harshavarman Isanavarman II Jayavarman IV Harshavarman II Rajendravarman Jayavarman V	Saktivarman Bhavavarman II Indravarman III Jaya Indravarman I Paramesvaravarman I Harivarman II
1000–1100		Rajendra Chola I Rajadhiraja Chola Rajendra Chola II Virarajendra Chola Athirajendra Chola Kulottunga Chola I	Udayadityavarman I Suryavarman I Udayadityavarman II Harshavarman III Jayavarman VI	Harivarman III Vikrantavarman IV Jaya Simhavarman II Jaya Paramesvaravarman I Bhadravarman III Rudravarman III Harivarman IV Jaya Indravarman II Paramabhodhisatva Jaya Indravarman II

1100–1200		Vikrama Chola Kulottunga Chola II Rajaraja Chola II Rajadhiraja Chola II Kulottunga Chola III	Dharanindravarman I Suryavarman II Dharanindravarman II Jayavarman VII	Harivarman V Jayavarman III Rudravarman IV Jaya Harivarman I Jaya Harivarman II Jaya Indravarman IV Suryajayavarman (Khmer king in Vijaya) Jaya Indravarman V (Champa king in Vijaya) Suryavarman or Vidyanandana (Khmer king in Panduranga)
1200–1300		Rajaraja Chola III Rajendra Chola III	Indravarman II Jayavarman VIII Srindravarman	Jaya Paramesvaravarman II Jaya Indravarman VI Indravarman V Jaya Simhavarman III

Source: Author's analysis

Karandai plates record that Suryavarman (1002–1050) of Kambuja Desa sought friendly relation with the Cholas.[2] It is also important to understand that this could not have been a one-off nor the first attempt because the trust and comfort exhibited by the Kambuja Desa king could only have been a result of a continuous relationship. There is speculation that Rajendra could have met and engaged with the Kambuja king during his earlier trip to Malaya and Indonesia in around 1024–25.[3] The subsequent interactions between the two kingdoms also indicates that this was not a one-off event. It is also important to understand that the Brihadisvara temple in Tanjore was built in 1010, which was approximately 2–3 years after Suryavarman I came into power in Kambuja Desa.

Koluttunga I and Jayavarman VI

An example of the interactions between these kingdoms was the one that took place between Koluttunga I and his contemporary, Jayavarman VI. The Karandai plates state that a precious stone was sent as a gift to the Cholas and it was placed in the wall of a hall in front of the famed Chidambaram temple.[4] This indicates a fairly continuous diplomatic relationship between the two kingdoms.

Koluttunga I and Suryavarman II

Inscriptional evidence shows that when Koluttunga I was expanding the Chidambaram Nataraja–Shiva temple, Suryavarman II offered to send a stone block as a gift for the construction. Koluttunga accepted the gift and installed the stone in the temple, mentioning that it was a gift from Kambuja Desa. This is yet another example of the strong relationship between the two kingdoms. Lastly, a gold chariot was presented by a Khmer king to the Cholas around twelfth century which is still there in a museum in Singapore. Figure 8.1 is a larger sample replica of the chariot mentioned.

FIGURE 8.1 Gold Chariot

Source: https://commons.wikimedia.org/wiki/File:12th_century_Airavatesvara_Temple_at_Darasuram,_dedicated_to_Shiva,_built_by_the_Chola_king_Rajaraja_II_Tamil_Nadu_India_(30).jpg

Temple Architecture

Two marvels constructed during the era were the Brihadisvara temple in Tanjore and the Angkor Wat in Kambuja Desa. Their designs have striking similarities and also some subtle differences as well. This surely indicates a much more pervasive cultural communication between these empires due to which these marvels could be built and sustained for such a long time.

The consensus among historians who have studied the Kambuja Desa temples is that they followed the Dravidian style of architecture (i.e., the style adopted by southern Bharatiya temples) with local variations that were customized to their needs. Though they look similar to the Nagar style in Northern Bharat, the similarities with Southern temples seem to predominate. The regular contact that Southern Bharatiya kings had with the kings of Kambuja Desa also is a reflection of this. For example, there were references to a close association between Rajaraja Chola and Suryavarman I around the time of the construction of the Brihadisvara temple. Similarly, during the construction of Angkor Wat, there were interactions between Koluttunga I and Suryavarman II, as mentioned earlier.[5]

On the actual structural similarities, a recent study suggests that there were 16 similarities, 15 variations and 18 interpretative similarities out of the 49 parameters tested for similarities between the Brihadisvara and the Angkor Wat temples.[6] Some of the innovations included the introduction of the Roluos style which had two distinct innovations on the gopura and libraries in the temple. Both of them were added around the Indravarman I era (877–889). Moreover, the Angkor temple was based on the philosophy of Mount Meru, which Bharatiya temples don't necessarily follow. For instance, in Angkor Wat, the central quincunx of the towers symbolize five peaks of the mountain, and the walls and the moats symbolize the surrounding mountain ranges and oceans.[7]

All these are anecdotal evidence of the confluence of architecture and the variations based on these confluences in temples built during those times in the two countries.

Economic Structures

In the earlier sections, I discussed some of the economic principles that were used in these kingdoms. Within these principles, there were also broad structures in terms of monetary and fiscal policies. On fiscal policies, there was consistent similarity in taxes between the Chola empire and the Kambuja Desa or Champa. The taxes were more or less similar in these kingdoms.

On the other hand, monetary policy was altogether different. While the monetary policy was not by any means as comprehensive as what we have today, in some countries, the need to deal with currencies and coins, their circulation and their impact on prices was a necessity. Even during Kautilya's times in the third century BCE, there were government staff at the village level who would gather information about the prices of commodities and send the information to the ruler. In all the kingdoms that I have discussed in this book, the Southern Bharatiya ones surely had some kind of monetary policy that focused on price stability. In countries like Kambuja Desa, the presence of currencies or coins is itself questionable.[8] So the concept of monetary policy may have been of relatively less interest to these civilizations.

Inscriptional and Empirical Evidence of Dharmanomics through the Years

Table 8.2 summarizes the key themes based on the evidence presented in this book on the economic models of the Common Era kingdoms. While this might not be all the evidence that has been discovered so far, the table tries to capture the essence of the discussions in the earlier chapters.

Assessment of Dharmanomics for All the Kingdoms Covered

Table 8.3 summarizes the broad trends that I see in the evidence that I have presented in this book which is inclusive of the inscriptive and analytical evidence as well as anecdotal evidence. There are two distinct features of the evidence I have provided—inscriptive evidence and correlated or interpreted evidence. A summation of these is shown in Table 8.3 in terms of colour gradation, where green represents more than conclusive nature of both the evidence mentioned, orange represents one of the pieces of evidence is definitive and the other is interpretative and

TABLE 8.2 Summary of Evidence Discussed in This Book

	Saraswati–Sindhu Civilization (3500 bce)	**Cholas (9th–13th Century)**	**Pallavas, Pandyas, Vijayanagar (2nd–8th Century, post 13th Century)**	**Kambuja Desa (6th–11th Century)**	**Champa, Java, Siam (9th–14th Century)**
KDC	Common principles related to ethics, trade and economic growth but lack of institutional insight.	Solid evidence to suggest KDC-related principles in governance, Srenis and communities. Examples include Uthiramerur inscriptions, democratized governance and flourishing trade. Also, candidate selection, sabhas, mahasabhas which facilitated commerce.	Similar to the Cholas albeit with some minor variations.	Inscriptions as well as practical evidence related to Kautilya's KDC model, with similarities in trade, commerce and governance mechanisms.	Similar to the Cholas and Kambuja Desa albeit with some variations specific to these countries.
Dharmic Ecosystem	Implicit evidence, but not conclusive enough.	Evidence of the largest temples built in Bharat during this era. Central to the socio-economic eco system.	Like the Cholas, these rulers made sure the Dharmic ecosystem was enhanced as much as possible.	Central to the economic model, since it was a temple-based economic model. Several evidence and theoretical references for this.	These countries developed the Dharmic ecosystem significantly, but if it was central to their model like Kambuja Desa is still an open question in my view.

Sreni Dharma	Examples of Dharma saṁjña and बलुतेदार balutēdāra which showed well established systems during the S–S period.	Plethora of Srenis, including Ainnuruvar, Anjuvannam, Manigraamam and Naandesi, which were centres of economic growth and catalyst for massive maritime trade. Most of them, if not all, were following Sreni Dharma with substantial evidence to back it.	Similar to the Srenis that were there during the Chola time, hence the presence of Sreni Dharma was there.	Trade was an important component and Sreni Dharma was an important operational strength, especially when dealing with traders from southern Bharat.	Similar to Cholas since these countries were not inland like Kambuja desa. As such, there was a greater variety and diversity of Srenis; most of whom followed some form of Sreni Dharma.

no colour or white means both these forms of evidence are not available.

TABLE 8.3 Summary of Evidence

	Saraswati–Sindhu Civilization	**Cholas**	**Pallavas, Pandyas, Vijayanagar**	**Kambuja Desa**	**Champa, Java, Siam**
KDC					
Dharmic Ecosystem					
Sreni Dharma					

Inscriptional, empirical and anecdotal evidence (represents the colour green mentioned on page 234)

Anecdotal but less inscriptional or empirical evidence (represents the colour orange mentioned on page 234)

Source: Author's analysis

There are a few caveats or observations that I need to make here. First, it is imperative to note that there was no uniform emphasis across all the components of Dharmanomics in all these kingdoms. While the kingdoms kept Dharmic values and ideas as their base, they had their own variations in the way they managed their economies. For example, Kambuja Desa essentially modelled its economy around the Dharmic ecosystem with the temple at the core of its economic model. On the other hand, some of the other kingdoms had the temple or the Dharmic ecosystem as a very important socioeconomic construct, but everything in the economy did not necessarily revolve around it. When we look at *Arthashastra* itself, there is barely any mention of the temple ecosystem in the text.

Second, we also need to be cognizant of the extent of adaptations that the kingdoms made in the older frameworks. For example, when we compare the inscriptions and the evidence, the Cholas had a flourishing Sreni system, with Srenis being integral to their economic and political policies, so much so that they would cross oceans to fight a war to support them. On the other hand, for the Pallavas, while trading and Srenis were an important part of their economic systems, the Srenis were not as ubiquitous or as powerful as in the times of the Cholas. There was definitely a variation in the emphasis given to the components of Dharmanomics in these kingdoms.

Third, and most interestingly, irrespective of the landscape, terrain and climatic conditions of these kingdoms, the underlying principle of Dharma and its values were completely built into the economic models and principles. We would expect that the geographical and topographic changes may have diluted the role of Dharmanomics in their ecosystems. But the evidence seen thus far does not suggest that. This fact reiterates the enduring and eternal relevance of Dharma and, as an extension Dharmanomics, to the well-being of these civilizations.

Last, it is important to understand that across all these civilizations, there was no barbaric quest for just power alone or just economic prosperity alone. There was a well-rounded developmental model and thinking that structurally ensured that economic growth and prosperity alone were not the end-all of everything. A holistic developmental model—which I believe what Dharmanomics is—encompasses a wider array of aspects which include community, society, arts, values, spirituality and inclusivity at its core. For example, even though the great Cholas conquered so many lands across the seas, when Rajendra Chola returned victorious from reaching the Ganges in the north, he did not think he was bigger than the universe, by any means. In fact, despite such success, he built Gangaikonda Cholapuram and essentially ensured that all the subsequent kings had to bow down to Lord Shiva because Lord Shiva was seen as the driver of his success. Such profound humility and understanding of the broader holistic developmental narrative were very important yet under-appreciated features of not just the Cholas but of the other kingdoms mentioned in this book as well.

Relevance for Today and Viksit Bharat–Completing the Trilogy!

To establish a relevance for Viksit Bharat, one has to establish credibility of the Dharma-based economic theories through research and books. My books *Kautilyanomics for Modern Times and Dharmanomics* attempt to establish a qualitative time series for thousands of years to earn the credibility to use such Dharmic-based framework ideas for the future. The question that people, who have read and studied the vast economic history we have accrued as a civilization, often ask, incredibly, is—*so what?* While it amuses me that such a question keeps popping up, as a researcher it is my obligation to provide the explanations to the reader—as much as possible. Briefly, I would like to address four key points of relevance of Dharma-based economic frameworks—Kautilyanomics, Dharmanomics and the third part of the trilogy on Dharma-based economic ideas for Viksit Bharat which I am working on— to today's Bharat and the socioeconomic challenges it faces.

First, in its rapid rise towards becoming a global superpower, Bharat needs to provide a philosophical foundation for the world to aspire to. While the Protestant ethic served as the fulcrum for the capitalistic world, what is the philosophical underpinning for Bharat as it captures the global socioeconomic space gradually, but firmly? There is no doubt in my mind that a Dharma-based economic world, which bats for Vasudhaiva Kutumbakam, Samanya Dharma with components that include Kautilyan Dharmic Capitalism, Dharmic ecosystem and the principles of Sreni Dharma, will play an integral part in such a socioeconomic dispensation. In simpler terms, Dharmanomics, with purusharthas and sustainability at its core, will serve as the philosophical foundation for Bharat to provide an alternate socioeconomic narrative to the Anglo-Saxon world's status quo. The weight, experience and wisdom of a model such as Dharmanomics, which is more than 5,000 years old, is the perfect remedy that Bharat can offer to the world at large.

Second, Dharmanomics would provide a much-needed anchor to modern economic policy's biggest challenges, with climate change and sustainability being top on the priority list. The essence of Dharmanomics—with Dharma beyond the binary of the state and market—would seek to reposition, in a sustainable manner, the way the world economy progresses. The ability to look beyond the self-centred consumer-driven economic choices of yesteryears and towards a collective Dharmic global outreach would serve to address the issue of sustainability bottom-up, rather than just through top-down solutions. This awareness—to be intrinsically conscious of the environment and its ethos while making fundamental economic choices for individuals—would help to create a bottom-up revolution in addressing the issue of sustainability with Dharmic awareness at its core. This Dharmic awareness would go a long way in ensuring that sustainability is always the focus rather than being subject to top-down interventions alone, and nothing more beyond that, as always. Dharmanomics would provide that behavioural alternative to the consumer which can address the issue of sustainability in a coherent and sustainable manner.

Third, in an increasingly polarized world, the universal ethos of Dharmanomics is central to not just world peace but also global economic prosperity. The ideas of engaging with the world for commercial trade, a rule-enforcing yet non-intervening state and sustainable growth and welfare will be important pillars of this global economic prosperity. Moreover, as the world grapples with new challenges such as artificial intelligence, it is imperative that the moral fabric of the society and the state are in the right place to address these challenges. A Dharmic growth model which places moral values as the foundation of economic prosperity would be an important factor in sustaining economic growth in an inclusive and holistic manner.

Fourth, it is also clear that economic growth alone will not make the world sustainable and inclusive. Through the examples of various kingdoms, we have seen in this book that the balance between economic growth and holistic development—in other words, the Dharmic balance—is an important component of progress. In the next few decades, Bharat's leadership in building such a Dharmic balance would be an example for the rest of the world to emulate.

While I have come to the end of this book, I hope to expand on these points in the next book—the third and the last book of this series—which would focus on the contours of a Dharma-based economic ideas for Viksit Bharat in Amrit Kaal, achievable by 2047. Researching and writing for this book has been a great learning experience, and I am looking forward to progressing on the next one.

Since you have read the book thus far, I am also grateful for your support in reading and reviewing my work. I am very passionate about the intrinsic role of Dharma and its possibilities to play a central role in global economic prosperity. All my efforts are aimed to providing historical reference points on this through my books—and to showcase a vision based on the eternal ideas they contain. The success of my books is always secondary; the primary motive is to get the message across to readers like you and trigger your thoughts on the ideas presented and to further enhance research on this subject. I do hope this book has made you contemplate on Dharmanomics.

I leave you with a quotation from the Bhagavad Gita (Chapter 2, Verse 47)[9] that is close to my heart and which symbolizes my approach to writing this book:

कर्मण्येवाधिकारस्ते मा फलेषु कदाचन।
मा कर्मफलहेतुर्भूर्मा ते सङ्गोऽस्त्वकर्मणि।। २-४७
You have the right to work only, but never to its fruits.
Let not the fruits of action be your motive, nor let
your attachment be to inaction.

I hope you enjoyed reading *Dharmanomics*!

Notes

Introduction

1 https://www.indiabudget.gov.in/budget2020-21/doc/Budget_Speech.pdf, accessed on 30 May 2024.

Chapter 1: Sreni Dharma

1 Vikramaditya Khanna, 'The Economic History of the Corporate Form in Ancient India', 2006, http://www.law.harvard.edu/programs/corp_gov/papers/2006sp-Speakers Paper03_02-21_Khanna.pdf, accessed on 2 April 2024.

2 Vikramaditya Khanna, 'The Economic History of the Corporate Form in Ancient India', p. 47.

3 Vikramaditya Khanna, 'The Economic History of the Corporate Form in Ancient India', p. 39.

4 Vikramaditya Khanna, 'The Economic History of the Corporate Form in Ancient India'.

5 http://bharatkalyan97.blogspot.com/2020/01/roots-of-sreni-seni-guild-dharma-traced.html, accessed on 30 May 2024.

6 Brihaspati Smriti, xiv 3–4, 'The Minor Law Books', Julius Jolly, ed. & tran., in *Sacred Books of the East*, vol. 33 (1965), *supra* note 46, viii at 9, 26; *Katyayanasmriti*, verses 668–69, 675–77 (Panduranga Vamana Kane, ed. & tran.) (1933) *supra* note 46, verse 254.

7 Brihaspati Smriti, xiv 3–4; 'The Minor Law Books', Julius Jolly, ed. & trans., in *Sacred Books of the East*, vol. 33 (1965), *supra* note 46, xvii at 20; 'Vyavahara Mayukha or Hindu Law, including Smritis of Yajnavalkya', 230 (verses 186–92 of Chapter 2), 239 (Verses 259–60 of Chapter 2), Vishwanath Narayan Mandlik, trans., (1982), *supra* note 46, II, p. 186–87.

8 R. Shamasastry, *Arthashastra of Chanakya Translated by R. Shamasastry*, 1915.

9 https://iks.iitgn.ac.in/wp-content/uploads/2017/01/Guilds_in_Ancient_India.pdf, accessed on 30 May 2024.

10 Kiran Kumar Thapliyal, Guilds in Ancient India: Study of Guild Organization in Northern India and West Deccan from 600 BC to 600 AD, 1996.

11 https://tamilnation.org/heritage/saraswathi, accessed on 30 May 2024.

Chapter 2: Dharmanomics

1 https://theomtemple.org/what-is-dharma-as-per-vedic-teachings/, accessed on 2 April 2024.

2 Kanchi H.H. Sri Chandrasekarandra Saraswati, *Hindu Dharma: The Universal Way of Life* (Bhavans Publications, 2008).

3 Swami Tejomayananda, *Dharma Shastra: Way to Peace, Prosperity and Purity* (Chinmaya Prakashan, 2022), https://www.chinmayapublications.com/swami-tejomayananda.

4 My pranams to Swami Advayananda from Chinmaya Mission for guiding me to this book and also Sukumarji (Chinmaya Mission, San Diego) and Sunita Grandiji (Chinmaya Mission, Ernakulam) for facilitating this.

5 Do note that the definitions and explanations have been simplified for a common reader. I have done the best to retain the essence of the meanings as much as possible.

6 https://www.wisdomlib.org/hinduism/book/manusmriti-with-the-commentary-of-medhatithi/d/doc200246.html, accessed on 2 April 2024.

7 Swami Tejomayananda, *Dharma Shastra: Way to Peace, Prosperity and Purity*, p. 39; https://www.chinmayapublications.com/swami-tejomayananda, accessed on 30 May 2024.

8 Burton Stein, 'The state, the Temple and Agricultural Development: A Study in Medieval South India', *The Economic Weekly Annual*, 1961.

9 A. Appadorai, *Economic Conditions in Southern India* (University of Madras, 1936).

Chapter 3: Saraswati–Sindhu Civilization

1 https://archive.org/details/TheIndusScript.TextConcordanceAndTablesIravathanMahadevan/

Corpus%20of%20Indus%20Seals%20and%20Inscriptions.%20Collections%20in%20India/, accessed on 19 June 2024.

2 https://books.google.com/books/about/Indus_Script.html?id=KAIaAQAAIAAJ, accessed on 19 June 2024.

3 https://www.youtube.com/watch?v=FRsVMhYQQI-Y&t=1s, accessed on 19 June 2024.

4 https://www.youtube.com/watch?v=tV7pi2QrvAo&t=5794s, accessed on 20 June 2024.

5 S. Kalyanaraman, *Vedic River Sarasvati and Hindu Civilization* (Aryan Books, 2008).

6 https://humanjourney.us/ideas/connecting-with-the-gods/early-civilizations-harappa/, accessed on 3 April 2024.

7 https://www.hindustantimes.com/cities/pune-news/new-evidence-suggests-harappan-civilization-is-7-000-to-8-000-years-old-101703182904001.html, accessed on 3 April 2024.

8 https://humanjourney.us/ideas/connecting-with-the-gods/early-civilizations-harappa/, accessed on 3 April 2024.

9 B. Ansumali Mukhopadhyay, 'Semantic Scope of Indus Inscriptions Comprising Taxation, Trade and Craft licensing, Commodity Control and Access Control: Archaeological and Script—Internal Evidence', *Humanities and Social Science Communications*, 10, 972 (2023), https://doi.org/10.1057/s41599-023-02320-7, accessed on 3 April 2024.

10 Dr Kalyanaraman, who is a co-author of this chapter, is a pioneer in deciphering the Indus script and his work has helped in understanding many of the nuances of these scripts.

11 R.C. Majumdar, *Corporate Life in Ancient India.*

12 S. Kalyanaraman, 'Stoneware Bangles Are Assigned Responsibilities in Sreni Guild, Corporate Form', June 2023, https://www.academia.edu/102787853, accessed on 23 June 2024.

13 S. Kalyanaraman, 'Stoneware Bangles Are Assigned Responsibilities in Sreni Guild, Corporate Form', p. 5.

14 S. Kalyanaraman, *Economic History of Veda Times*, https://www.academia.edu/36759458, accessed on 30 May 2024.

15 http://bharatkalyan97.blogspot.com/2018/06/economic-history-of-veda-times-tribute.html, accessed on 31 March 2024.

16 Sanjeev Sanyal, *The Ocean of Churn: How the Indian Ocean Shaped Human History* (Penguin Random House, 2016), https://www.amazon.com/Ocean-Churn-Indian-Shaped-History/dp/0670087327, accessed on 30 May 2024.

17 https://www.academia.edu/82503984, accessed on 30 May 2024.

18 R. Maddin, T.S. Wheeler and J.D. Muhly, 'Tin in the Ancient Near East: Old Questions and New Finds', *Expedition*, 1977, 19 (2), p. 35–47.

19 Jane McIntosh, *The Ancient Indus Valley: New Perspectives* (ABC-CLIO, 2008), p. 210, 229.

20 https://www.academia.edu/103277521, accessed on 18 March 2024.

21 https://www.academia.edu/37367694, accessed on 1 June 2024.

22 Barry Eichengreen and Rui Pedro Esteves, 'International Finance', *The Cambridge Economic History of the Modern World: Volume 2: 1870 to the Present*, edited by Kyoji Fukao and Stephen Broadberry (Cambridge University Press, 2021), vol. 2, p. 501–525.

23 https://www.academia.edu/100830813, accessed on 30 May 2024.

24 https://www.academia.edu/100830813, accessed on 30 May 2024.

25 I am not getting into the debate on the continuity here, which would be a book by itself. However, it is important to highlight some of the common traits which indicate possible continuation of some of these concepts into the Chola era. Here I am referring to the continuity of some of the techniques, skills and mechanisms and not Dharmic principles themselves, which are quite clear from my perspective.

26 Kauṭilya, 'The Duties of Government Superintendents', *Arthashastra Book 2*, translated by R. Shamasastry, (Government Press, 1915), p. 511–585.

27 https://www.telangana360.com/2017/01/telangana-damascus-or-wootz-steel.html, accessed on 5 June 2024.

28 https://www.academia.edu/43831170, accessed on 5 June 2024.

29 https://indiankanoon.org/doc/66044776/?type=print, accessed on 1 June 2024.

CHAPTER 4: CHOLAS

1 My sincere thanks to Sri Jeyesunder, IFS and Dr Chitra Madhavan for their inputs on this section on the Cholas.

2 Wilfred Harvey Schoff, *The Periplus of the Erythraen Sea* (Forgotten Books, 1912), p. 187.

3 Kanakalatha Mukund, *The World of the Tamil Merchant* (Penguin, 2012).

4 N.P. Chakravarti, ed., *Epigraphia Indica*, vol. 22, 1933, p. 146, https://archive.org/details/in.ernet.dli.2015.69621/page/n195/mode/2up, accessed on 4 April 2024.

5 https://www.elections.tn.gov.in/Factsheet.aspx, accessed on 30 May 2024; https://iastoppers.com/articles/kudavolai-electoral-system, accessed on 30 May 2024.

6 http://know-your-heritage.blogspot.com/2014/07/uthiramerur-inscriptions-on-chola.html, accessed on 18 March 2024.

7 http://know-your-heritage.blogspot.com/2014/07/uthiramerur-inscriptions-on-chola.html, accessed on 30 May 2024.

8 Burton Stein, 'A History of India', edited by David Arnold, *The Blackwell History of the World*, general editor R.I. Moore (Wiley-Blackwell,1998), https://hkrdb.kar.nic.in/documents/Downloads/Good%20Reads/A%20History%20of%20India%202nd%20ed.pdf, accessed on 30 May 2024.

9 Kanakalatha Mukund, *The World of the Tamil Merchant*, p. 126.

10 Kanakalatha Mukund, *The World of the Tamil Merchant.*

11 N. Karashima, Y. Subbarayalu and P. Shanmugam, 'Nagaram during the Chola and Pandyan Period: Commerce and Towns in the Tamil Country A.D. 850–1350', *Indian Historical Review 2008*, 35 (1), p. 1–33, https://journals.sagepub.com/action/showCitFormats?doi=10.1177%2F037698360803500101&mobileUi=0, accessed on 1 June 2024.

12 R. Jayasurya, *The Trading Community in Early Tamil Society up to 900 AD*, 2008, http://www.languageinindia.com/nov2008/jeyasuryamphil.pdf, accessed on 30 May 2024.

13 https://www.tnarch.gov.in/epigraphy/guild-inscriptions, accessed on 20 June 2024.

14 https://tamilnation.org/heritage/chola/deivanayagam.htm, accessed on 18 March 2024.

15 https://www.valanjiyar.com/article/the-ancient-south-Bharatn-merchant-guild/.

16 https://www.valanjiyar.com/article/the-ancient-south-Bharatn-merchant-guild/.

17 Hermann Kulke, K. Kesavapany and Vijay Sakhuja (eds.), *Nagapattinam to Suvarnadwipa: Reflections on the Chola Naval Expeditions to Southeast Asia* (Iseas-Yusof Ishak Institute, 2009), p. 511, https://www.amazon.com/Nagapattinam-Suvarnadwipa-Reflections-Expeditions-Southeast/dp/9812309373, accessed on 1 June 2024.

18 P. Ravi and M. Venkatachalapathy, 'A Brief Study of Trade Guilds in Andhra from 1300 AD TO 1600 AD', https://www.fepbl.com/index.php/ijarss/article/view/22/225, accessed on 1 June 2024.

19 Hermann Kulke, K. Kesavapany and Vijay Sakhuja (eds.), *Nagapattinam to Suvarnadwipa*, p. 511.

20 Hermann Kulke, K. Kesavapany and Vijay Sakhuja (eds.), *Nagapattinam to Suvarnadwipa*, p. 149.

21 K.A. Nilakanta Sastri, *The Colas* (University of Madras, 1913: 2013 reprint), p. 598.

22 Kamini Dandapani, *Rajaraja Chola, King of Kings* (Aleph Book Company, 2022), p. 134.

23 Kamini Dandapani, *Rajaraja Chola, King of Kings*, p. 126.

24 A. Appadorai, *Economic Conditions in Southern India (1000–1500 A.D)*, p. 274.

25 Dayalan, *Early Temples of Tamil Nadu: Their Role in Socio-Economic Life (c. A.D 550–925)* (New Delhi: Harman Publishing House, 1992), p. 162.

26 https://www.whatisindia.com/inscriptions/south_indian_inscriptions/volume_2/no_66_68_outside_of_north_enclosure.html, accessed on 19 March 2024.

27 *South Indian Inscriptions* (SII) VIII, p. 151, https://archive.org/details/dli.jZY9lup2kZl6TuXGlZQdjZIdlZYy, accessed on 5 June 2024.

28 Kanakalatha Mukund, *The World of the Tamil Merchant*, p. 115.

29 https://www.whatisindia.com/inscriptions/south_indian_inscriptions/volume_3/no_101_105_parakesarivarman_parantaka_i.html, accessed on 19 March 2024.

30 M. Kavitha, 'Socio-Economic Functions of Temples during Medieval Tamil Country 11th–16th Century A.D.', *International Journal of Business and Management Invention*, 6 (7), July 2017, p. 18–23.

31 Kanakalatha Mukund, *The World of the Tamil Merchant*, p. 119.

32 https://journals.sagepub.com/doi/10.1177/001946466800500304, accessed on 1 June 2024.

33 Burton Stein, 'The state, the Temple and Agricultural Development'.

34 Kanakalatha Mukund, *The World of the Tamil Merchant*, p. 113.

35 Kavitha, 'Socio-Economic Functions of Temples during Medieval Tamil Country 11th–16th Century A.D.', p. 18–23.

36 https://www.academia.edu/72483888, accessed on 1 June 2024.

37 https://journals.sagepub.com/doi/10.1177/001946466800500304, accessed on 1 June 2024.

38 https://www.academia.edu/72483888, accessed on 1 June 2024.

39 https://www.academia.edu/72483888, accessed on 2 June 2024.

40 https://www.whatisindia.com/inscriptions/south_indian_inscriptions/volume_2/no_24_25_inner_gopura_left_entrance.html, accessed on 2 June 2024.

41 https://www.academia.edu/72483888, accessed on 2 June 2024.

42 K.A. Nilakanta Sastri, *The Colas*, p. 567.

43 https://gacbe.ac.in/pdf/ematerial/18MHI22C-U1.pdf, accessed on 20 June 2024.

44 K.A. Nilakanta Sastri, *The Colas*, p. 584.

45 'Chola Art and Architecture: Brilliant Bronze Sculptures and Magnificent Stone Temples', https://www.exoticindiaart.

com/blog/chola-art-and-architecture-brilliant-bronze-sculptures-and-magnificent-stone-temples/, accessed on 19 March 2024.

46 K.A. Nilakanta Sastri, *The Colas*, p. 594.

47 Wilfred Harvey Schoff, *The Periplus of the Erythraen Sea* , p. 242.

48 K.A. Nilakanta Sastri, *The Colas*.

49 K.A. Nilakanta Sastri, *The Colas*, p. 594.

50 *Ostasiatische Zeitschrift*, 1933, p. 5–11, https://www.abebooks.com/Ostasiatische-Zeitschrift-1933-Auftrage-Gesellschaft-Kunst/30914991746/bd, accessed on 30 May 2024.

51 https://www.valanjiyar.com/article/the-ancient-south-Bharatn-merchant-guild/.

52 https://en.wikipedia.org/wiki/Economy_of_ancient_Tamil_country, accessed on 20 March 2024.

53 Nagaswamy, *Tamil Nadu: The Land of Vedas* (Tamil Arts Academy, 2016), p. 401.

54 Kanakalatha Mukund, *The World of the Tamil Merchant*, p. 144.

55 Sriram Balasubramanian, *Kautilyanomics for Modern Times*.

56 https://journals.sagepub.com/doi/10.1177/001946466800500304, accessed on 2 June 2024.

57 https://journals.sagepub.com/doi/10.1177/001946466800500304, p. 291.

Chapter 5: Pallavas, Pandyas and Vijayanagar Empire

1 C. Minakshi, 'Administration and Social Life under the Pallavās', (University of Madras, 1938) p. 19.

2 C. Minakshi, 'Administration and Social Life under the Pallavās', p. 23.

3 https://en.wikipedia.org/wiki/Pallava_dynasty#Origins, accessed on 21 March 2024.

4 R.C. Majumdar, *Kambuja Desa* (Hassel Street Press, 2021), https://www.amazon.com/Kambuja-Desa-R-C-Majumdar/dp/101417788X, accessed on 26 June 2024.

5 https://storytrails-walks.in/blog/the-cambodi-an-king-of-kanchipuram, accessed on 22 March 2024.

6 Ngô Văn Doanh, *Mỹ Sơn Relics*, p. 66 ff.; p.183 ff. An English translation of the inscription is at p.197 ff, https://books.google.com/books/about/Mỹ_Sơn_Relics.html?id=ieNu-AAAAMAAJ, accessed on 2 June 2024.

7 C. Minakshi, 'Administration and Social Life under the Pallavās', p. 61.

8 C. Minakshi, 'Administration and Social Life under the Pallavās', p. 82.

9 *Epigraphica India*, vol. XI, p. 225. https://archive.org/details/in.ernet.dli.2015.115919/page/n285/mode/2up, accessed on 31 May 2024.

10 Toung Pao II, 5, https://www.jstor.org/stable/4526467.

11 C. Minakshi, 'Administration and Social Life under the Pallavās', p. 138.

12 C. Minakshi, 'Administration and Social Life under the Pallavās', p. 149.

13 C. Minakshi, 'Administration and Social Life under the Pallavās', p. 97.

14 C. Minakshi, 'Administration and Social Life under the Pallavās', p. 108.

15 C. Minakshi, 'Administration and Social Life under the Pallavās', p. 139.

16 K.A. Nilakanta Sastri, *The Pandyan Kingdom* (Luzac, 1929), https://archive.org/details/dli.csl.5955, accessed on 3 June 2024.

17 The lineages of the kings provided here are based on K.A. Nilakanta Sastri's books. I acknowledge that Pandya kings could have existed earlier, especially prior to the Sangam period. But for the sake of consistency, in this book I will stay with the lineage mentioned here.

18 https://en.wikipedia.org/wiki/Pandya_dynasty#cite_note-:3-7, accessed on 3 June 2024.

19 https://en.wikipedia.org/wiki/Pandya_dynasty#cite_note-:3-7, accessed on 3 June 2024.

20 https://www.academia.edu/43831170, accessed on 3 June 2024.

21 S. Dhammika, *The Edicts of King Ashoka: An English Rendering* (Buddhist Publication Society: Kandy, 1994).

22 https://prepp.in/news/e-492-pandya-kingdom-ancient-history-notes#Economy, accessed on 5 June 2024.

23 https://a.co/d/fimnzcf, accessed on 5 June 2024.

24 R. Champakalakshmi, *Trade, Ideology and Urbanization* (Oxford, 1999), p. 180, https://www.amazon.com/

Trade-Ideology-Urbanization-Oxford-Paperbacks/dp/0195648757, accessed on 5 June 2024.

25 R. Champakalakshmi, *Trade, Ideology and Urbanization*, p. 190.

26 N. Karashima, Y. Subbarayalu and P. Shanmugam, 'Nagaram during the Chola and Pandyan Period', p. 1–33.

27 Wilfred Harvey Schoff, *The Periplus of the Erythraen Sea.*

28 R. Champakalakshmi, 'Ornaments in the Sangam Age', *Journal of Indian History*, 1968, vol XLVII, p. 281–292.

29 R. Champakalakshmi, *Trade, Ideology and Urbanization*, p. 186.

30 Kanakalatha Mukund, *The World of the Tamil Merchant*, p. 34.

31 R.C. Majumdar, *Corporate Life in Ancient India.*

32 Harihara I had nominated Bukka as a joint ruler from 1344 and eventually died in 1357.

33 Between 1614 and 1618, they were at war and there was no single, consistent and established leader.

34 Devaraya II was the son of Vijayraya I, and he had jointly ruled with this father during 1422–26 before taking over the reins completely.

35 The Saluva dynasty was there for only a brief period, so I decided to mention it only in a footnote. The rulers were Saluva Narasimha (1485–1491), Thimma Buppala (1491) and Narasimha Raya II (1491–1505).

36 R. Jyothi, 'The Trade and Trade-Guilds in Vijayanagar Empire', *International Journal of Research in Economics and Social Sciences*, 9 (6), June 2019, https://www.academia.edu/43894766, accessed on 27 June, 2024.

37 N.C. Sujatha, *Vijayanagara as Reflected through Its Numismatics,* VI (22), April–June 2017, p. 2, http://cijhar.in/pdf/2017_v6i22.pdf, accessed on 31 May 2024.

38 A.V. Narasimha Murthy, *The Coins of Karnataka* (Geetha Book House, 1975), p. 389, https://primo.getty.edu/primo-explore/fulldisplay?vid=GRI&docid=GETTY_ALMA21123561800001551&context=L, accessed on 27 June 2024.

39 Sriram Balasubramanian, *Kautilyanomics for Modern Times.*

40 Kathleen D. Morrison and Carla M. Sinopoli, 'Economic Diversity and Integration in a Pre-Colonial Indian Empire', in 'Archaeology of Empires', *World Archaeology*, 23(3), February 1992, p. 335–352.

41 Kathleen D. Morrison and Carla M. Sinopoli, 'Economic Diversity and Integration in a Pre-Colonial Indian Empire', p. 343.

42 *Annual Report on South Indian Epigraphy for 1913/1922* (Archaeological Survey of India: New Delhi).

43 R. Jyothi, 'The Trade and Trade-Guilds in Vijayanagar Empire'.

44 M. Kavitha, 'Socio-Economic Functions of Temples during Medieval Tamil Country 11th–16th Century A.D.', p. 18–23.

45 https://www.tourmyindia.com/blog/tirupati-balaji-temple-interesting-facts/, accessed on 4 June 2024.

46 https://www.tirupatibalajipackage.com/10-fascinating-facts-about-tirumala-venkateswara-temple/, accessed on 4 June 2024.

47 https://www.tirumala.org/TTDTempleHistory.aspx, accessed on 4 June 2024.

48 https://www.tourmyindia.com/blog/tirupati-balaji-temple-interesting-facts/, accessed on 4 June 2024.

49 https://english.jagran.com/spiritual/tirumala-tirupati-devasthanam-7-interesting-facts-you-should-know-about-the-second-richest-temple-in-india-10156281, accessed on 4 June 2024.

50 Burton Stein, 'The state, the Temple and Agricultural Development'.

51 Burton Stein, 'The state, the Temple and Agricultural Development'.

52 Appadorai, 'Economic Conditions in Southern India', University of Madras, 1936.

53 This was a term that I had used first in my book, *Kautilyanomics for Modern Times*. In a simple sense, it is a term to identify a nudge which uses the Dharmic way of life to catalyse more efficient economic outcomes.

54 R. Jyothi, 'The Trade and Trade-Guilds in Vijayanagar Empire'.

55 R. Jyothi, 'The Trade and Trade-Guilds in Vijayanagar Empire'.

Chapter 6: Kambuja Desa

1 R.C. Majumdar, *Kambuja Desa*, p. 10.

2 G. Coedes, *Indianized States of Southeast Asia*, p. 36.

3 G. Coedes, *Indianized States of Southeast Asia*, p. 38.

4 R.C. Majumdar, *Kambuja Desa*, p. 49.

5 Author's visit to the Angkor National Museum, where this was written.

6 It is important to mention again the earlier reference of Nandivarman II and how he was brought back to Bharat by the Pallavas, reaching out to Hiranyavarman who was considered a Kambuja Desa king. Actually, he was a local ruler in Champa (today's Vietnam) during that time (around 730 CE). Champa was ruled by Khmers and was considered a part of Kambuja Desa.

7 https://www.cambridge.org/core/journals/antiquity/article/mahendraparvata-an-early-angkorperiod-capital-defined-through-airborne-laser-scanning-at-phnom-kulen/CAC3E93D6046CC27D862C1E333FD0713, accessed on 4 June 2024.

8 R.C. Majumdar, *Inscriptions of Kambuja*, p. xi, https://ia802908.us.archive.org/10/items/in.ernet.dli.2015.181497/2015.181497.Inscriptions-Of-Kambuja.pdf, accessed on 28 June 2024.

9 https://www.prekshaa.in/article/dharmashastra-roots-cambodia-puranic-traditions-and-culture, accessed on 26 March 2024.

10 R.C. Majumdar, *Inscriptions of Kambuja*, p. xi.

11 D. Evans, C. Pottier, R. Fletcher, S. Hensley, I. Tapley, A. Milne, and M. Barbetti, 'A Comprehensive Archaeological Map of the World's Largest Preindustrial Settlement Complex at Angkor, Cambodia', *Proceedings of the National Academy of Sciences of the United States of America*, 104(36), 2007, p. 14277–14282, https://www.pnas.org/doi/10.1073/pnas.0702525104, accessed on 26 March 2024.

12 R.C. Majumdar, *Inscriptions of Kambuja*.

13 L.A. Sedov, 'Angkor: Society and State', *The Early State*, edited by H.J.M. Claessen and Peter Skalnik (Mouton Publishers, 1978), p. 111–130.

14 E. Lusting, *Power and Pragmaticism in the Political Economy of Angkor*, p. 70.
15 R.C. Majumdar, Inscriptions of Kambuja, Inscription No. 145, p. 347.
16 https://www.prekshaa.in/article/dharmashastra-roots-cambodia-puranic-traditions-and-culture, accessed on 4 June 2024.
17 R.C. Majumdar, *Kambuja Desa*, p. 59.
18 R.C. Majumdar, *Hindu Colonies in the Far East* (Hassell Street Press, 2021).
19 R.C. Majumdar, *Kambuja Desa*, p. 134.
20 https://a.co/d/4loNNw2, accessed on 31 May 2024.
21 https://a.co/d/4loNNw2, accessed on 5 June 2024.
22 E. Lusting, *Power and Pragmaticism in the Political Economy of Angkor*, p. 91.
23 E. Lusting, *Power and Pragmaticism in the Political Economy of Angkor*', p. 91–101.
24 https://www.penguinrandomhouse.com/books/206182/the-great-transformation-by-karl-polanyi/, accessed on 27 March 2024.
25 Morris Silver, 'Karl Polanyi and Markets in the Ancient Near East: The Challenge of the Evidence', *The Journal of Economic History*, vol. 43, no. 4, 1983, p. 795–829, http://www.jstor.org/stable/2121050, accessed on 24 April 2024. A summary of the critique can be found at https://www.libertarianism.org/blog/karl-polanyis-battle-economic-history, accessed on 27 March 2024.
26 E. Lusting, *Power and Pragmaticism in the Political Economy of Angkor*, p. 54.
27 H. Kulke, 'The Early and Imperial Kingdom in Southeast Asian History', *Southeast Asia in the 9th to 14th Centuries*, edited by D. G. Hall and A. C. Milner (Institute of Southeast Asian Studies, 1986), p. 1–22; H. Kulke, 'The Early and the Imperial Kingdom: A Processual Model of Integrative State Formation in Early Medieval India', *The State in India 1000–170* (Oxford University Press, 1995), p. 233–262.
28 Kenneth R. Hall, *Maritime Trade and Development in Southeast Asia* (University of Hawaii Press, 1985), https://scholarspace.manoa.hawaii.edu/server/api/core/

bitstreams/04159870-42f8-4dc6-8789-54c0b79496b0/content, accessed on 27 March 2024.

29 Example: A local temple in Suryavarman I's reign received 25,000 kg of hulled rice annually but shared only 90 kg out of it with the corresponding central temple. In addition, 6 kg of vegetable oil, 25 kg of sesame seeds, 25 kg of chick peas, 2 banners and 2 measures of cloth were annually provided by the local temple to the central temple; George Coedès, 'La stèle de Ta-prohm', *BEFEO* 6 (1,2), 1906, p. 44–81, https://www.jstor.org/stable/43729616, accessed on 28 June 2024.

30 https://theangkorguide.net/temple-information-detail.html?name=angkor-wat-temple, accessed on 4 June 2024; https://www.livescience.com/23841-angkor-wat.html, accessed on 4 June 2024.

31 https://whc.unesco.org/en/list/668, accessed on 4 June 2024.

32 https://www.livescience.com/24440-angkor-wat-canals.html, accessed on 4 June 2024.

33 Jon Ortner, *Angkor: Celestial Temples of the Khmer Empire* (Abbeville Press, 2002).

34 Charles Higham, *Early Cultures of Mainland Southeast Asia* (Art Media Resources, 2003).

35 https://skift.com/2023/03/17/cambodia-relocates-angkor-wat-communities-in-controversial-tourism-touch-up/, accessed on 4 June 2024.

36 https://thegoguy.com/why-right-now-is-the-best-time-to-visit-angkor-wat-in-siem-reap-cambodia/, accessed on 4 June 2024.

37 K.R. Hall, 'The Temple-Based Mainland Political Economies of Angkor Cambodia and Pagan Burma, ca. 889–1300', *A History of Early Southeast Asia: Maritime Trade and Societal Development, 100–1500* (Rowman & Littlefield, 2011); E. Lusting, *Power and Pragmaticism in the Political Economy of Angkor*; L.A. Sedov, 'On the Problem of the Economic System in Angkor Cambodia in the IX XII Centuries', *Narody Asii I Afriki, Istoria, Ekonomika, Kul'tura*, trans. by A. Glasse, vol. 6, 1963, p. 73–81, Akademija Nauk SSR.

38 Sarah Klassen, Scott G. Ortman, José Lobo and Damian Evans, 'Provisioning an Early City: Spatial Equilibrium in

the Agricultural Economy at Angkor, Cambodia, *Journal of Archaeological Method and Theory*, vol. 29, 2022, p. 763–794, https://doi.org/10.1007/s10816-021-09535-5, accessed on 27 March 2024.

39 https://cdn.angkordatabase.asia/libs/docs/publications/water-management-in-angkor/The_water_management_network_of_Angkor_C.pdf, accessed on 27 March 2024.

40 https://cdn.angkordatabase.asia/libs/docs/publications/water-management-in-angkor/The_water_management_network_of_Angkor_C.pdf, accessed on 27 March 2024.

41 Sarah Klassen, Scott G. Ortman, José Lobo and Damian Evans, 'Provisioning an Early City' p. 763–794.

42 A. Reid, 'Southeast Asia in the Age of Commerce, 1450–1680', *Volume One: The Lands below the Winds* (Yale University Press: New Haven, 1988), p. 18.

43 https://www.nla.gov.au/digital-classroom/year-8/asia-pacific-world/angkorkhmer-empire-c802-c1431/themes/way-life-khmer, accessed on 27 March 2024.

44 Mitch Hendrickson, 'Industries of Angkor Project: Preliminary Investigation of Iron Production at Boeng Kroam, Preah Khan of Kompong Svay', https://journals.lib.washington.edu/index.php/JIPA/article/view/15257, accessed on 27 March 2024.

45 Mitch Hendrickson, Stéphanie Leroy, 'Sparks and Needles: Seeking Catalysts of State Expansions: A Case Study of Technological Interaction at Angkor, Cambodia (9–13 Century)', *Journal of Anthropological Archaeology*, vol. 57, 2020, https://doi.org/10.1016/j.jaa.2019.101141, accessed on 27 March 2024.

46 Peter Grave, Lisa Kealhofer, Kaseka Phon, Piphal Heng, Miriam T. Stark, Ben Marsh, Darith Ea, Rachna Chhay, Gary P. Marriner, 'Centralized Power/Decentralized Production? Angkorian Stoneware and the Southern Production Complex of Cheung Ek, Cambodia', *Journal of Archaeological Science*, vol. 125, 2021, 105270, ISSN 0305-4403, https://doi.org/10.1016/j.jas.2020.105270, accessed on 31 May 2024.

47 Kenneth R. Hall, *Maritime Trade and State Development in Early Southeast Asia*, p. 178.

48 R.C. Majumdar, *Inscriptions of Kambuja.*

49 Kenneth R. Hall, *Maritime Trade and State Development in Early Southeast Asia*, p. 179.

50 Kenneth R. Hall, *Maritime Trade and State Development in Early Southeast Asia*, p. 179.

Chapter 7: Other Dharmic Southeast Asian Kingdoms

1 https://www.opindia.com/2020/09/kingdom-of-champa-and-the-chams-hinduism-in-vietnam/, accessed on 29 March 2024.

2 Ky Phuong Tran and Nguyen Thi Thu anh, tran., 'A Proposed Relationship between Champa and Chola Dynasties During the 11th and 13th Centuries: A View from the Historical Sources and Artistic Evidences', *SPAFA Journal* 5, 2021, https://doi.org/10.26721/spafajournal.2021.v5.673, accessed on 31 May 2024.

3 Ky Phuong Tran and Nguyen Thi Thu anh, tran., 'A Proposed Relationship between Champa and Chola Dynasties During the 11th and 13th Centuries'.

4 Kenneth R. Hall, *Maritime Trade and State Development in Early Southeast Asia*, p. 223.

5 Kenneth R. Hall, *Maritime Trade and State Development in Early Southeast Asia*, p. 222.

6 Ky Phuong Tran and Nguyen Thi Thu anh, tran., 'A Proposed Relationship between Champa and Chola Dynasties During the 11th and 13th Centuries'.

7 R.C. Majumdar, *Hindu Colonies in the Far East*, p. 89.

8 https://www.academia.edu/44754283, accessed on 5 June 2024.

9 https://ismaili.net/Source/0104c.html, accessed on 5 June 2024.

10 https://www.hindustantimes.com/lifestyle/how-thailands-ayutthaya-is-related-to-ayodhya-and-lord-ram-101702021337371.html, accessed on 5 June 2024.

11 http://www.icm.gov.mo/rc/viewer/20013/945, accessed on 5 June 2024.

12 https://whc.unesco.org/en/list/576/, accessed on 5 June 2024.

13 Charnvit Kasetsiri, *The Rise of Ayudhya: A History of Siam in the Fourteenth and Fifteenth Centuries, East Asia Historical Monographs* (Oxford University Press, 1976).

14 João de Barros, *Da Ásia. Década Terceira, Parte Primeira [From Asia. Third Decade, First Part]* (Na Regia Officina Typografica, 1777), 2, p. 169, https://archive.org/details/A209005, accessed on 5 June 2024.

15 Tomé Pires, *The Suma Oriental,* trans and ed. Armando Cortesão, 2 vols (Hakluyt Society, 1944), 1, p. 103; http://www.icm.gov.mo/rc/viewer/20013/945, accessed on 5 June 2024.

16 https://www.asj.upd.edu.ph/mediabox/archive/ASJ-15-1977/francisco-indian-prespanish-philippines.pdf, accessed on 20 June 2024; https://www.ancient-origins.net/ancient-places-asia/pre-colonial-philippines-0010781, accessed on 20 June 2024.

17 https://timesofindia.indiatimes.com/india/Hindu-gods-forgotten-in-India-revered-in-Japan/articleshow/50525067.cms, accessed on 20 June 2024.

Chapter 8: Dharmanomics through 5,000 Years

1 The 5,000 years in the title of this chapter includes the Saraswati–Sindhu civilization which is dated around 3500 BCE. Even if we exclude this, it would still be more than 2,000 years.

2 *Economic History of India (from the Earliest Time to 1707 AD)*, http://epgp.inflibnet.ac.in/epgpdata/uploads/epgp_content/S000829IC/P001687/M024945/ET/1510563797P12-M19-Cholas-TradeandCommerce-ET.pdf, accessed on 30 March 2024.

3 https://ignca.gov.in/Asi_data/87893.pdf, accessed on 30 March 2024.

4 https://ignca.gov.in/Asi_data/87893.pdf, p. 16, accessed on 30 March 2024.

5 https://angkordatabase.asia/books/cambodia-india-out-side-india-decoding-khmer-architecture, accessed on 30 March 2024.

6 https://angkordatabase.asia/books/cambodia-india-out-side-india-decoding-khmer-architecture, accessed on 30 March 2024.

7 https://en.wikipedia.org/wiki/Angkor_Wat#Architecture, accessed on 27 March 2024.

8 As mentioned earlier, Kambuja Desa probably did not have a currency or coinage for many years, especially during the Kambuja Desa era.

9 http://swamivivekanandaquotesgarden.blogspot.com/2014/05/bhagavad-gita-chapter-2-verse-47.html, accessed on 30 March 2024.

Index

About the Author

Sriram Balasubramanian is a well-known economist and bestselling author based at one of the leading international monetary institutions in the world. He has worked for several global organizations including the International Monetary Fund (IMF) in the past. His areas of expertise include global macroeconomics, socioeconomic trends in emerging markets and iconic Indic and dharmic culture in the context of economics. He has written for several international publications such as *Bloomberg*, *Foreign Policy*, *The Wall Street Journal* and *Vox EU* as an independent columnist and has been an independent panellist on CNBC TV18. Besides authoring the path-breaking bestseller *Kautilyanomics for Modern Times*, he has authored two other books, *JAMBA: The Joint Family* (shortlisted for the Third Annual IAAC Literary Festival organized by the Indo-American Arts Council) and *The Wizards*, which has been featured in varied publications, including *The Hindu*.

He is an alumnus of Columbia University, New York. He lives in Washington DC/Maryland area in the USA with his family.

About the Author